T0142452

Advances in Computer Vision and Pattern Recognition

More information about this series at http://www.springer.com/series/4205

Kaspar Riesen

Structural Pattern Recognition with Graph Edit Distance

Approximation Algorithms and Applications

 Springer

Kaspar Riesen
Institut für Wirtschaftsinformatik
Fachhochschule Nordwestschweiz
Olten
Switzerland

ISSN 2191-6586   ISSN 2191-6594   (electronic)
Advances in Computer Vision and Pattern Recognition
ISBN 978-3-319-80101-8   ISBN 978-3-319-27252-8   (eBook)
DOI 10.1007/978-3-319-27252-8

Printed on acid-free paper

This Springer imprint is published by SpringerNature
The registered company is Springer International Publishing AG Switzerland

To Madeleine, Emilie, and Maxime

Preface

The present book is concerned with the use of graphs in the field of structural pattern recognition. In fact, graphs are recognized as versatile alternative to feature vectors and thus, they found widespread application in pattern recognition and related fields (yet, the present book is actually focused on the field of pattern recognition only). In the last four decades, a huge number of procedures for graph distance computation, which is actually a basic requirement for pattern recognition, have been proposed in the literature. *Graph edit distance*, introduced about 30 years ago, is still one of the most flexible graph distance models available and subject of various recent research activities.

The objective of the present book is twofold. First, it gives a general and thorough introduction into the field of structural pattern recognition with a particular focus on graph edit distance (including a survey of graph edit distance applications that emerged during the last decade). Second, it presents a comprehensive compilation of diverse novel methods related to graph edit distance that have been developed and researched in the course of a recent research project that has been conducted under my supervision. In particular, the second part of the present book summarizes and consolidates the results of the following articles.[1]

1. Kaspar Riesen, Horst Bunke: Improving Bipartite Graph Edit Distance Approximation using Various Search Strategies. Pattern Recognition 48(4): 1349–1363 (2015).
2. Kaspar Riesen, Andreas Fischer, Horst Bunke: Estimating Graph Edit Distance Using Lower and Upper Bounds of Bipartite Approximations. IJPRAI 29(2) (2015).
3. Miquel Ferrer, Francesc Serratosa, Kaspar Riesen: Improving Bipartite Graph Matching by Assessing the Assignment Confidence. Pattern Recognition Letters, 2015. Accepted for Publication.

---

[1]We reuse several text excerpts, tables, and figures from the corresponding original publications with permission from *Elsevier*, *World Scientific*, and *IEEE*.

4. Kaspar Riesen, Miquel Ferrer: Predicting the Correctness of Node Assignments in Bipartite Graph Matching. Pattern Recognition Letters, 2015. Accepted for Publication.
5. Kaspar Riesen, Miquel Ferrer, Horst Bunke: Approximate Graph Edit Distance in Quadratic Time. IEEE/ACM Transactions on Computational Biology and Bioinformatics (TCBB), 2015. Accepted for Publication.

Bern   Kaspar Riesen
September 2015

Acknowledgments

I am deeply grateful to Horst Bunke for introducing me to the world of graphs and pattern recognition about 10 years ago. His excellent advice and open attitude towards new ideas have strongly influenced my scientific development.

Although only one author is mentioned on the front cover of this book, various colleagues contributed invaluable parts to this work. In particular, I would like to thank the co-authors of the papers, which actually build the basis of this book, viz., Andreas Fischer, Miquel Ferrer, Rolf Dornberger, Francesc Serratosa, and Horst Bunke.

Moreover, I would like to thank Thomas Strahm for his support in all administrative concerns as well as for encouraging me for writing the present book.

I would also like to acknowledge the funding by the Hasler Foundation Switzerland and the Swiss National Science Foundation (Project 200021 153249).

Furthermore, I would like to thank Simon Rees and Wayne Wheeler from Springer for their guidance and support.

Last but not least, I am very grateful to my family for their understanding and encouragement.

Contents

Part I
Foundations and Applications
of Graph Edit Distance

Chapter 1
Introduction and Basic Concepts

Abstract In this chapter we first introduce pattern recognition as a computer science discipline and then outline the major differences between statistical and structural pattern recognition. In particular, we discuss the advantages and drawbacks of both approaches. Eventually, graph-based pattern representation is formally introduced and complemented by a list of applications where graphs are actually employed. The remaining parts of this chapter are then dedicated to formal introductions of diverse graph matching definitions. We particularly delve into the difference between exact and inexact graph matching. Last but not least, we give a brief survey of existing graph matching methodologies that somehow differ from the approach that is actually pursued in the present book.

1.1 Pattern Recognition

The ability of recognizing patterns has been essential for our survival and thus, evolution has led to highly sophisticated neural and cognitive systems in humans for solving pattern recognition tasks [1]. In fact, humans are faced with a great diversity of pattern recognition problems in their everyday life. Examples of pattern recognition tasks—which are in the majority of cases intuitively solved—include the recognition of a written or a spoken word, the face of a friend, an object on the table, a traffic sign on the road, and many others. These simple examples illustrate the essence of pattern recognition. In the world there exist classes of patterns which are recognized by humans according to certain knowledge learned before [2].

The terminology *pattern* refers to any observation in the real world (e.g., an image, an object, a symbol, or a word, to name just a few). The overall aim of *pattern recognition* as a computer science discipline is to develop methods that are able to (partially) imitate the human capacity of perception and intelligence. In other words, pattern recognition aims at defining algorithms that automate or (at least) support the process of recognizing patterns stemming from the real world.

However, pattern recognition refers to a highly complex process which cannot be solved by means of explicitly specified algorithms in general. For instance, to date one is not able to write an analytic algorithm to recognize, say, a face in a photo [3].

© Springer International Publishing Switzerland 2015
K. Riesen, *Structural Pattern Recognition with Graph Edit Distance*,
Advances in Computer Vision and Pattern Recognition,
DOI 10.1007/978-3-319-27252-8_1

In order to overcome this problem, machine-based pattern recognition is based on the so-called *learning paradigm*. That is, pattern recognition algorithms are commonly designed such that they can be trained on labeled data (referred to as *training data*). By means of this training data, a pattern recognition system is able to derive a model, which in turn can be used to solve the given pattern recognition task. Hence, the purpose of any pattern recognition system is to learn from examples such that it becomes able to make predictions about new, i.e., unseen, data.

Pattern recognition emerged as a very important and active discipline in computer science. This becomes also evident by the high number of scientific journals that are concerned with this research area (e.g., *Pattern Analysis and Applications* (Springer), *Pattern Recognition* and *Pattern Recognition Letters* (both Elsevier), and the *IEEE Transactions on Pattern Analysis and Machine Intelligence*, to name just a few examples). Moreover, pattern recognition methodologies are nowadays employed in various areas of science and industry. Handwriting recognition [4–9] and document analysis [10–15] are well-known examples of pattern recognition applications. Other prominent examples of pattern recognition applications include (biometric) person identification and authentication [16–24], activity predictions for molecular compounds [25–28], and function predictions for proteins [29–33].

1.1.1 Statistical and Structural Pattern Recognition

The question how to represent patterns in a formal way such that they can automatically be processed by machine is a key issue in pattern recognition and related fields. In general, there are two major ways to tackle this crucial step, viz., the *statistical* and the *structural approach*.

In the statistical approach, feature vectors are employed for representing the underlying patterns. That is, a pattern is formally represented as a vector $\mathbf{x} = (x_1, \ldots, x_n) \in \mathbb{R}^n$ of n numerical features. Representing patterns by feature vectors offers a number of useful properties, in particular, the mathematical wealth of efficient operations available in a vector space, which has eventually resulted in a rich repository of algorithmic tools for statistical pattern recognition [1, 3, 34].

However, the use of feature vectors implicates the two following limitations.

1. As vectors always represent a predefined set of features, all vectors in a given application have to preserve the same length regardless the size or complexity of the corresponding pattern.
2. Vectors do not provide a direct possibility to describe binary (or higher order) relationships that might exist among different parts of a pattern.

These two drawbacks are severe, particularly when the patterns under consideration are characterized by complex structural relationships rather than the statistical distribution of a fixed set of pattern features.

Both limitations can be overcome by *graph-based pattern representation*, which is commonly used in a structural pattern recognition. Basically, graphs consist of finite sets of (labeled) nodes and edges, where the edges connect pairs of nodes.

Table 1.1 Complementary
properties of feature vectors
and graphs

	Vectors	Graphs
Representational power	Low	High
Efficiency	High	Low

Hence, graphs are able to not only describe properties of a pattern, but also (binary) relationships among different parts of the underlying pattern, or arrangement of patterns. Moreover, graphs are not constrained to a fixed size, i.e., the number of nodes and edges is not limited a priori but can be adapted to the size and the complexity of each individual pattern under consideration.

However, one drawback of graphs, when compared to feature vectors, is the significant increase of the complexity of many algorithms. Regard, for instance, the algorithmic comparison of two patterns. In a statistical pattern recognition, every vector has equal dimension, and moreover, the ith entry in any vector describes the same numerical property of the underlying pattern. Due to this homogeneous nature, comparison of two patterns is straightforward and can be accomplished in linear time with respect to the length of the two vectors (e.g., by means of the Euclidean distance). The same task for graphs, however, is much more complex, as the sets of nodes and edges are generally unordered and of arbitrary size. More formally, when comparing two graphs with each other, one has to identify common parts of the graphs by considering all of their subsets of nodes. Regarding that there are $O(2^n)$ subsets of nodes in a graph with n nodes, the inherent difficulty of graph comparison becomes obvious.

We have to conclude that the flexibility of graphs handicap their general applicability in pattern recognition. In summary and from a high-level perspective, we observe quite complementary properties of feature vectors and graphs (cf. Table 1.1). The present book is concerned with the use of graphs in pattern recognition and particularly addresses the efficiency problem of graph comparison.

Readers who are aware of the recent rise of *graph kernels* [35–37] and *graph embedding methods* [38–40] might interject that the traditional gap between statistical and structural pattern recognition has been bridged. In fact, both graph kernels and graph embeddings provide a powerful vectorial description of the underlying graphs. While graph kernels produce an implicit embedding of graphs into a Hilbert space, graph embeddings result in an explicit feature vector in a real vector space. Yet, both approaches crucially depend on similarity or dissimilarity computation on graphs. That is, in spite of the recent paradigm shift in structural pattern recognition, the topic of (efficient) graph comparison is still of high importance.

1.2 Graph and Subgraph

The following definition allows us to handle arbitrarily structured graphs with unconstrained labeling functions.

Definition 1.1 *(Graph)* Let L_V and L_E be finite or infinite label sets for nodes and edges, respectively. A *graph* g is a four-tuple $g = (V, E, \mu, \nu)$, where

- V is the finite set of nodes,
- $E \subseteq V \times V$ is the set of edges,
- $\mu : V \rightarrow L_V$ is the node labeling function, and
- $\nu : E \rightarrow L_E$ is the edge labeling function.

The set of all graphs over the label alphabets L_V and L_E (also referred to as *graph domain*) is denoted by $\mathscr{G}$. The size of a graph g is denoted by $|g|$ and is defined as the number of nodes, i.e., $|g| = |V|$.

The labels for both nodes and edges can be given by the set of integers $L = \{1, 2, 3, \ldots\}$, the vector space $L = \mathbb{R}^n$, a set of symbolic labels $L = \{\alpha, \beta, \gamma, \ldots\}$, or a combination of various label alphabets from different domains. Given that the nodes and/or the edges are labeled, the graphs are referred to as *labeled graphs*.[1] *Unlabeled graphs* are obtained as a special case by assigning the same (empty) label $\varnothing$ to all nodes and edges, i.e., $L_V = L_E = \{\varnothing\}$. In some algorithms and applications it is necessary to include *empty "nodes"* and/or *empty "edges"* (also referred to as *null nodes* and *null edges*). We denote both empty nodes and empty edges by ε. Note the difference between an unlabeled and an empty node. An empty node ε is non-existing (i.e., *null*) while an unlabeled node u is an existing node from V with empty label $\mu(u) = \varnothing$ (the same accounts for the edges).

Edges are given by pairs of nodes (u, v), where $u \in V$ denotes the source node and $v \in V$ the target node of a directed edge. Commonly, the two nodes u and v connected by an edge (u, v) are referred to as *adjacent*. A graph is termed *complete* if all pairs of nodes are adjacent. The *degree* of a node $u \in V$ is the number of adjacent nodes to u, i.e., the number of *incident* edges of u.

Directed graphs directly correspond to the above-stated definition of a graph. However, by inserting a reverse edge $(v, u) \in E$ for every edge $(u, v) \in E$ with an identical label, i.e., $\nu(u, v) = \nu(v, u)$, the class of *undirected graphs* can be modeled as well. Since there are always edges in both directions in this case, the direction of an edge can be safely ignored.

A common approach to describe the edge structure of a graph $g = (V, E, \mu, \nu)$ is to define the adjacency matrix of g.

Definition 1.2 *(Adjacency Matrix)* Let $g = (V, E, \mu, \nu)$ be a graph with $|g| = n$. The $n \times n$ *adjacency matrix* $\mathbf{A} = (a_{ij})_{n \times n}$ of graph g is defined by

$$a_{ij} = \begin{cases} (v_i, v_j) & \text{if } (v_i, v_j) \in E \\ \varepsilon & \text{otherwise} \end{cases}$$

where $v_i, v_j \in V$ and ε refers to the empty edge.

---

[1]*Attributes* and *attributed graphs* are sometimes synonymously used for *labels* and *labeled graphs*, respectively.

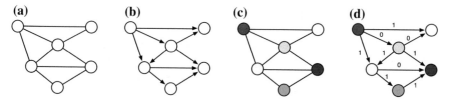

Fig. 1.1 Different kinds of graphs: **a** undirected and unlabeled, **b** directed and unlabeled, **c** undirected with labeled nodes (different shades of *grey* refer to different labels), **d** directed with labeled nodes and edges (edges are labeled with binary numbers)

If there actually is an edge between the ith node $v_i \in V$ and the jth node $v_j \in V$, entry a_{ij} of the adjacency matrix $\mathbf{A}$ points to the respective edge (v_i, v_j). Otherwise a_{ij} refers to the empty edge ε. Clearly, one can use the labeling function $\nu : E \to L_E$ to access the label of nonempty edges $a_{ij} \in \mathbf{A}$. Formally, if $a_{ij} \neq \varepsilon, \nu(a_{ij}) = \nu((v_i, v_j))$. Note that if the underlying graph is undirected, the corresponding adjacency matrix will be symmetric with respect to the labeling of the edges (i.e., $\nu(a_{ij}) = \nu(a_{ji})$ accounts for all $i, j = 1, \ldots, n$).

Example 1 In Fig. 1.1 some example graphs (directed/undirected, labeled/unlabeled) are shown. The adjacency matrix $\mathbf{A}$ of the graph shown in Fig. 1.1a is defined by

$$
\mathbf{A} = \begin{bmatrix}
\varepsilon & (v_1, v_2) & (v_1, v_3) & (v_1, v_4) & \varepsilon & \varepsilon \\
(v_2, v_1) & \varepsilon & (v_2, v_3) & \varepsilon & \varepsilon & \varepsilon \\
(v_3, v_1) & (v_3, v_2) & \varepsilon & (v_3, v_4) & (v_3, v_5) & \varepsilon \\
(v_4, v_1) & \varepsilon & (v_4, v_3) & \varepsilon & (v_4, v_5) & (v_4, v_6) \\
\varepsilon & \varepsilon & (v_5, v_3) & (v_5, v_4) & \varepsilon & (v_5, v_6) \\
\varepsilon & \varepsilon & \varepsilon & (v_6, v_4) & (v_6, v_5) & \varepsilon
\end{bmatrix}
$$

Note that the nodes $V = \{v_1, \ldots, v_6\}$ of this graph are enumerated from top to bottom and from left to right in this example.

A large variety of specific graph types are included in Definition 1.1. The following list outlines some of these special types.

- *Weighted graphs*: For this type of graphs the node and edge label alphabets are restricted by $L_V = \{\varnothing\}$ and $L_E = \{x \in \mathbb{R} \mid 0 \leq x \leq 1\}$, respectively.
- *Graphs with unique node labels*: The node labels for this kind of graphs are also restricted such that each node is labeled with a distinct label [41–43]. Formally, for all nodes $u, v \in V$ with $u \neq v$ it follows $\mu(u) \neq \mu(v)$.
- *Valence graphs*: For this type of graph every node's degree is bounded by, or fixed to, a given value (known as *bounded-valence graphs* or *fixed-valence graphs*, respectively [44, 45]).
- *Planar graphs*: Planar graphs can be drawn on the plane in such a way that its edges intersect only at their endpoints [46, 47].

- *Trees*: Trees are acyclic graphs with directed edges such that every node is the start node of zero or more edges and the target node of at most one edge. In other words, every node has zero or more *children nodes* and at most one *parent node* [48–52].
- *Ordered Graphs*: An ordered graph is a directed graph with *topologically ordered* node sets V. A topological ordering of the nodes means that for every directed edge $(u, v) \in E$, u is sorted before v in V [53].

In analogy to the subset relation in set theory, we define parts of a graph as follows.

Definition 1.3 (*Subgraph*) Let $g_1 = (V_1, E_1, \mu_1, \nu_1)$ and $g_2 = (V_2, E_2, \mu_2, \nu_2)$ be graphs. Graph g_1 is a *subgraph* of g_2, denoted by $g_1 \subseteq g_2$, if

1. $V_1 \subseteq V_2$,
2. $E_1 \subseteq E_2$,
3. $\mu_1(u) = \mu_2(u)$ for all $u \in V_1$, and
4. $\nu_1(e) = \nu_2(e)$ for all $e \in E_1$.

By replacing the second condition by the more stringent condition

(2') $E_1 = E_2 \cap V_1 \times V_1$,

g_1 becomes an *induced subgraph* of g_2. A complete subgraph is referred to as a *clique*.

Obviously, a subgraph g_1 is obtained from a graph g_2 by removing some nodes and their incident (as well as possibly some additional) edges from g_2. For g_1 to be an induced subgraph of g_2, some nodes including their incident edges are removed from g_2 only, i.e., no additional edge removal is allowed.

Example 2 Figure 1.2b, c show an induced and a non-induced subgraph of the graph in Fig. 1.2a, respectively.

Due to their power and flexibility, graphs have found widespread application in pattern recognition and related fields [54]. A prominent example of a class of patterns, which can be formally represented in a more suitable and natural way by means of graphs rather than with feature vectors, are chemical compounds [26–28, 55, 56]. Such compounds consist of atoms and covalent bonds which can be readily converted into nodes and edges, respectively.

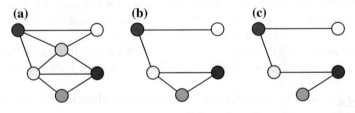

Fig. 1.2 Graph (**b**) is an induced subgraph of (**a**), and graph (**c**) is a non-induced subgraph of (**a**)

Fig. 1.3 The chemical
compound of *Aspirin*
$(C_9 H_8 O_4)$ represented by
means of an undirected
labeled graph

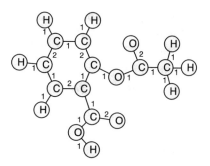

Example 3 In Fig. 1.3, for instance, the chemical compound of *Aspirin* $(C_9 H_8 O_4)$ represented by means of an undirected labeled graph is shown. The nodes and edges are labeled with the chemical symbol of the corresponding atom and the valence of the bond, respectively.

Other examples of patterns where graphs turn out to be an appropriate representation formalism are binary executables [57–63], documents [64–67], proteins [29, 30, 68, 69], networks [42, 70–73], handwritten symbols and characters [74–78], and many others. In Chap. 9 several standard data sets for graph-based pattern recognition are described [79]. Moreover, Sect. 3.4 gives an overview of recent graph-based pattern representations that are somehow related to the graph distance paradigm to be used throughout the present book.

1.3 Graph Matching

The availability of a dissimilarity or similarity measure is a basic requirement for pattern recognition and analysis. Obviously, the concepts of similarity and dissimilarity are closely related to each other, as both a small dissimilarity value and a large similarity value indicate a close proximity. Moreover, there exist several methods for transforming similarities into dissimilarities, and vice versa. From now on we will focus on the concept of dissimilarity. The computation of a dissimilarity between two patterns formally described by means of n-dimensional feature vectors $\mathbf{x} = (x_1, \ldots, x_n)$ and $\mathbf{y} = (y_1, \ldots, y_n)$ is often based on the *Minkowski distance*

$$||\mathbf{x} - \mathbf{y}||_p = \left(\sum_{i=1}^{n} |x_i - y_i|^p \right)^{1/p}$$

with order $p \geq 1$. The Minkowski distance is a generalization of both the *Euclidean distance* $(p = 2)$ and the *Manhattan distance* $(p = 1)$. In fact, the Minkowski distance can be seen as a standard model for measuring dissimilarities between statistical patterns.

For graph dissimilarity computation, however, no standard model has been established to date. The problem of computing graph proximity is commonly referred to as *graph comparison problem* [80].

Definition 1.4 (*Graph Comparison Problem*) Given two graphs g_1 and g_2 from a graph domain $\mathcal{G}$, the *graph comparison problem* is given by defining a function

$$d : \mathcal{G} \times \mathcal{G} \to \mathbb{R}$$

such that $d(g_1, g_2)$ quantifies the dissimilarity of g_1 and g_2.

The graph comparison problem is commonly solved via a particular *graph matching* algorithm, which maps similar substructures of graph g_1 to similar substructures of graph g_2. That is, the major goal of graph matching is to find a correspondence between the nodes and the edges of two graphs that satisfies some, more or less, stringent constraints [81]. Given this correspondence of nodes and edges, a dissimilarity score $d(g_1, g_2)$ can eventually be computed in various ways.

Graph matching has been the topic of numerous studies in computer science over the last few decades [82, 83]. Two main categories of graph matching can be distinguished, viz., *exact graph matching* and *inexact graph matching* (also referred to as *error-tolerant graph matching*). Roughly speaking, in exact graph matching one aims at finding a strict correspondence between the two graphs being matched, or at least among their subparts. That is, exact matching is basically concerned with the question whether or not two graphs (or subgraphs of them) are identical in terms of both their labeling and their edge structure. Rather than merely checking whether graphs are (in large parts) identical, the latter approach allows also matchings between completely nonidentical graphs. Hence, error-tolerant graph matching is a more general problem than exact graph matching (in fact, exact graph matching can be interpreted as special case of error-tolerant graph matching). The quality of an error-tolerant graph matching can be quantified by means of a specific objective function (which can eventually be optimized by different algorithms).

In the next two subsections both exact and error-tolerant graph matching are formally defined. Moreover, we give a brief survey on standard methods for both paradigms. For a more extensive review on graph matching methods emerged during the last 40 years, the reader is referred to [81, 84, 85].

1.3.1   Exact Graph Matching

The identity of two graphs g_1 and g_2 is commonly established by defining a bijective function, termed *graph isomorphism*, mapping the nodes of g_1 to the nodes of g_2 such that the *edge structure* of the graphs is preserved. If two nodes from g_1 are mapped to two nodes in g_2, an *edge-preserving* node mapping ensures that if, and only if, there is an edge between the nodes in g_1 there is also an edge between the nodes in g_2.

Definition 1.5 (*Graph Isomorphism*) Let us consider two graphs $g_1 = (V_1, E_1, \mu, \nu)$ and $g_2 = (V_2, E_2, \mu, \nu)$. A *graph isomorphism* is a bijective mapping $f : V_1 \to V_2$ satisfying

1. $\mu_1(u) = \mu_2(f(u)) \quad \forall u \in V_1$,
2. $e_1 = (u, v) \in E_1 \Rightarrow e_2 = (f(u), f(v)) \in E_2$ such that $\nu_1(e_1) = \nu_2(e_2) \quad \forall e_1 \in E_1$,
3. $e_2 = (u, v) \in E_2 \Rightarrow e_1 = (f^{-1}(u), f^{-1}(v)) \in E_1$ such that $\nu_1(e_1) = \nu_2(e_2) \quad \forall e_2 \in E_2$

Two graphs g_1 and g_2 are called *isomorphic* if there exists an isomorphism f between their respective node sets V_1 and V_2.

Subgraph isomorphism is a weaker form of a node mapping function in terms of only requiring that an isomorphism holds between a graph g_1 and an (induced) subgraph of g_2. Intuitively, a subgraph isomorphism between two graphs indicates that the smaller graph is contained in the larger graph, and thus, subgraph isomorphism can be interpreted as a concept for subgraph equality.

Definition 1.6 (*Subgraph Isomorphism*) Let $g_1 = (V_1, E_1, \mu_1, \nu_1)$ and $g_2 = (V_2, E_2, \mu_2, \nu_2)$ be graphs. A *subgraph isomorphism* is an injective function $f : V_1 \to V_2$ from g_1 to g_2 if there exists a subgraph $g \subseteq g_2$ such that f is a graph isomorphism between g_1 and g.

Subgraph isomorphism is a harder problem than graph isomorphism, as we have to not only check whether a permutation of g_1 is identical to g_2, but also decide whether g_1 is isomorphic to any of the subgraphs of g_2 with equal size as g_1. One can show that subgraph isomorphism is a generalization of two NP-complete problems, viz., the *maximum clique problem* and the problem of testing whether a graph contains a *Hamiltonian cycle* [86]. Hence, in contrast with the problem of graph isomorphism (whose complexity remains unresolved to date), subgraph isomorphism is known to be NP-complete [87].

Example 4 In Fig. 1.4a, b two isomorphic graphs are shown, while in Fig. 1.4a, c an example of a subgraph isomorphism is given.

Standard procedures for testing graphs for isomorphism are based on tree search techniques with backtracking. These search algorithms are often endowed with elaborated heuristics to avoid a complete exploration of the space of all possible matchings [88–94]. Yet, there are also graph isomorphism algorithms available which are not based on tree search methods. For instance *Nauty* [95], which addresses the isomorphism problem by using results from group theory, or algorithms that are based on *random walks* [96] and *decision trees* [97, 98], to name just three alternative approaches.

The process of exact graph matching primarily aims at identifying corresponding substructures in the two graphs under consideration. Given this correspondence, an associated dissimilarity score can be readily inferred. More formally, graph

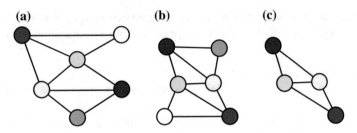

Fig. 1.4 Graph (**b**) is isomorphic to (**a**), and graph (**c**) is isomorphic to a subgraph of (**a**). Node attributes are indicated by different shades of *gray*, while edges are unlabeled

isomorphism as well as subgraph isomorphism provides us with a coarse dissimilarity measure, which is 0 (minimum dissimilarity) or 1 (maximum dissimilarity) for (sub)graph isomorphic or non-isomorphic graphs, respectively. Hence, two graphs must be completely identical, or the smaller graph must be identically contained in the other graph, to be deemed similar.

More refined dissimilarity models, which still fall into the category of exact graph matching, are based on the formal concept of the largest common part of two graphs.

Definition 1.7 (*Maximum common subgraph*) Let $g_1 = (V_1, E_1, \mu_1, \nu_1)$ and $g_2 = (V_2, E_2, \mu_2, \nu_2)$ be graphs. A common subgraph of g_1 and g_2 is a graph $g = (V, E, \mu, \nu)$ such that there exist subgraph isomorphisms from g to g_1 and from g to g_2. We call g a *maximum common subgraph* of g_1 and g_2 ($mcs(g_1, g_2)$) if there exists no other common subgraph of g_1 and g_2 that has more nodes than g.

A maximum common subgraph of two graphs represents the maximal part of both graphs that is identical in terms of structure and labels. In general, the maximum common subgraph is not uniquely defined. In other words, there may be more than one common subgraph with a maximal number of nodes.

Example 5 In Fig. 1.5c the maximum common subgraph is shown for the two graphs in Fig. 1.5a, b.

A standard approach for the computation of the maximum common subgraph of two graphs g_1 and g_2 is based on solving the *maximum clique problem* in the *association graph* of g_1 and g_2 [99, 100]. The association graph of two graphs represents the

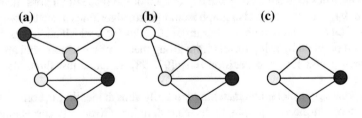

Fig. 1.5 Graph (**c**) is a maximum common subgraph of graph (**a**) and (**b**)

complete set of possible node-to-node mappings that preserve the edge structure and labels of both graphs. Finding a maximum clique in the association graph, that is, a fully connected maximal subgraph is then equivalent to finding a maximum common subgraph. In [101] the reader can find an experimental comparison of algorithms for maximum common subgraph computation on randomly connected graphs.

Given the maximum common subgraph of two graphs, various graph dissimilarity measures can be derived [83]. Roughly speaking, these dissimilarity measures are reciprocally proportional to the size of the maximum common subgraph of the two graphs (i.e., the larger the maximum common subgraph, the smaller the dissimilarity and vice versa). The distance measure introduced in [102], for instance, is defined by

$$d_{MCS}(g_1, g_2) = 1 - \frac{|mcs(g_1, g_2)|}{\max\{|g_1|, |g_2|\}}.$$

It has been shown that d_{MCS} is a metric and produces distances in [0, 1]. That is, if two graphs are isomorphic, their d_{MCS} distance is 0, while d_{MCS} equals 1, if two graphs have no part in common.

Another distance measure, which is also based on the maximum common subgraph, has been proposed in [103] and is formally defined by

$$d_{WGU}(g_1, g_2) = 1 - \frac{|mcs(g_1, g_2)|}{|g_1| + |g_2| - |mcs(g_1, g_2)|}.$$

The denominator $|g_1| + |g_2| - |mcs(g_1, g_2)|$ represents the size of the union of the two graphs in the set-theoretic sense. The motivation of using graph union in the denominator is to allow for changes in the smaller graph to exert some influence on the distance measure, which does not happen with d_{MCS}. This distance measure behaves similarly to d_{MCS}, i.e., for d_{WGU} it was also demonstrated to be a metric and it also creates distance values in [0, 1]. A further distance measure [104], which is not normalized to the interval [0, 1], is defined by

$$d_{UGU}(g_1, g_2) = |g_1| + |g_2| - 2|mcs(g_1, g_2)|.$$

Both distance models d_{WGU} and d_{UGU} can be reformulated by means of the minimum common supergraph. The *minimum common supergraph* can be interpreted as the complementary concept of the maximum common subgraph.

Definition 1.8 (*Minimum common supergraph*) Let $g_1 = (V_1, E_1, \mu_1, \nu_1)$ and $g_2 = (V_2, E_2, \mu_2, \nu_2)$ be graphs. A common supergraph of g_1 and g_2 is a graph $g = (V, E, \mu, \nu)$ such that there exist subgraph isomorphisms from g_1 to g and from g_2 to g. We call g a *minimum common supergraph* of g_1 and g_2 ($MCS(g_1, g_2)$) if there exists no other common supergraph of g_1 and g_2 that has less nodes than g.

Example 6 In Fig. 1.6a the minimum common supergraph of the graphs in Fig. 1.6b, c is given.

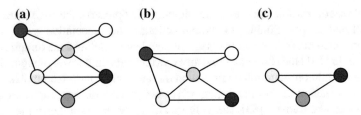

Fig. 1.6 Graph (**a**) is a minimum common supergraph of graph (**b**) and (**c**)

The computation of a minimum common supergraph can be reduced to the problem of computing a maximum common subgraph [105]. In particular, the size of the minimum common supergraph can be computed via the size of maximum common subgraph. Formally, we have

$$|MCS(g_1, g_2)| = |g_1| + |g_2| - |mcs(g_1, g_2)|. \tag{1.1}$$

Using Eq. 1.1, the dissimilarity $d_{UGU}(g_1, g_2)$ can now be rewritten with the aid of the minimum common supergraph (as proposed in [106]) as follows.

$$\begin{aligned} d_{UGU}(g_1, g_2) &= |g_1| + |g_2| - 2|mcs(g_1, g_2)| \\ &= |MCS(g_1, g_2)| - |mcs(g_1, g_2)| \end{aligned}$$

This reformulation gives rise to another intuition behind this distance measure. The maximum common subgraph provides a "lower bound" and the minimum supergraph an "upper bound" on the similarity of two graphs. If two graphs are identical, then both their maximum common subgraph and minimum common supergraph are the same as the original graphs. That is, $|g_1| = |g_2| = |MCS(g_1, g_2)| = |mcs(g_1, g_2)|$, which leads to $d_{MMCS}(g_1, g_2) = 0$. As the graphs become more dissimilar, the size of the maximum common subgraph decreases, while the size of the minimum supergraph increases. This in turn leads to increasing values of $d_{MMCS}(g_1, g_2)$. For two graphs with an empty maximum common subgraph, the distance will become $|MCS(g_1, g_2)| = |g_1| + |g_2|$. The distance $d_{MMCS}(g_1, g_2)$ has also been shown to be a metric, but it does not produce values normalized to the interval [0, 1]. We can also create a normalized version of this distance measure by [83]

$$d_{MMCSN}(g_1, g_2) = 1 - \frac{|mcs(g_1, g_2)|}{|MCS(g_1, g_2)|},$$

which is identical with d_{WGU} because of Eq. 1.1.

1.3.2 Error-Tolerant Graph Matching

The main advantage of exact graph matching is its stringent definition and its solid mathematical foundation. However, in exact graph matching for finding two graphs g_1 and g_2 to be similar, it is required that a significant part of the topology together with the corresponding node and edge labels in g_1 and g_2 have to be identical. In fact, this constraint is too rigid in various real-world applications and thus, a large number of error-tolerant, or inexact, graph matching methods have been proposed in the last few decades [81, 84, 85].

Error-tolerant graph matching is to dealing with a more general matching problem than the one of (sub)graph isomorphism or maximum common subgraph. In particular, error-tolerant graph matching relaxes and extends the concept of graph isomorphism (as stated in Definition 1.4) in three major points.

- First, mappings of nodes $u \in V_1$ to nodes $f(u) \in V_2$ with different labels ($\mu_1(u) \neq \mu_2(f(u))$) are possible in the error-tolerant case. The same accounts for the edges.
- Second, error-tolerant graph matching also allows node mappings that possibly violate the edge structure (while exact graph matching is edge-preserving in general).
- Third, error-tolerant graph matching explicitly allows the deletion of some nodes (and edges) of the first graph and/or the insertion of some nodes (and edges) of the second graph (rather than matching all nodes (and edges) of the involved graphs with a bijective function).

Definition 1.9 (*Error-tolerant Graph Matching*) Let $g_1 = (V_1, E_1, \mu_1, \nu_1)$ and $g_2 = (V_2, E_2, \mu_2, \nu_2)$ be two graphs. An *error-tolerant graph matching* is a mapping $f : V_1 \cup \{\varepsilon\} \rightarrow V_2 \cup \{\varepsilon\}$, where ε refers to the empty node. With respect to nonempty nodes in V_1 and V_2, mapping f is bijective. However, f allows that several nodes from V_1 are simultaneously mapped to the empty node ε, and likewise, ε can be mapped to several nodes from V_2. Formally, mapping f satisfies

1. $f(u_1) \neq \varepsilon \Rightarrow f(u_1) \neq f(u_2) \quad \forall u_1, u_2 \in V_1$
2. $f^{-1}(v_1) \neq \varepsilon \Rightarrow f^{-1}(v_1) \neq f^{-1}(v_2) \quad \forall v_1, v_2 \in V_2$

In an error-tolerant graph matching f, each node of g_1 is either mapped to ε (i.e., deleted) or uniquely matched with a node in g_2. Likewise, every node in g_2 is either a map of ε (i.e., inserted) or matched with a unique node in g_1. Note that the matching f is not restricted by the labeling of the nodes. Moreover, in contrast with graph isomorphism (and related concepts), where the edge structure as well as the edge labeling are merely preserved, the edges are actually processed in an error-tolerant matching.

Note, however, that this edge processing is always defined by the matching on their adjacent nodes. That is, whether an edge (u, v) is matched with an existing edge from the other graph or with the empty edge ε depends on the operations actually performed on both adjacent nodes u and v.

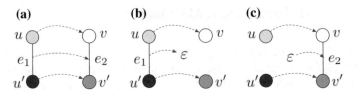

Fig. 1.7 Matchings on edges are uniquely defined by the matchings actually applied on both of their adjacent nodes. Three cases can be distinguished. **a** Case 1. **b** Case 2. **c** Case 3

Formally, let $u, u' \in V_1 \cup \{\varepsilon\}$ and $v, v' \in V_2 \cup \{\varepsilon\}$, and assume that both mappings $f(u) = v$ and $f(u') = v'$ are present in matching f. Depending on whether or not there is an edge $(u, u') \in E_1$ and/or an edge $(v, v') \in E_2$, the following three cases can be distinguished[2] (see also Fig. 1.7).

1. If there are edges $e_1 = (u, u') \in E_1$ and $e_2 = (v, v') \in E_2$, the edge mapping $e_1 \mapsto e_2$ is implied by $f(u) = v$ and $f(u') = v'$.
2. If there is an edge $e_1 = (u, u') \in E_1$ but no edge $e_2 = (v, v') \in E_2$, the edge deletion $e_1 \mapsto \varepsilon$ is implied by $f(u) = v$ and $f(u') = v'$. Obviously, if v and/or v' refer to the empty node ε there cannot be any edge $(v, v') \in E_2$ and thus the edge deletion $e_1 \mapsto \varepsilon$ becomes necessary.
3. If there is no edge $e_1 = (u, u') \in E_1$ but an edge $e_2 = (v, v') \in E_2$, the edge insertion $\varepsilon \mapsto e_2$ is implied by $f(u) = v$ and $f(u') = v'$. Similar to case 2, if $u = \varepsilon$ and/or $u' = \varepsilon$ there cannot be any edge $(u, u') \in E_1$.

Major advantage of error-tolerant graph matching (when compared to exact graph matching) is the integration of a certain tolerance to errors and noise in the matching process. This error tolerance particularly allows the definition of dissimilarities in a more general way than with the exact matching approaches. For instance, rather than merely evaluating whether or not two nodes are equal, an error-tolerant graph matching is able to measure the dissimilarity of the respective nodes (with respect to their labels). By assigning a high cost to mappings where the labels are dissimilar, and likewise, a low cost to mappings where the labels are similar, the matching process can be guided to match similar substructures of both graphs with each other.

Formally, error-tolerant graph matching algorithms aim at finding a mapping f from one graph to another such that the overall cost $c(f)$ of f is minimized. This *overall cost* $c(f)$ can be defined, for instance, by

---

[2]Note that these three cases are defined with respect to undirected edges. Yet, the generalization to directed edges can be readily accomplished.

$$
c(f) = \overbrace{\sum_{\substack{u \in V_1 \\ f(u) \neq \varepsilon}} c(u, f(u))}^{\textit{node mappings}} + \overbrace{\sum_{\substack{u \in V_1 \\ f(u) = \varepsilon}} c(u, \varepsilon)}^{\textit{node deletions}} + \overbrace{\sum_{\substack{v \in V_2 \\ f^{-1}(v) = \varepsilon}} c(\varepsilon, v)}^{\textit{node insertions}} +
$$

$$
\underbrace{\sum_{\substack{(u, v) \in E_1 \\ (f(u), f(v)) \in E_2}} c((u, v), (f(u), f(v)))}_{\textit{edge mappings}} + \underbrace{\sum_{\substack{(u, v) \in E_1 \\ (f(u), f(v)) \notin E_2}} c((u, v), \varepsilon)}_{\textit{edge deletions}} +
$$

$$
\underbrace{\sum_{\substack{(f(u), f(v)) \in E_2 \\ (u, v) \notin E_1}} c(\varepsilon, (f(u), f(v)))}_{\textit{edge insertions}}
$$

Note that this rather cumbersome definition of the overall cost $c(f)$ of matching f will be redefined in a more compact and elegant manner in the next chapter. Moreover, the definition of an adequate cost for individual node and edge mappings is revisited in Sect. 2.1.2.

The problem of optimizing the cost $c(f)$ of an error-tolerant graph matching f is known to be NP-complete. This means that the run time for minimizing $c(f)$ may be huge even for rather small graphs. Yet, in recent years several *approximate*, or *suboptimal*, algorithms for error-tolerant graph matching have been proposed [107–115]. These algorithms offer polynomial, rather than exponential, run times. Yet, in contrast to *optimal* error-tolerant graph matching, approximate algorithms do not guarantee to find the global minimum of the matching cost $c(f)$, but only a local one. Usually this approximation is not very far from the global one, but there are no guarantees [81].

A common way to make error-tolerant graph matching more efficient is to restrict considerations to special classes of graphs. Examples include the classes of ordered graphs [53], planar graphs [46], trees [52], or graphs with unique node labels [41].

Definition 1.9 is well established and widely used as a basis for the development of error-tolerant graph matching algorithms. However, various alternative approaches and definitions have been proposed in the literature [81, 84]. Three prominent families of error-tolerant graph matching algorithms that somehow differ in their basis to Definition 1.9, are briefly reviewed in the following (non-exhaustive) list.

- *Spectral methods* constitute an important class of error-tolerant graph matching procedures with a quite long tradition [116–128]. The general idea of this approach is based on the following observation. The eigenvalues and the eigenvectors of the adjacency or the *Laplacian matrix* of a graph (also known as *structural matrices*) are invariant with respect to node permutations. Hence, if two graphs are isomorphic, their structural matrices will have the same eigendecomposition. The

converse, i.e., deducing from the equality of eigendecompositions to graph isomorphism, is not true in general. However, by representing the underlying graphs
by means of the eigendecomposition of their structural matrices, the dissimilarity
computation on graphs can be conducted on specific features derived from their
eigendecomposition.

- *Graph kernels* constitute a second family of error-tolerant matching procedures
that partially differ in their foundation from Definition 1.9. Kernel methods were
originally developed for vectorial representations, but the kernel framework can
be extended to graphs in a very natural way [3, 129–131]. Graph kernels are special matching procedures in the sense of providing not only a graph dissimilarity
value but an implicit embedding of the graphs in a *Hilbert space*. This particular
embedding makes powerful kernel machines (e.g., *support vector machines* [132])
applicable to graphs.

  Various families of graph kernels emerged during the last decade. A seminal contribution is the work on *convolution kernels*, which provides a general framework
  for dealing with complex objects [133–138]. *Random walk kernels* measure the
  similarity of two graphs by the number of random walks in both graphs that have
  all or some labels in common [30, 55, 69, 131, 139–143]. *Diffusion kernels* are
  defined with respect to a base similarity measure which is then used to construct
  a valid kernel matrix [37, 144–148]. Various other kernels are discussed in [28,
  149–152]. These kernels are based on finding identical substructures in two graphs,
  such as common subgraphs, subtrees, and cycles.

- Clearly, the graph matching problem constitutes a *discrete optimization problem*.
  Yet, several attempts have been made to reformulate the graph matching problem to
  a *continuous optimization problem* (basically by relaxing some constraints). Major
  benefit of such a reformulation is that the transformed problem can be solved by
  means of existing algorithms stemming from the large arsenal of continuous optimization algorithms [153]. These algorithms typically provide a time complexity
  which is polynomial in the size of the problem (often with low exponent). Yet,
  they do not ensure the computation of an optimal solution (although there exist
  some techniques to avoid local optima). Furthermore, the solution found needs to
  be converted back from the continuous into the initial discrete problem domain by
  a process, which might introduce an additional level of approximation error [81].
  Based on the pioneering work presented in [154], the idea of continuous optimization for graph matching has been refined and extended in several contributions [51,
  155–166].

The present book is concerned with the graph matching paradigm of *graph edit
distance* [167, 168]. In fact, graph edit distance directly corresponds to the definition
of an error-tolerant graph matching as stated in Definition 1.9. Furthermore, with the
concept of graph edit distance we are able to cope with directed and undirected, as
well as with labeled and unlabeled graphs. If there are labels on nodes, edges, or both,
no constraints on the respective label alphabets have to be considered. Moreover,
through the use of application specific cost functions, graph edit distance can be
adapted and tailored to various problem specifications. Hence, the basic concept of

graph edit distance can be considered as one of the most flexible and versatile graph matching models available. The following chapter is concerned with a thorough and formal introduction to the concept of graph edit distance.

1.4 Outline of the Book

The present book is organized in two parts. Part I is concerned with the theoretic foundations, the basic concepts, and some recent applications of graph edit distance in pattern recognition.

- Chapter 2 formally introduces the concept of graph edit distance and shows some basic properties of this graph matching paradigm. In particular, it is shown how the cost function for graph edit distance can be appropriately defined. Moreover, it outlines a general algorithmic procedure for the exact computation of graph edit distance (based on a tree search). Finally, three different pattern recognition methodologies, which make use of graph edit distance, are presented (nearest neighbor classification, graph edit distance based kernels, and graph embedding via graph edit distance computation).
- In Chap. 3 we provide a proper reformulation of graph edit distance to a quadratic assignment problem. This reformulation builds the basis for a recent algorithmic framework for approximating the graph edit distance in cubic time [114]. This approximation framework in turn builds the basis for the remainder of the present book. During the last 5 years, several pattern recognition applications have emerged that make use of this graph edit distance approximation framework. The last section of this chapter gives a survey on these applications (including applications from biometric person authentication, chemoinformatics, document analysis, image and object recognition in various fields, keyword spotting, handwriting recognition, malware detection, ontology matching, and many others).

The graph edit distance approximation presented in Chap. 3 suffers from two major problems, viz., an overestimation of the true edit distance and a run time which may still be too high in certain applications. Part II of the present book is concerned with recent solutions for these two problems.

- The first problem has been recently addressed in various publications [169–175]. The corresponding line of research is reviewed in Chap. 4. In particular, various procedures for reducing the distance overestimation resulting from the approximation framework are presented. These procedure are either based on the post-processing search procedures or the integration of node centrality measures in the graph matching process.
- In Chap. 5 another possibility for the reduction of the overestimation is presented. This approach is based on machine learning. Precisely, we show how the true graph edit distance can be estimated by means of regression analysis that takes different approximations into account [176]. Moreover, it is shown how statistical classifiers

can be used to learn which of the node assignments returned by the approximation framework are incorrect with respect to an optimal graph matching [177].

- Although the existing approximation allows the computation of graph edit distance in cubic time, the time complexity of the complete approximation framework might still be too high, in particular for large-scale graphs and/or large-scale graph data sets. Chapter 6 reviews some recent attempts in making the algorithm for graph edit distance approximation substantially faster [178–181]. These extensions allow the approximation of graph edit distance in quadratic, rather than cubic, time.
- Finally, Chap. 7 summarizes the content and the main findings of the book and outlines the several options for future work.

References

1. R.O. Duda, P.E. Hart, D.G. Stork, *Pattern Classification* (Wiley-Interscience, New York, 2001)
2. M. Nadler, E.P. Smith, *Pattern Recognition Engineering* (Wiley, New York, 1992)
3. J. Shawe-Taylor, N. Cristianini, *Kernel Methods for Pattern Analysis* (Cambridge University Press, Cambridge, 2004)
4. U.-V. Marti, H. Bunke, Using a statistical language model to improve the performance of an HMM-based cursive handwriting recognition system. Int. J. Pattern Recognit. Artif. Intell. **15**, 65–90 (2001)
5. M. Liwicki, H. Bunke, Handwriting recognition of whiteboard notes—studying the influence of training set size and type. Int. J. Pattern Recognit. Artif. Intell. **21**(1), 83–98 (2007)
6. M. Liwicki, E. Indermühle, H. Bunke, On-line handwritten text line detection using dynamic programming, in *Proceedings of the 11th International Workshop on Frontiers in Handwriting Recognition*, pp. 186–191 (2008)
7. M. Zimmermann, J.-C. Chappelier, H. Bunke, Offline grammar-based recognition of handwritten sentences. IEEE Trans. Pattern Anal. Mach. Intell. **28**(5), 818–821 (2006)
8. R. Bertolami, S. Uchida, M. Zimmermann, H. Bunke, Non-uniform slant correction for handwritten text line recognition, in *Proceedings of the Ninth International Conference on Document Analysis and Recognition*, vol. 1, pp. 18–22 (2007)
9. M. Liwicki, S. Ebert, A. Dengel, Bridging the gap between handwriting recognition and knowledge management. Pattern Recognit. Lett. **35**, 204–213 (2014)
10. F. Sebastiani, Machine learning in automated text categorization. ACM Comput. Surv. **34**(1), 1–47 (2002)
11. A. Vinciarelli, Noisy text categorization, in *Proceedings of the 17th International Conference on Pattern Recognition*, vol. 2, pp. 554–557 (2004)
12. A. Juan, E. Vidal, On the use of Bernoulli mixture models for text classification. Pattern Recognit. **35**(12), 2705–2710 (2002)
13. R. Manmatha, T.M. Rath, Indexing of handwritten historical documents—recent progress. Symposium on document image understanding technology, pp. 77–85 (2003)
14. T.M. Rath, R. Manmatha, Word image matching using dynamic time warping, in *Proceedings of the International Conference on Computer Vision and Pattern Recognition*, pp. 521–527 (2003)
15. T.M. Rath, R. Manmatha, Word spotting for historical documents. Int. J. Doc. Anal. Recognit. **9**, 139–152 (2007)
16. A. Schlapbach, H. Bunke, A writer identification and verification system using HMM based recognizers. Pattern Anal. Appl. **10**(1), 33–43 (2007)

17. A. Schlapbach, H. Bunke, Off-line writer identification and verification using gaussian mixture models, in *Machine Learning in Document Analysis and Recognition*, vol. 90, ed. by S. Marinai, H. Fujisawa (Springer, Berlin, 2008)
18. A.K. Jain, S. Prabhakar, L. Hong, A multichannel approach to fingerprint classification. IEEE Trans. Pattern Anal. Mach. Intell. **21**(4), 348–359 (1999)
19. M. Neuhaus, H. Bunke, A graph matching based approach to fingerprint classification using directional variance, in *Proceedings of the 5th International Conference on Audio- and Video-Based Biometric Person Authentication*, LNCS, ed. by T. Kanade, A. Jain, N.K. Rath (Springer, New York, 2005), pp. 191–200
20. A. Serrau, G.L. Marcialis, H. Bunke, F. Roli, An experimental comparison of fingerprint classification methods using graphs, in *Proceedings of the 5th International Workshop on Graph-based Representations in Pattern Recognition*. LNCS, vol. 3434 (Springer, New York, 2005), pp. 281–290
21. L. Hong, A.K. Jain, Integrating faces and fingerprints for personal identification. IEEE Trans. Pattern Anal. Mach. Intell. **20**(12), 1295–1307 (1998)
22. N. Yager, A. Amin, Fingerprint classification: a review. Pattern Anal. Appl. **7**(1), 77–93 (2004)
23. G.L. Marcialis, F. Roli, A. Serrau, Fusion of statistical and structural fingerprint classifiers, in *4th International Conference Audio- and Video-Based Biometric Person Authentication*, LNCS, ed. by J. Kittler, M.S. Nixon (Springer, New York, 2003), pp. 310–317
24. E. Griechisch, M.I. Malik, M. Liwicki, Online signature verification based on kolmogorov-smirnov distribution distance, in *Proceedings of 14th International Conference on Frontiers in Handwriting Recognition*, pp. 738–742 (2014)
25. R.D. Brown, Y.C. Martin, Use of structure-activity data to compare structure-based clustering methods and descriptors for use in compound selection. J. Chem. Inf. Comput. Sci. **36**(3), 572–584 (1996)
26. P. Mahé, N. Ueda, T. Akutsu, Graph kernels for molecular structures-activity relationship analysis with support vector machines. J. Chem. Inf. Model. **45**(4), 939–951 (2005)
27. L. Brun, D. Conte, P. Foggia, M. Vento, Symbolic learning versus graph kernels: an experimental comparison in a chemical application, in *Proceedings of the Fourteenth East-European Conference on Advances in Databases and Information Systems*, ed. by I. Ivanovic, B. Thalheim, B. Catania, Z. Budimac (2010), pp. 31–40
28. B. Gaüzère, L. Brun, D. Villemin, Two new graphs kernels in chemoinformatics. Pattern Recognit. Lett. **33**(15), 2038–2047 (2012)
29. K. Borgwardt, H.-P. Kriegel, Graph kernels for disease outcome prediction from protein-protein interaction networks. Pacific symposium on biocomputing, pp. 4–15 (2007)
30. K. Borgwardt, C. Ong, S. Schönauer, S. Vishwanathan, A. Smola, H.-P. Kriegel, Protein function prediction via graph kernels. Bioinformatics **21**(1), 47–56 (2005)
31. C. Leslie, E. Eskin, W. Noble, The spectrum kernel: a string kernel for SVM protein classification, in *Proceedings of the Pacific Symposium on Biocomputing* (World Scientific, Singapore, 2002), pp. 564–575
32. C. Leslie, E. Eskin, A. Cohen, J. Weston, W. Noble, Mismatch string kernels for discriminative protein classification. Bioinformatics **20**(4), 467–476 (2004)
33. M. Song, C.M. Breneman, J. Bi, N. Sukumar, K.P. Bennett, S. Cramer, N. Tugcu, Prediction of protein retention times in anion-exchange chromatography systems using support vector machine regression. J. Chem. Inf. Comput. Sci. **42**(6), 1347–1357 (2002)
34. C. Bishop, *Pattern Recognition and Machine Learning* (Springer, New York, 2008)
35. T. Gärtner, *Kernels for Structured Data* (World Scientific, Singapore, 2008)
36. M. Neuhaus, H. Bunke, *Bridging the Gap Between Graph Edit Distance and Kernel Machines* (World Scientific, Singapore, 2007)
37. A. Smola, R. Kondor, Kernels and regularization on graphs, in *Proceedings of the 16th International Conference on Comptuational Learning Theory*. LNAI, vol. 2777 (Springer, Berlin, 2003), pp. 144–158
38. Y. Fu, Y. Ma (eds.), *Graph Embedding for Pattern Analysis* (Springer, New York, 2013)

39. P. Foggia, M. Vento, Graph embedding for pattern recognition, in *Proceedings of Recognizing Patterns in Signals, Speech, Images and Videos*. LNCS, vol. 6388 (2010), pp. 75–82
40. K. Riesen, H. Bunke, *Graph Classification and Clustering Based on Vector Space Embedding* (World Scientific, Singapore, 2010)
41. P. Dickinson, H. Bunke, A. Dadej, M. Kraetzl, On graphs with unique node labels, in *Proceedings of the 4th International Workshop on Graph Based Representations in Pattern Recognition*, vol. 2726, LNCS, ed. by E. Hancock, M. Ven (Springer, New York, 2003), pp. 13–23
42. P.J. Dickinson, H. Bunke, A. Dadej, M. Kraetzl, Matching graphs with unique node labels. Pattern Anal. Appl. **7**(3), 243–254 (2004)
43. P.J. Dickinson, M. Kraetzl, H. Bunke, M. Neuhaus, A. Dadej, Similarity measures for hierarchical representations of graphs with unique node labels. Int. J. Pattern Recognit. Artif. Intell. **18**(3), 425–442 (2004)
44. E.M. Luks, Isomorphism of graphs of bounded valence can be tested in polynomial time. J. Comput. Syst. Sci. **25**, 42–65 (1982)
45. P. Foggia, C. Sansone, M. Vento, A database of graphs for isomorphism and subgraph isomorphism benchmarking, in *Proceedings of the 3rd International Workshop on Graph Based Representations in Pattern Recognition*, pp. 176–187 (2001)
46. M. Neuhaus, H. Bunke, An error-tolerant approximate matching algorithm for attributed planar graphs and its application to fingerprint classification, in *Proceedings of the 10th International Workshop on SSPR*, vol. 3138, LNCS, ed. by A. Fred, et al. (2004), pp. 180–189
47. J.E. Hopcroft, J. Wong, Linear time algorithm for isomorphism of planar graphs, in *Proceedings of the 6th Annual ACM Symposium on Theory of Computing*, pp. 172–184 (1974)
48. K. Zhang, R. Statman, D. Shasha, On the editing distance between unordered labelled trees. Inf. Process. Lett. **42**(3), 133–139 (1992)
49. M. Pelillo, K. Siddiqi, S. Zucker, Matching hierarchical structures using association graphs. IEEE Trans. Pattern Anal. Mach. Intell. **21**(11), 1105–1120 (1999)
50. M. Pelillo, Matching free trees, maximal cliques and monotone game dynamics. IEEE Trans. Pattern Anal. Mach. Intell. **24**(11), 1535–1541 (2002)
51. A. Torsello, E. Hancock, Computing approximate tree edit distance using relaxation labeling. Pattern Recognit. Lett. **24**(8), 1089–1097 (2003)
52. A. Torsello, D. Hidovic-Rowe, M. Pelillo, Polynomial-time metrics for attributed trees. IEEE Trans. Pattern Anal. Mach. Intell. **27**(7), 1087–1099 (2005)
53. X. Jiang, H. Bunke, Optimal quadratic-time isomorphism of ordered graphs. Pattern Recognit. **32**(17), 1273–1283 (1999)
54. D. Conte, P. Foggia, C. Sansone, M. Vento, Graph matching applications in pattern recognition and image processing, in *Proceedings of the 2003 International Conference on Image Processing*, vol. 3, pp. II–21–24 (2003)
55. L. Ralaivola, S.J. Swamidass, H. Saigo, P. Baldi, Graph kernels for chemical informatics. Neural Netw. **18**(8), 1093–1110 (2005)
56. J.W. Raymond, P. Willett, Maximum common subgraph isomorphism algorithms for the matching of chemical structures. J. Comput.-Aided Mol. Des. **16**(7), 521–533 (2002)
57. J. Kinable, O. Kostakis, Malware classification based on call graph clustering. J. Comput. Virol. **7**(4), 233–245 (2011)
58. M. Bourquin, A. King, E. Robbins, Binslayer: accurate comparison of binary executables, in *Proceedings of the 2nd ACM SIGPLAN Program Protection and Reverse Engineering Workshop* (2013)
59. A.A.E. Elhadi, M.A. Maarof, A.H. Osman, Malware detection based on hybrid signature behaviour application programming interface call graph. Am. J. Appl. Sci. **9**(3), 283–288 (2012)
60. O. Kostakis, H. Mahmoudi, J. Kinable, K. Mustonen, Improved call graph comparison using simulated annealing, in *Proceedings of the 2011 ACM Symposium on Applied Computing*, pp. 1516–1523 (2011)
61. O. Kostakis, Classy: fast clustering streams of call-graphs. Data Min. Knowl. Discov. **28**(5–6), 1554–1585 (2014)

62. M. Zhang, Y. Duan, H. Yin, Z. Zhao, Semantics-aware android malware classification using weighted contextual api dependency graphs, in *Proceedings of the 2014 ACM SIGSAC Conference on Computer and Communications Security*, pp. 1105–1116 (2014)
63. M.L. Kammer, Plagiarism detection in haskell programs using call graph matching. Master's thesis, Utrecht University (2011)
64. H. Bunke, K. Riesen, Recent advances in graph-based pattern recognition with applications in document analysis. Pattern Recognit. **44**(5), 1057–1067 (2011)
65. A. Schenker, M. Last, H. Bunke, A. Kandel, Classification of web documents using graph matching. Int. J. Pattern Recognit. Artif. Intell. **18**(3), 475–496 (2004)
66. A. Schenker, H. Bunke, M. Last, A. Kandel, *Graph-Theoretic Techniques for Web Content Mining* (World Scientific, Singapore, 2005)
67. A. Brügger, H. Bunke, P. Dickinson, K. Riesen, Generalized graph matching for data mining and information retrieval, in *Advances in Data Mining*, vol. 5077, Medical Applications, E-Commerce, Marketing, and Theoretical Aspects, LNCS, ed. by P. Perner (Springe, New York, 2008), pp. 298–312
68. K. Baxter, J. Glasgow, Protein structure determination, combining inexact graph matching and deformable templates, in *Proceedings of the Vision, Interface*, pp. 179–186 (2000)
69. K. Borgwardt, H.-P. Kriegel, Shortest-path kernels on graphs, in *Proceedings of the 5th IEEE International Conference on Data Mining* (IEEE, Los Alamitos, 2005), pp. 74–81
70. H. Bunke, M. Kraetzl, P. Shoubridge, W.D. Wallis, Detection of abnormal change in time series of graphs. J. Interconnect. Netw. **3**(1–2), 85–101 (2002)
71. H. Bunke, P. Dickinson, A. Humm, C.H. Irniger, M. Kraetzl, Computer network monitoring and abnormal event detection using graph matching and multidimensional scaling, in *Advances in Data Mining Proceedings of the 6th Industrial Conference on Data Mining, ICDM*, vol. 4065, LNAI, ed. by P. Perner (Springer, New York, 2006), pp. 576–590
72. M.E.J. Newman, *Networks—An Introduction* (Oxford University Press, Oxford, 2010)
73. M.E.J. Newman, A measure of betweenness centrality on random walks. Soc. Netw. **27**, 39–54 (2005)
74. A. Fischer, K. Riesen, H. Bunke, Graph similarity features for HMM-based handwriting recognition in historical documents, in *Proceedings of the International Conference on Frontiers in Handwriting Recognition*, pp. 253–258 (2010)
75. A. Fischer, C.Y. Suen, V. Frinken, K. Riesen, H. Bunke, A fast matching algorithm for graph-based handwriting recognition, in *Proceedings of the 8th International Workshop on Graph Based Representations in Pattern Recognition*, vol. 7877, LNCS, ed. by W. Kropatsch, N. Artner, Y. Haxhimusa, X. Jiang (2013), pp. 194–203
76. J. Lladós, E. Martí, J. Villanueva, Symbol recognition by error-tolerant subgraph matching between region adjacency graphs. IEEE Trans. Pattern Anal. Mach. Intell. **23**(10), 1137–1143 (2001)
77. J. Lladós, G. Sánchez, Graph matching versus graph parsing in graphics recognition. Int. J. Pattern Recognit. Artif. Intell. **18**(3), 455–475 (2004)
78. M. Ferrer, E. Valveny, F. Serratosa, Spectral median graphs applied to graphical symbol recognition, in *Proceedings of the 11th Iberoamerican Congress in Pattern Recognition, CIARP*. LNCS, vol. 4225 (2006), pp. 774–783
79. K. Riesen and H. Bunke. IAM graph database repository for graph based pattern recognition and machine learning, in *Structural, Syntactic, and Statistical Pattern Recognition*, vol. 5342, LNCS, ed by N. da Vitoria Lobo et al. (2008), pp. 287–297
80. K. Borgwardt, Graph kernels. Ph.D. thesis, Ludwig-Maximilians-University Munich (2007)
81. D. Conte, P. Foggia, C. Sansone, M. Vento, Thirty years of graph matching in pattern recognition. Int. J. Pattern Recognit. Artif. Intell. **18**(3), 265–298 (2004)
82. H. Bunke, Recent developments in graph matching, in *Proceedings of the 15th International Conference on Pattern Recognition*, vol. 2, pp. 117–124 (2000)
83. K. Riesen, X. Jiang, H. Bunke, Exact and Inexact Graph Matching: Methodology and Applications, *Managing and Mining Graph Data* (Springer, New York, 2010)

84. P. Foggia, G. Percannella, M. Vento, Graph matching and learning in pattern recognition in the last 10 years. Int. J. Pattern Recognit. Artif. Intell. **28**(1), 40 (2014)
85. L. Livi, A. Rizzi, The graph matching problem. Pattern Anal. Appl. **16**, 253–283 (2013)
86. R.M. Karp, Reducibility among combinatorial problems, in *Complexity of Computer Computations*, ed. by R.E. Miller, J.W. Thatcher, pp. 85–103 (1972)
87. M.R. Garey, D.S. Johnson., *Computers and Intractability: A Guide to the Theory of NP-Completeness* (Freeman and Co., New York, 1979)
88. J.R. Ullmann, An algorithm for subgraph isomorphism. J. Assoc. Comput. Mach. **23**(1), 31–42 (1976)
89. L.P. Cordella, P. Foggia, C. Sansone, M. Vento, Performance evaluation of the VF graph matching algorithm, in *International Conference on Image Analysis and Processing*, pp. 1172–1177 (1999)
90. L.P. Cordella, P. Foggia, C. Sansone, M. Vento, Fast graph matching for detecting CAD image components, in *Proceedings of the 15th International Conference on Pattern Recognition*, vol. 2, pp. 1038–1041 (2000)
91. J. Larrosa, G. Valiente, Constraint satisfaction algorithms for graph pattern matching. Math. Struct. Comput. Sci. **12**(4), 403–422 (2002)
92. S. Zampelli, Y. Deville, C. Solnon, Solving subgraph isomorphism problems with constraint programming. Constraints **15**, 327–353 (2010)
93. J.R. Ullmann, Bit-vector algorithms for binary constraint satisfaction and subgraph isomorphism. J. Exp. Algorithm. **15**, 1.6:1.1–1.6:1.64 (2011)
94. C. Solnon, All different-based filtering for subgraph isomorphism. Artif. Intell. **174**, 850–864 (2010)
95. B.D. McKay, Practical graph isomorphism. Congressus Numerantium **30**, 45–87 (1981)
96. M. Gori, M. Maggini, L. Sarti, Exact and approximate graph matching using random walks. IEEE Trans. Pattern Anal. Mach. Intell. **27**(7), 1100–1111 (2005)
97. B.T. Messmer, H. Bunke, A decision tree approach to graph and subgraph isomorphism detection. Pattern Recognit. **32**, 1979–1998 (1008)
98. M. Weber, M. Liwicki, A. Dengel, Indexing with well-founded total order for faster subgraph isomorphism detection, in *Proceedings of Graph-Based Representations in Pattern Recognition*, LNCS, ed. by X. Jiang, M. Ferrer, A. Torsello (2011), pp. 185–194
99. G. Levi, A note on the derivation of maximal common subgraphs of two directed or undirected graphs. Calcolo **9**, 341–354 (1972)
100. J.J. McGregor, Backtrack search algorithms and the maximal common subgraph problem. Softw. Pract. Exp. **12**, 23–34 (1982)
101. H. Bunke, P. Foggia, C. Guidobaldi, C. Sansone, M. Vento, A comparison of algorithms for maximum common subgraph on randomly connected graphs, in *Structural, Syntactic, and Statistical Pattern Recognition*, vol. 2396, LNCS, ed. by T. Caelli, A. Amin, R. Duin, M. Kamel, D. de Ridder (Springer, New York, 2002), pp. 85–106
102. H. Bunke, K. Shearer, A graph distance metric based on the maximal common subgraph. Pattern Recognit. Lett. **19**(3–4), 255–259 (1998)
103. W.D. Wallis, P. Shoubridge, M. Kraetzl, D. Ray, Graph distances using graph union. Pattern Recognit. Lett. **22**(6), 701–704 (2001)
104. H. Bunke, On a relation between graph edit distance and maximum common subgraph. Pattern Recognit. Lett. **18**, 689–694 (1997)
105. H. Bunke, X. Jiang, A. Kandel, On the minimum common supergraph of two graphs. Computing **65**(1), 13–25 (2000)
106. M.-L. Fernandez, G. Valiente, A graph distance metric combining maximum common subgraph and minimum common supergraph. Pattern Recognit. Lett. **22**(6–7), 753–758 (2001)
107. M.C. Boeres, C.C. Ribeiro, I. Bloch, A randomized heuristic for scene recognition by graph matching, in *Proceedings of the 3rd Workshop on Efficient and Experimental Algorithms*, vol. 3059, LNCS, ed. by C.C. Ribeiro, S.L. Martins (Springer, New York, 2004), pp. 100–113
108. S. Sorlin, C. Solnon, Reactive tabu search for measuring graph similarity, in *Proceedings of the 5th International Workshop on Graph-based Representations in Pattern Recognition*, vol. 3434, LNCS, ed. by L. Brun, M. Vento (Springer, New York, 2005), pp. 172–182

109. M. Neuhaus, K. Riesen, H. Bunke, Fast suboptimal algorithms for the computation of graph edit distance, in *Proceedings of the 11th International Workshop on Strucural and Syntactic Pattern Recognition*, vol. 4109, LNCS, ed. by D.-Y. Yeung, J.T. Kwok, A. Fred, F. Roli, D. de Ridder (2006), pp. 163–172

110. D. Justice, A. Hero, A binary linear programming formulation of the graph edit distance. IEEE Trans. Pattern Anal. Mach. Intell. **28**(8), 1200–1214 (2006)

111. M.A. Eshera, K.S. Fu, A graph distance measure for image analysis. IEEE Trans. Syst. Man Cybern. (Part B) **14**(3), 398–408 (1984)

112. M.A. Eshera, K.S. Fu, A similarity measure between attributed relational graphs for image analysis, in *Proceedings of the 7th International Confernece on Pattern Recognition*, pp. 75–77 (1984)

113. K. Riesen, M. Neuhaus, H. Bunke, Bipartite graph matching for computing the edit distance of graphs, in *Proceedings of the 6th International Workshop on Graph Based Representations in Pattern Recognition*, vol. 4538, LNCS, ed. by F. Escolano, M. Vento (2007), pp. 1–12

114. K. Riesen, H. Bunke, Approximate graph edit distance computation by means of bipartite graph matching. Image Vis. Comput. **27**(4), 950–959 (2009)

115. F. Serratosa, Fast computation of bipartite graph matching. Pattern Recognit. Lett. **45**, 244–250 (2014)

116. S. Umeyama, An eigendecomposition approach to weighted graph matching problems. IEEE Trans. Pattern Anal. Mach. Intell. **10**(5), 695–703 (1988)

117. T. Caelli, S. Kosinov, Inexact graph matching using eigen-subspace projection clustering. Int. J. Pattern Recognit. Artif. Intell. **18**(3), 329–355 (2004)

118. T. Caelli, S. Kosinov, An eigenspace projection clustering method for inexact graph matching. IEEE Trans. Pattern Anal. Mach. Intell. **26**(4), 515–519 (2004)

119. A. Shokoufandeh, D. Macrini, S. Dickinson, K. Siddiqi, S.W. Zucker, Indexing hierarchical structures using graph spectra. IEEE Trans. Pattern Anal. Mach. Intell. **27**(7), 1125–1140 (2005)

120. B. Luo, R. Wilson, E. Hancock, Spectral feature vectors for graph clustering, in *Structural, Syntactic, and Statistical Pattern Recognition*, vol. 2396, LNCS, ed. by T. Caelli, A. Amin, R. Duin, M. Kamel, D. de Ridder (Springer, New York, 2002), pp. 83–93

121. A. Robles-Kelly, E.R. Hancock, String edit distance, random walks and graph matching. Int. J. Pattern Recognit. Artif. Intell. **18**(3), 315–327 (2004)

122. A. Robles-Kelly, E.R. Hancock, Graph edit distance from spectral seriation. IEEE Trans. Pattern Anal. Mach. Intell. **27**(3), 365–378 (2005)

123. S. Kosinov, T. Caelli, Inexact multisubgraph matching using graph eigenspace and clustering models, in *Structural, Syntactic, and Statistical Pattern Recognition*, vol. 2396, LNCS, ed. by T. Caelli, A. Amin, R. Duin, M. Kamel, D. de Ridder (Springer, New York, 2002), pp. 133–142

124. R.C. Wilson, E.R. Hancock, B. Luo, Pattern vectors from algebraic graph theory. IEEE Trans. Pattern Anal. Mach. Intell. **27**(7), 1112–1124 (2005)

125. A. Robles-Kelly, E.R. Hancock, A Riemannian approach to graph embedding. Pattern Recognit. **40**, 1024–1056 (2007)

126. H. Qiu, E.R. Hancock, Graph matching and clustering using spectral partitions. Pattern Recognit. **39**(1), 22–34 (2006)

127. H. Qiu, E.R. Hancock, Graph simplication and matching using commute times. Pattern Recognit. **40**(10), 2874–2889 (2007)

128. R.C. Wilson, P. Zhu, A study of graph spectra for comparing graphs and trees. Pattern Recognit. **41**(9), 2833–2841 (2008)

129. B. Schölkopf, A. Smola, *Learning with Kernels* (MIT Press, Cambridge, 2002)

130. T. Gärtner, A survey of kernels for structured data. SIGKDD Explor. **5**(1), 49–58 (2003)

131. T. Gärtner, P. Flach, S. Wrobel, On graph kernels: hardness results and efficient alternatives, in *Proceedings of the 16th Annual Conference on Learning Theory*, ed. by B. Schölkopf, M. Warmuth (2003), pp. 129–143

132. C. Burges, A tutorial on support vector machines for pattern recognition. Data Min. Knowl. Discov. **2**(2), 121–167 (1998)
133. D. Haussler, Convolution kernels on discrete structures. Technical report UCSC-CRL-99-10, University of California, Santa Cruz (1999)
134. C. Watkins, Dynamic alignment kernels, in *Advances in Large Margin Classifiers*, ed. by A. Smola, P.L. Bartlett, B. Schölkopf, D. Schuurmans (MIT Press, Cambridge, 2000), pp. 39–50
135. C. Watkins, Kernels from matching operations. Technical report CSD-TR-98-07, Royal Holloway College (1999)
136. K. Borgwardt, T. Petri, H.-P. Kriegel, S. Vishwanathan, An efficient sampling scheme for comparison of large graphs, in *Proceedings of the 5th. International Workshop on Mining and Learning with Graphs*, ed. by P. Frasconi, K. Kersting, K. Tsuda (2007)
137. L. Rossi, A. Torsello, E. Hancock, A continuous-time quantum walk kernel for unattributed graphs, in *Proceedings of the 9th International Workshop on Graph Based Representations in Pattern Recognition*, ed. by W. Kropatsch, N. Artner, Y. Haxhimusa, X. Jiang (2013), pp. 101–110
138. L. Bai, L. Rossi, A. Torsello, E.R. Hancock, A quantum Jensen–Shannon graph kernel for unattributed graphs. Pattern Recognit. **48**(2), 344–355 (2015)
139. T. Gärtner, Exponential and geometric kernels for graphs, in *NIPS Workshop on Unreal Data: Principles of Modeling Nonvectorial Data* (2002)
140. H. Kashima, A. Inokuchi, Kernels for graph classification, in *Proceedings of the ICDM Workshop on Active Mining* (2002), pp. 31–36
141. H. Kashima, K. Tsuda, A. Inokuchi, Marginalized kernels between labeled graphs, in *Proceedings of the 20th International Conference on Machine Learning* (AAAI Press, 2003), pp. 321–328
142. S.V.N. Vishwanathan, K. Borgwardt, N.N. Schraudolph, Fast computation of graph kernels, in *Proceedings of the 20th Annual Conference on Neural Information Processing Systems* (MIT Press, Cambridge, 2006), pp. 1449–1456
143. J. Lebrun, P.H. Gosselin, S. Philipp-Foliguet, Inexact graph matching based on kernels for object retrieval in image databases. Image Vis. Comput. **29**(11), 716–729 (2011)
144. R.I. Kondor, J. Lafferty, Diffusion kernels on graphs and other discrete input spaces, in *Proceedings of the 19th International Conference on Machine Learning* (2002), pp. 315–322
145. J. Kandola, J. Shawe-Taylor, N. Cristianini, Learning semantic similarity. Neural Inf. Process. Syst. **15**, 657–664 (2002)
146. J. Lafferty, G. Lebanon, Information diffusion kernels, in *Advances in Neural Information Processing Systems*, vol. 15 (MIT Press, Cambridge, 2003), pp. 375–382
147. J.-P. Vert, M. Kanehisa, Graph-driven features extraction from microarray data using diffusion kernels and kernel CCA, in *Advances in Neural Information Processing Systems* (MIT Press, Cambridge, 2003), pp. 1425–1432
148. J. Lafferty, G. Lebanon, Diffusion kernels on statistical manifolds. J. Mach. Learn. Res. **6**, 129–163 (2005)
149. J. Ramon, T. Gärtner, Expressivity versus efficiency of graph kernels, in *Proceedings of the First International Workshop on Mining Graphs, Trees and Sequences* (2003), pp. 65–74
150. T. Horvath, T. Gärtner, S. Wrobel, Cyclic pattern kernels for predictive graph mining, in *Proceedings of the International Conference on Knowledge Discovery and Data Mining* (ACM Press, New York, 2004), pp. 65–74
151. B. Gauzere, L. Brun, D. Villemin, Two new graph kernels and applications to chemoinformatics, in *Proceedings of the 8th International Workshop on Graph Based Representations in Pattern Recognition*, ed. by X. Jiang, M. Ferrer, A. Torsello (2011), pp. 112–121
152. B. Gauzere, P.A. Grenier, L. Brun, D. Villemin, Treelet kernel incorporating cyclic, stereo and inter pattern information in chemoinformatics. Pattern Recognit. **48**(2), 356–367 (2015)
153. N. Gould, An introduction to algorithms for continuous optimization. Oxford University Computing Laboratory Notes (2006)
154. M.A. Fischler, R.A. Elschlager, The representation and matching of pictorial structures. IEEE Trans. Comput. **22**(1), 67–92 (1973)

155. J. Kittler, E.R. Hancock, Combining evidence in probabilistic relaxation. Int. J. Pattern Recognit. Artif. Intell. **3**(1), 29–51 (1989)
156. S. Gold, A. Rangarajan, A graduated assignment algorithm for graph matching. IEEE Trans. Pattern Anal. Mach. Intell. **18**(4), 377–388 (1996)
157. E.R. Hancock, J. Kittler, Discrete relaxation. Pattern Recognit. **23**(7), 711–733 (1990)
158. W.J. Christmas, J. Kittler, M. Petrou, Structural matching in computer vision using probabilistic relaxation. IEEE Trans. Pattern Anal. Mach. Intell. **17**(8), 749–764 (1995)
159. R.C. Wilson, E. Hancock, Structural matching by discrete relaxation. IEEE Trans. Pattern Anal. Mach. Intell. **19**(6), 634–648 (1997)
160. R. Myers, R.C. Wilson, E.R. Hancock, Bayesian graph edit distance. IEEE Trans. Pattern Anal. Mach. Intell. **22**(6), 628–635 (2000)
161. H. Wang, E.R. Hancock, Probabilistic relaxation labelling using the Fokker–Planck equation. Pattern Recognit. **41**(11), 3393–3411 (2008)
162. M.A. van Wyk, T.S. Durrani, B.J. van Wyk, A RKHS interpolator-based graph matching algorithm. IEEE Trans. Pattern Anal. Mach. Intell. **24**(7), 988–995 (2003)
163. M.A. van Wyk, J. Clark, An algorithm for approximate least-squares attributed graph matching. Probl. Appl. Math. Comput. Intell., 67–72 (2000)
164. B. Huet, E.R. Hancock, Shape recognition from large image libraries by inexact graph matching. Pattern Recognit. Lett. **20**(11–13), 1259–1269 (1999)
165. M. Zaslavskiy, F. Bach, J.-P. Vert, A path following algorithm for the graph matching problem. IEEE Trans. Pattern Anal. Mach. Intell. **31**(12), 2227–2242 (2009)
166. B. Luo, E. Hancock, Structural graph matching using the EM algorithm and singular value decomposition. IEEE Trans. Pattern Anal. Mach. Intell. **23**(10), 1120–1136 (2001)
167. H. Bunke, G. Allermann, Inexact graph matching for structural pattern recognition. Pattern Recognit. Lett. **1**, 245–253 (1983)
168. A. Sanfeliu, K.S. Fu, A distance measure between attributed relational graphs for pattern recognition. IEEE Trans. Syst. Man Cybern. (Part B), **13**(3), 353–363 (1983)
169. K. Riesen, A. Fischer, H. Bunke, Improving graph edit distance approximation by centrality measures, in *Proceedings of the 22nd International Conference on Pattern Recognition* (2014), pp. 3910–3914
170. K. Riesen, R. Dornberger, H. Bunke, Iterative bipartite graph edit distance approximation, in *Proceedings of the 11th IAPR International Workshop on Document Analysis Systems*, ed. by J.Y. Ramel, M. Liwicki, J.-M. Ogier, K. Kise, R. Smith (2014), pp. 61–65
171. K. Riesen, H. Bunke, Improving approximate graph edit distance by means of a greedy swap strategy, in *Proceedings of the ICISP*, vol. 8509, LNCS, ed. by A. Elmoataz, O. Lezoray, F. Nouboud, D. Mammass (2014), pp. 314–321
172. K. Riesen, A. Fischer, H. Bunke, Improving approximate graph edit distance using genetic algorithms, in *Proceedings of the International Workshop on Structural and Syntactic Pattern Recognition*, vol. 8621, LNCS, ed. by P. Fränti, G. Brown, M. Loog, F. Escolano, M. Pelillo (2014), pp. 63–72
173. K. Riesen, A. Fischer, H. Bunke, Combining bipartite graph matching and beam search for graph edit distance approximation, in *Proceedings of the International Workshop on Artificial Neural Networks in Pattern Recognition*, ed. by N.E. Gayar, F. Schwenker, Ch. Suen (2014), pp. 117–128
174. K. Riesen, H. Bunke, Improving bipartite graph edit distance approximation using various search strategies. Pattern Recognit. **48**(4), 1349–1363 (2015)
175. M. Ferrer, F. Serratosa, K. Riesen, A first step towards exact graph edit distance using bipartite graph matching, in *Proceedings of the 10th International Workshop on Graph Based Representations in Pattern Recognition*, vol. 9069, LNCS, ed. by C.L. Liu, B. Luo, W. Kropatsch, J. Cheng (2015), pp. 77–86
176. K. Riesen, A. Fischer, H. Bunke, Estimating graph edit distance using lower and upper bounds of bipartite approximations. Int. J. Pattern Recognit. Artif. Intell. **29**(2), 1550011 (2015)
177. M. Ferrer, F. Serratosa, K. Riesen, Learning heuristics to reduce the overestimation of bipartite graph edit distance approximation, in *Proceedings of the 11th International Conference on*

Machine Learning and Data Mining in Pattern Recognition, vol. 9166, LNAI, ed. by P. Perner (2015), pp. 1–15

178. K. Riesen, M. Ferrer, A. Fischer, H. Bunke, Approximation of graph edit distance in quadratic time, in *Proceedings of the 10th International Workshop on Graph Based Representations in Pattern Recognition*, vol. 9069, LNCS, ed. by C.L. Liu, B. Luo, W. Kropatsch, J. Cheng (2015), pp. 3–12

179. K. Riesen, M. Ferrer, R. Dornberger, H. Bunke, Greedy graph edit distance, in *Proceedings of the 11th International Conference on Machine Learning and Data Mining in Pattern Recognition*, vol. 9166, LNAI, ed. by P. Perner (2015), pp. 1–14

180. K. Riesen, M. Ferrer, H. Bunke, Approximate graph edit distance in quadratic time. Accepted for publication in IEEE/ACM Transactions on Computational Biology and Bioinformatics

181. K. Riesen, M. Ferrer, H. Bunke, Suboptimal graph edit distance based on sorted local assignments, in *Proceedings of the 12th International Workshop on Multiple Classifier Systems*, ed. by F. Schwenker, F. Roli, J. Kittler (2015), pp. 147–156

Chapter 2
Graph Edit Distance

Abstract Graph edit distance measures distances between two graphs g_1 and g_2 by the amount of distortion that is needed to transform g_1 into g_2. The basic distortion operations of graph edit distance can cope with arbitrary labels on both nodes and edges as well as with directed or undirected edges. Therefore, graph edit distance is one of the most flexible dissimilarity models available for graphs. The present chapter gives a formal definition of graph edit distance as well as some basic properties of this distance model. In particular, it presents an overview of how the cost model can be chosen in a certain graph edit distance application. Moreover, the exact computation of graph edit distance based on a tree search algorithm is outlined. In the last section of this chapter, three general approaches for graph edit distance-based pattern recognition are briefly reviewed.

2.1 Basic Definition and Properties

The basic idea of *edit distance* is to derive a dissimilarity measure from the number as well as the strength of the distortions that have to be applied to transform a source pattern into a target pattern. Originally, the concept of edit distance has been proposed for string representations [1, 2]. Eventually, the edit distance has been extended from strings to more general data structures such as trees [3] and graphs [4–8] (see [9] for a recent survey on the development of graph edit distance).

Given two graphs, the source graph $g_1 = (V_1, E_1, \mu_1, \nu_1)$ and the target graph $g_2 = (V_2, E_2, \mu_2, \nu_2)$, the basic idea of graph edit distance is to transform g_1 into g_2 using some edit operations. A standard set of edit operations is given by *insertions*, *deletions*, and *substitutions* of both nodes and edges. Note that other edit operations such as *merging* or *splitting* of both nodes and edges might be useful in some applications but not considered in the present book (we refer to [10] for an application of additional edit operations). We denote the substitution of two nodes $u \in V_1$ and $v \in V_2$ by $(u \rightarrow v)$, the deletion of node $u \in V_1$ by $(u \rightarrow \varepsilon)$, and the insertion of node $v \in V_2$ by $(\varepsilon \rightarrow v)$, where ε refers to the empty node. For edge edit operations we use a similar notation.

© Springer International Publishing Switzerland 2015
K. Riesen, *Structural Pattern Recognition with Graph Edit Distance*,
Advances in Computer Vision and Pattern Recognition,
DOI 10.1007/978-3-319-27252-8_2

Definition 2.1 (*Edit Path*) A set $\{e_1, \dots, e_k\}$ of k edit operations e_i that transform g_1 completely into g_2 is called a *(complete) edit path* $\lambda(g_1, g_2)$ between g_1 and g_2. A *partial edit path*, i.e., a subset of $\{e_1, \dots, e_k\}$, edits proper subsets of nodes and/or edges of the underlying graphs.

Note that the definition of an edit path perfectly corresponds to the definition of an error tolerant graph matching stated in Chap. 1 (see Definition 1.9). Remember that the matching of the edge structure is uniquely defined via operations which are actually carried out on the nodes (see the discussion about implicit edge mappings derived from node mappings in Sect. 1.3.2). The same applies for edit operations. That is, it is sufficient that an edit path $\lambda(g_1, g_2)$ covers the nodes from V_1 and V_2 only. Thus, from now on we assume that an edit path $\lambda(g_1, g_2)$ explicitly describes the correspondences found between the graphs' nodes V_1 and V_2, while the edge edit operations are implicitly given by these node correspondences.

Example 7 In Fig. 2.1 an edit path $\lambda(g_1, g_2)$ between two undirected and unlabeled graphs g_1 and g_2 is illustrated. Obviously, this edit path is defined by

$$\lambda = \{(u_1 \to \varepsilon), (u_2 \to v_3), (u_3 \to v_2), (u_4 \to v_1)\}.$$

This particular edit path implies the following edge edit operations:

$$\{((u_1, u_2) \to \varepsilon), ((u_2, u_3) \to (v_3, v_2)), ((u_3, u_4) \to (v_2, v_1)), ((u_2, u_4) \to \varepsilon)\}.$$

Let $\Upsilon(g_1, g_2)$ denote the set of all complete edit paths between two graphs g_1 and g_2. To find the most suitable edit path out of $\Upsilon(g_1, g_2)$, one introduces a cost $c(e)$ for every edit operation e, measuring the strength of the corresponding operation. The idea of such a cost is to define whether or not an edit operation e represents a strong modification of the graph. Clearly, between two similar graphs, there should exist an inexpensive edit path, representing low-cost operations, while for dissimilar graphs an edit path with high cost is needed. Consequently, the edit distance of two graphs is defined as follows.

Definition 2.2 (*Graph Edit Distance*) Let $g_1 = (V_1, E_1, \mu_1, \nu_1)$ be the source and $g_2 = (V_2, E_2, \mu_2, \nu_2)$ the target graph. The *graph edit distance* $d_{\lambda_{\min}}(g_1, g_2)$, or $d_{\lambda_{\min}}$ for short, between g_1 and g_2 is defined by

$$d_{\lambda_{\min}}(g_1, g_2) = \min_{\lambda \in \Upsilon(g_1, g_2)} \sum_{e_i \in \lambda} c(e_i), \tag{2.1}$$

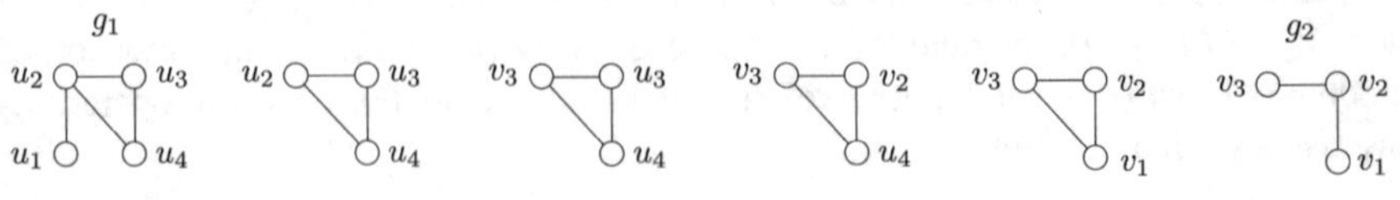

Fig. 2.1 An edit path λ between two graphs g_1 and g_2

where $\Upsilon(g_1, g_2)$ denotes the set of all complete edit paths transforming g_1 into g_2, c denotes the cost function measuring the strength $c(e_i)$ of node edit operation e_i (including the cost of all edge edit operations implied by the operations applied on the adjacent nodes of the edges), and $\lambda_{\min}$ refers to the minimal cost edit path found in $\Upsilon(g_1, g_2)$.

Clearly, there might be two (or more) edit paths with equal minimal cost in $\Upsilon(g_1, g_2)$. That is, the minimal cost edit path $\lambda_{\min} \in \Upsilon(g_1, g_2)$ is not necessarily unique.

2.1.1 Conditions on Edit Cost Functions

From the theoretical point of view, it is possible to extend a complete edit path $\{e_1, \dots, e_k\} \in \Upsilon(g_1, g_2)$ with an arbitrary number of additional insertions $(\varepsilon \rightarrow v_1), \dots, (\varepsilon \rightarrow v_n)$ followed by their corresponding deletions $(v_1 \rightarrow \varepsilon), \dots, (v_n \rightarrow \varepsilon)$ (where $\{v_i\}_{i=1,\dots,n}$ are arbitrary nodes). Hence, the size of the set of possible edit paths $\Upsilon(g_1, g_2)$ is infinite. In practice, however, three weak conditions on the cost function c are sufficient such that only a finite number of edit paths have to be evaluated to find the minimum cost edit path among all valid paths between two given graphs. First, we define the cost function to be nonnegative, i.e.,

$$c(e) \geq 0, \quad \text{for all node and edge edit operations } e. \tag{2.2}$$

We refer to this condition as *non-negativity*. Next we aim at assuring that only substitution operations of both nodes and edges have a zero cost, i.e.,

$$c(e) > 0, \quad \text{for all node and edge deletions and insertions } e. \tag{2.3}$$

Given this condition, edit paths containing an insertion of a node or edge followed by its subsequent deletion can be safely omitted. Finally, we want to prevent unnecessary substitutions to be added to an edit path. This is achieved by asserting that the elimination of such unnecessary substitutions from edit paths will not increase the corresponding sum of edit operation cost [11]. Formally,

$$c(u \rightarrow w) \leq c(u \rightarrow v) + c(v \rightarrow w)$$
$$c(u \rightarrow \varepsilon) \leq c(u \rightarrow v) + c(v \rightarrow \varepsilon) \tag{2.4}$$
$$c(\varepsilon \rightarrow v) \leq c(\varepsilon \rightarrow u) + c(u \rightarrow v)$$

for all nodes u, v, w and corresponding node substitutions, deletions, and insertions. We refer to this condition as *triangle inequality*. For instance, instead of substituting u with v and then substituting v with w (line 1), one can safely replace the two

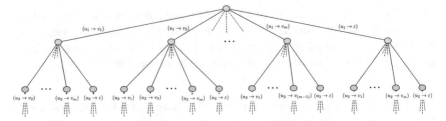

Fig. 2.2 The combinatorial explosion of edit paths between two graphs g_1 and g_2

right-hand side operations by the edit operation $(u \to w)$ on the left and will never miss out a minimum cost edit path. The same accounts for unnecessary substitutions of edges, of course. Therefore, each edit path $\{e_1, \ldots, e_k\} \in \Upsilon(g_1, g_2)$, containing superfluous substitutions of both nodes and edges, can be replaced by a shorter edit path with a total cost that is equal to, or lower than, the sum of cost of the former edit path.

Given the above stated conditions 2.2, 2.3, and 2.4 on the edit cost function, it is guaranteed that adding edit operations to an edit path $\{e_1, \ldots, e_k\} \in \Upsilon(g_1, g_2)$ containing operations on nodes or edges, which are neither involved in g_1 nor in g_2, will never decrease the overall edit cost of the edit path. Consequently, in order to find the minimum cost edit path $\lambda_{\min}$ among all possible edit paths $\Upsilon(g_1, g_2)$, we have to consider the $|V_1|$ node deletions, the $|V_2|$ node insertions, and the $|V_1| \times |V_2|$ possible node substitutions only.[1] In other words, the size of $\Upsilon(g_1, g_2)$ is bounded by a finite number of edit paths.

However, the upper bound on the number of edit paths in $\Upsilon(g_1, g_2)$ is exponential in the number of nodes of the involved graphs. Let us consider n nodes in g_1 ($V_1 = \{u_1, \ldots, u_n\}$) and m nodes in g_2 ($V_2 = \{v_1, \ldots, v_m\}$). By starting with an arbitrary node u_1 from V_1, $(m + 1)$ different edit operations have to be considered to build the following initial set of partial edit paths of size 1:

$$\{(u_1 \to v_1)\}, \{(u_1 \to v_2)\}, \ldots, \{(u_1 \to v_m)\}, \{(u_1 \to \varepsilon)\} \tag{2.5}$$

The next (arbitrarily chosen) node $u_2 \in V_1$ can now be substituted with one of the remaining nodes of V_2 or deleted. These edit operations applied on node $u_2 \in V_1$ can be appropriately combined with the $(m + 1)$ partial edit paths from list 2.5 resulting in $O(m^2)$ partial edit paths in total. This combinatorial process has to be continued until all nodes of both graphs are processed and thus, the set of possible edit paths $\Upsilon(g_1, g_2)$ contains $O(m^n)$ edit paths. In Fig. 2.2 the combinatorial explosion of possible edit paths between two graphs is illustrated.

Note that graph edit distance is not necessarily a metric. However, by adding the following two conditions to the above stated conditions of *non-negativity* and

---

[1]Remember that the source graph g_1 is edited such that it is transformed into the target graph g_2. Hence, the edit direction is essential and only nodes in g_1 can be deleted and only nodes in g_2 can be inserted.

triangle inequality (Conditions 2.2 and 2.4, respectively), the graph edit distance becomes metric [7]. First, we define identical substitutions to have zero cost, i.e.,

$$c(e) = 0, \tag{2.6}$$

if, and only if, edit operation e is an identical node or edge substitution (*identity of indiscernibles*). Second, we define the cost function c to be symmetric, i.e.,

$$c(e) = c(e^{-1}), \tag{2.7}$$

holds for any edit operation e on nodes and edges, where e^{-1} denotes the inverse edit operation to e (*Symmetry*).

2.1.2 Example Definitions of Cost Functions

The effectiveness of edit distance-based pattern recognition relies on the adequate definition of cost functions for the basic edit operations. In [12] an extensive review on different cost functions for graph edit distance can be found. In the present section, some important classes of cost functions for common label alphabets are defined.

In case of unlabeled graphs, the cost is usually defined via unit cost for all deletions and insertions of both nodes and edges, while substitutions are free of cost. Formally,

$$c(u \rightarrow \varepsilon) = c(\varepsilon \rightarrow u') = c((u, v) \rightarrow \varepsilon) = c(\varepsilon \rightarrow (u', v')) = 1$$
$$c(u \rightarrow u') = c((u, v) \rightarrow (u', v')) = 0$$

for all nodes $u, v \in V_1$ and $u', v' \in V_2$ as well as all edges $(u, v) \in E_1$ and $(u', v') \in E_2$.

In general, however, the cost $c(e)$ of a particular edit operation e is defined with respect to the underlying label alphabets L_V and L_E. For instance, for numerical node and edge labels, i.e., for label alphabets $L_V, L_E = \mathbb{R}^n$, a Minkowski distance can be used to model the cost of a substitution operation on the graphs (referred to as *Minkowski cost function* from now on). The Minkowski cost function defines the substitution cost proportional to the Minkowski distance of the two corresponding labels. The basic intuition behind this approach is that the more dissimilar the two labels are, the stronger is the distortion associated with the corresponding substitution.

Formally, given two graphs $g_1 = (V_1, E_1, \mu_1, \nu_1)$ and $g_2 = (V_2, E_2, \mu_2, \nu_2)$, where $\mu_1, \mu_2 : V_1, V_2 \rightarrow \mathbb{R}^n$, the cost for the three node edit operations can be defined by

$$c(u \to \varepsilon) = \tau$$
$$c(\varepsilon \to v) = \tau$$
$$c(u \to v) = ||\mu_1(u) - \mu_2(v)||_p$$

where $u \in V_1$, $v \in V_2$, and $\tau \in \mathbb{R}^+$ is a positive constant representing the cost of a node deletion/insertion.[2] Note that $||\mu_1(u) - \mu_2(v)||_p$ refers to the Minkowski distance of order p between two vectors $\mu_1(u), \mu_2(v) \in \mathbb{R}^n$. A similar cost model can be defined for edges, of course.

Note that any node substitution having a higher cost than 2τ can be safely replaced by a composition of a deletion and an insertion of the involved nodes (the same accounts for the edges). This behavior reflects the basic intuition that substitutions should be favored over deletions and insertions to a certain degree. A substitution cost for numerically labeled nodes (or edges) that is guaranteed to be in the interval $[0, 2\tau]$ can be defined, for instance, by

$$c(u \to v) = \frac{1}{\frac{1}{2\tau} + \exp(-\alpha||\mu_1(u) - \mu_2(v)||_p + \sigma)}.$$

That is, the substitution cost for two nodes $u \in V_1$ and $v \in V_2$ is defined via a *Sigmoid function* of the (weighted) Minkowski distance between the corresponding labels $\mu_1(u)$ and $\mu_2(v)$. Note that we have two meta parameters in this cost function, viz., α and σ, which control the gradient and the left–right shift of the Sigmoid curve, respectively.

In some applications, it might be that the edges are attributed by an angle that specifies an undirected orientation of a line. That is, the angle value $\nu(e)$ of every edge e might be in the interval $(-\pi/2, +\pi/2]$. Because of the cyclic nature of angular measurements, a Minkowski-based distance would not be appropriate for the definition of a substitution cost. The following cost model for edges $e \in E_1$ and $e' \in E_2$ could be used in this case

$$c(e \to e') = \min(\pi - |\nu(e) - \nu(e')|, |\nu(e) - \nu(e')|).$$

In other applications, the node and/or edge labels might be not numerical and thus nonnumerical distance functions have to be employed to measure the cost of a particular substitution operation. For instance, the label alphabet can be given by the set of all strings of arbitrary size over a finite set of symbols. In this case a distance model for strings, as for instance the *string edit distance* [1, 2], could be used for measuring the cost of a substitution. In other problem domains, the label alphabet might be given by a finite set of n symbolic labels $L_{V/E} = \{\alpha_1, \alpha_2, \ldots, \alpha_n\}$. In such case a substitution cost model using a *Dirac function*, which returns zero when the involved labels are identical and a nonnegative constant otherwise, could be the method of choice.

---

[2]For the sake of symmetry, an identical cost τ for deletions and insertions is defined here.

Note that also combinations of various cost functions are possible. This might be particularly interesting when the nodes (or edges) are labeled with more than one attribute, for instance with a type (i.e., a symbolic label) together with a numerical measurement. For identically typed nodes, a Minkowski cost function could then be employed, for instance. In case of nonidentical types on the nodes, however, the substitution cost could be set to 2τ, which reflects the intuition that nodes with different types of labels cannot be substituted but have to be deleted and inserted, respectively.

The definition of application-specific cost functions, which can be adopted to the peculiarity of the underlying label alphabet, accounts for the flexibility of graph edit distance. Yet, prior knowledge about the labels and their meaning has to be available. If in a particular case this prior knowledge is not available, automatic procedures for learning the cost model from a set of sample graphs are available as well [13–17].

In [13], for instance, a cost inference method that is based on a distribution estimation of edit operations has been proposed (this particular approach is based on an idea originally presented in [18]). An *Expectation Maximization* algorithm is then employed in order to learn mixture densities from a labeled sample of graphs and derive edit costs. In [14] a system of *self-organizing maps* (SOMs) is proposed. This system represents the distance measuring spaces of node and edge labels and the learning process is based on the concept of self-organization. That is, it adapts the edit costs in such a way that the similarity of graphs from the same class is increased, while the similarity of graphs from different classes decreases. In [15] the graph edit process is formulated in a stochastic context and a maximum likelihood parameter estimation of the distribution of edit operations is performed. The underlying distortion model is also learned using an expectation maximization algorithm. From this model the desired cost functions can be finally derived. The authors of [16] present an optimization method to learn the cost model such that the *Hamming distance* between an oracle's node assignment and the automatically derived correspondence is minimized. Finally, in [17] another method for the automatic definition of edit costs has been proposed. This approach is based on an assignment defined by a specialist and an interactive and adaptive graph recognition method in conjunction with human interaction.

2.2 Computation of Exact Graph Edit Distance

In order to compute the graph edit distance $d_{\lambda_{min}}(g_1, g_2)$ often A*-based search techniques using some heuristics are employed [19–23]. A* is a best-first search algorithm [24] which is *complete* and *admissible*, i.e. it always finds a solution if there is one and it never overestimates the cost of reaching the goal.

The basic idea of A*-based search methods is to organize the underlying search space as an ordered tree. The root node of the search tree represents the starting point of the search procedure, inner nodes of the search tree correspond to partial solutions, and leaf nodes represent complete—not necessarily optimal—solutions. In case of graph edit distance computation, inner nodes and leaf nodes correspond to partial and complete edit paths, respectively. Such a search tree is dynamically constructed at runtime by iteratively creating successor nodes linked by edges to the currently considered node in the search tree.

Algorithm 1 Exact Graph Edit Distance Algorithm

Input: Non-empty graphs $g_1 = (V_1, E_1, \mu, \nu)$ and $g_2 = (V_2, E_2, \mu, \nu)$,
            where $V_1 = \{u_1, \ldots, u_n\}$ and $V_2 = \{v_1, \ldots, v_m\}$
Output: A minimum cost edit path from g_1 to g_2
            e.g. $\lambda_{min} = \{u_1 \to v_3, u_2 \to \varepsilon, \ldots, \varepsilon \to v_2\}$

1: initialize $OPEN$ to the empty set $\{\}$
2: For each node $w \in V_2$, insert the substitution $\{u_1 \to w\}$ into $OPEN$
3: Insert the deletion $\{u_1 \to \varepsilon\}$ into $OPEN$
4: **loop**
5:    Remove $\lambda_{min} = \arg\min_{\lambda \in OPEN}\{g(\lambda) + h(\lambda)\}$ from $OPEN$
6:    **if** λ_{min} is a complete edit path **then**
7:       Return λ_{min} as the solution
8:    **else**
9:       Let $\lambda_{min} = \{u_1 \to v_{\varphi_1}, \cdots, u_k \to v_{\varphi_k}\}$
10:      **if** $k < n$ **then**
11:        For each $w \in V_2 \setminus \{v_{\varphi_1}, \cdots, v_{\varphi_k}\}$, insert $\lambda_{min} \cup \{u_{k+1} \to w\}$ into $OPEN$
12:        Insert $\lambda_{min} \cup \{u_{k+1} \to \varepsilon\}$ into $OPEN$
13:      **else**
14:        Insert $\lambda_{min} \cup \bigcup_{w \in V_2 \setminus \{v_{\varphi_1}, \cdots, v_{\varphi_k}\}} \{\varepsilon \to w\}$ into $OPEN$
15:      **end if**
16:    **end if**
17: **end loop**

In Algorithm 1, the A*-based method for optimal graph edit distance computation is given. The nodes of the source graph g_1 are processed in fixed, yet arbitrary, order $u_1, u_2, \ldots, u_n$. The substitution (line 11) and the deletion of a node (line 12) are considered simultaneously, which produces a number of successor nodes in the search tree. If all nodes of the first graph have been processed, the remaining nodes of the second graph are inserted in a single step (line 14). The set $OPEN$ contains the search tree nodes, i.e., (partial or complete) edit paths, to be processed in the next steps.

In order to determine the most promising (partial) edit path $\lambda \in OPEN$, i.e., the edit path to be used for further expansion in the next iteration, a heuristic function is usually used (line 5). Formally, for a (partial) edit path λ in the search tree, we use $g(\lambda)$ to denote the accumulated cost of the edit operations $e_i \in \lambda$, and we use $h(\lambda) \geq 0$ for denoting the estimated cost to complete the edit path λ (several heuristics for the computation of $h(\lambda)$ exist [19–23]). The sum $g(\lambda) + h(\lambda)$ gives the total cost assigned to an open node in the search tree. Given that the estimation of the future cost $h(\lambda)$ is lower than, or equal to, the real cost, the algorithm is admissible. Hence, this procedure guarantees that if the current edit path λ_{min} removed from $OPEN$ is complete (line 6), then λ_{min} is always optimal in the sense of providing minimal cost among all possible competing paths (line 7).

Note that the edge operations implied by the node edit operations can be derived from every partial or complete edit path λ during the search procedure given in Algorithm 1. The cost of these implied edge operations are dynamically added to the corresponding path $\lambda \in OPEN$ and are thus considered in the edit path assessment on line 5. Formally, for every node edit operation $(u \rightarrow v)$, which is included in λ, it is verified whether there are adjacent nodes to u and/or v which have been already edited in λ. If this is the case, the corresponding edge edit operations can be instantly triggered and the resulting edge edit cost added to the overall cost $g(\lambda)$ (the same accounts for the estimation $h(\lambda)$).

Example 8 In Fig. 2.3 a part of a search tree for graph edit distance computation between two undirected graphs g_1 and g_2 is shown. The nodes are labeled with integers, while the edges are unlabeled. We use unit cost for deletions and insertions of both nodes and edges. Edge substitutions are free of cost, while the cost for substituting a node $u \in V_1$ with a node $v \in V_2$ is defined via $c(u \rightarrow v) = |\mu_1(u) - \mu_2(v)|$.

The total cost $g(\lambda)$ of (partial) edit paths λ is computed by the node edit operation cost plus the cost of all edge operations that can be triggered according to the node operations carried out so far (we set $h(\lambda) = 0$ for all edit paths, i.e., no heuristic information is employed in this example). The accumulated edit costs are indicated in the tree search nodes.

Regard, for instance, the edit path displayed with dotted arrows. When $(u_1 \rightarrow v_2)$ and $(u_2 \rightarrow v_1)$ have been added to λ, the cost amounts to 2 (both node substitutions have a cost of 1 and the implied edge edit operation $((u_1, u_2) \rightarrow (v_1, v_2))$ has zero

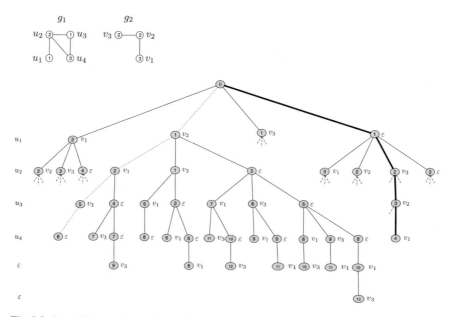

Fig. 2.3 Part of the search tree for graph edit distance computation between two graphs g_1 and g_2

cost). The next node substitution added to λ is $(u_3 \rightarrow v_3)$ with a cost of 1. This operation implies two edge edit operations, viz., the deletion of $(u_2, u_3) \in E_1$ and the insertion of $(v_2, v_3) \in E_2$. Hence, we have a total cost of 5 for this partial edit path. Finally, by adding $(u_4 \rightarrow \varepsilon)$ to the edit path, we add a cost of 3 to the overall cost (one node deletion and two implied edge deletions). That is, this edit path offers a total cost of 8.

The edit path displayed with bold arrows, i.e.,

$$\lambda_{\min} = \{(u_1 \rightarrow \varepsilon), (u_2 \rightarrow v_3), (u_3 \rightarrow v_2), (u_4 \rightarrow v_1)\}$$

corresponds to a minimal cost edit path with a total cost of 4.

2.3   Graph Edit Distance-Based Pattern Recognition

2.3.1   Nearest-Neighbor Classification

The traditional approach to graph edit distance-based pattern recognition is given by the *k-nearest-neighbor classification* (*k*-NN). In contrast with other classifiers such as artificial neural networks, Bayes classifiers, or decision trees [25], the underlying pattern space need not be rich in mathematical operations for nearest-neighbor classifiers to be applicable. More formally, in order to use the nearest-neighbor classifier, only a pattern dissimilarity measure must be available. Therefore, the *k*-NN classifier is perfectly suited for the graph domain, where several graph dissimilarity models, but only little mathematical structure, are available.

The *k*-NN classifier proceeds as follows. Let us assume that a graph domain $\mathscr{G}$, an appropriate definition of a graph edit distance $d : \mathscr{G} \times \mathscr{G} \rightarrow \mathbb{R}$, a set of labels Ω, and a labeled set of N training graphs $\{(g_i, \omega_i)\}_{1 \leq i \leq N} \subseteq \mathscr{G} \times \Omega$ is given. The 1-nearest-neighbor classifier (1-NN) is defined by assigning an input graph $g \in \mathscr{G}$ to the class of its most similar training graph. That is, the 1-NN classifier $f : \mathscr{G} \rightarrow \Omega$ is defined by

$$f(g) = \omega_j, \quad \text{where } j = \underset{1 \leq i \leq N}{\operatorname{argmin}} \, d(g, g_i).$$

If $k = 1$, the *k*-NN classifier's decision is based on just one graph from the training set, no matter if this graph is an outlier or a true class representative. That is, the decision boundary is largely based on empirical arguments. To render nearest-neighbor classification less prone to outlier graphs, it is common to consider not only the single most similar graph from the training set, but evaluate several of the most similar graphs. Formally, if $\{(g_{(1)}, \omega_{(1)}), \ldots, (g_{(k)}, \omega_{(k)})\} \subseteq \{(g_i, \omega_i)\}_{1 \leq i \leq N}$ are those k graphs in the training set that have the smallest distance $d(g, g_{(i)})$ to an input graph $g \in \mathscr{G}$, the *k*-NN classifier $f : \mathscr{G} \rightarrow \Omega$ is defined by

$$f(g) = \operatorname*{argmax}_{\omega \in \Omega} |\{(g_{(i)}, \omega_{(i)}) : \omega_{(i)} = \omega\}|.$$

Nearest-neighbor classifiers provide us with a natural way to classify graphs by means of graph edit distance. However, the major restriction of nearest-neighbor classifiers is that a sufficiently large number of training graphs covering a substantial part of the graph domain must be available.

2.3.2 Kernel-Based Classification

Kernel methods have become one of the most rapidly emerging subfields in pattern recognition and related areas (see [26, 27] for a thorough introduction to kernel theory). The reason for this is twofold. First, kernel theory makes standard algorithms for pattern recognition (originally developed for vectorial data) applicable to more complex data structures such as strings, trees, or graphs. That is, kernel methods can be seen as a fundamental theory for bridging the gap between statistical and structural pattern recognition. Second, kernel methods allow one to extend basic linear algorithms to complex nonlinear ones in a unified and elegant manner.

The key idea of kernel methods is based on an essentially different way how the underlying data is represented [28]. In the kernel approach, an explicit data representation is of secondary interest. That is, rather than defining individual representations for each pattern, the data is represented by pairwise comparisons via *kernel functions* [27, 29].

Definition 2.3 (*Positive Definite Kernel*) Given a pattern domain $\mathcal{X}$, a *kernel function* $\kappa : \mathcal{X} \times \mathcal{X} \rightarrow \mathbb{R}$ is a symmetric function, i.e., $\kappa(x_i, x_j) = \kappa(x_j, x_i)$, mapping pairs of patterns $x_i, x_j \in \mathcal{X}$ to real numbers. A kernel function κ is called positive definite[3] if, and only if, for all $N \in \mathbb{N}$,

$$\sum_{i,j=1}^{N} c_i c_j \kappa(x_i, x_j) \geq 0$$

for all $\{c_1, \ldots, c_N\} \subseteq \mathbb{R}$, and any choice of N objects $\{x_1, \ldots, x_N\} \subseteq \mathcal{X}$.

Kernel functions that are positive definite are often called *valid kernels, admissible kernels*, or *Mercer kernels*.

Kernels can be seen as pattern similarity measures satisfying the condition of symmetry and positive definiteness. Hence, graph edit distance becomes particularly interesting as it provides us with a symmetric graph dissimilarity measure, which can be readily turned into a similarity measure. In [30] monotonically decreasing transformations have been proposed which map low distance values to high similarity

---

[3]Note that positive definite functions according to the definition given in this section are sometimes called positive semi-definite since $\sum_{i,j=1}^{n} c_i c_j \kappa(x_i, x_j)$ can be zero and need not be strictly positive.

values and vice versa. Formally, given the edit distance $d(g, g')$ of two graphs g and g', the following similarity kernels can be defined, for instance (the list makes no claim to be complete).

- $\kappa(g, g') = -d(g, g')^2$
- $\kappa(g, g') = -d(g, g')$
- $\kappa(g, g') = tanh(-d(g, g'))$
- $\kappa(g, g') = \exp(-\gamma d(g, g')^2)$, where $\gamma > 0$

In [31] the fourth similarity kernel from the above-listed similarity functions is explicitly suggested for classifying distance-based data. Note that these kernel functions are not positive definite in general. However, there is theoretical and empirical evidence that using indefinite kernels may be reasonable if some conditions are fulfilled [11, 31].

Note that other, in particular more sophisticated, graph kernels have been proposed in conjunction with graph edit distance [11]. For instance, kernel functions that measure the similarity of two graphs by considering the node and edge substitutions from an optimal edit path $\lambda_{\min}$ only (i.e., omitting the deletions/insertions of both nodes and edges). The similarity of the substituted nodes and edges is then individually quantified and appropriately combined (by means of a multiplication). Moreover, also standard graph kernels such as *convolution kernels*, *random walk kernels*, or *diffusion kernels* have been substantially extended by means of graph edit distance in [11].

The following theorem gives a good intuition what kernel functions actually are (for proofs we refer to [26, 27]).

Theorem 2.1 [26, 27] *Let $\kappa : \mathcal{X} \times \mathcal{X} \to \mathbb{R}$ be a valid kernel on a pattern space $\mathcal{X}$, then there exists a possibly infinite-dimensional Hilbert space $\mathcal{F}$ and a mapping $\phi : \mathcal{X} \to \mathcal{F}$ such that*

$$\kappa(x, x') = \langle \phi(x), \phi(x') \rangle,$$

for all $x, x' \in \mathcal{X}$ where $\langle \cdot, \cdot \rangle$ denotes the dot product in $\mathcal{F}$.

In other words, kernels κ can be thought of as a dot product $\langle \cdot, \cdot \rangle$ in some (implicitly existing) feature space $\mathcal{F}$, and thus, instead of mapping patterns from the original pattern space $\mathcal{X}$ to the feature space $\mathcal{F}$ and computing their dot product there, one can simply evaluate the value of the kernel function in $\mathcal{X}$ [11].

In recent years, a huge amount of important algorithms has been *kernelized*, i.e., entirely reformulated in terms of dot products. These algorithms include support vector machine, nearest-neighbor classifier, perceptron algorithm, principal component analysis, Fisher discriminant analysis, canonical correlation analysis, k-means clustering, self-organizing map, partial least squares regression, and many others [26, 27]. Kernelized algorithms are commonly referred to as *kernel machines*.

Clearly, any kernel machine can be turned into an alternative algorithm by merely replacing the dot product $\langle \cdot, \cdot \rangle$ by a valid kernel $\kappa(\cdot, \cdot)$. This procedure is commonly referred to as *kernel trick* [26, 27]. The kernel trick is especially interesting for graph-based pattern representation since a graph kernel value (for instance the transformed graph edit distances defined above) can be fed into any kernel machine (e.g., a support vector machine). In other words, the graph kernel approach makes many powerful pattern recognition algorithms instantly applicable to graphs.

2.3.3   Classification of Vector Space Embedded Graphs

The motivation of *graph embedding* is similar to that of the kernel approach, viz., making the arsenal of algorithmic tools originally developed for vectorial data applicable to graphs. Yet, in contrast with kernel methods, which provide an implicit graph embedding only, graph embedding techniques result in an explicit vectorial description of the graphs.

The idea of a recent graph embedding framework [32] is based on the seminal work done by Pekalska and Duin [33]. The key idea of this graph embedding approach is to use the distances of an input graph to a number of training graphs, termed *prototype graphs*, as a vectorial description of the graph. That is, one makes use of the *dissimilarity representation* for pattern recognition rather than the original graph-based representation.

Definition 2.4   (*Graph Embedding*) Let us assume that a graph domain $\mathscr{G}$ is given. If $\mathscr{T} = \{g_1, \ldots, g_N\} \subseteq \mathscr{G}$ is a set with N graphs and $\mathscr{P} = \{p_1, \ldots, p_n\} \subseteq \mathscr{T}$ is a prototype set with $n \leq N$ graphs, the mapping

$$\phi_n^{\mathscr{P}} : \mathscr{G} \to \mathbb{R}^n$$

is defined as the function

$$\phi_n^{\mathscr{P}}(g) = (d(g, p_1), \ldots, d(g, p_n)),$$

where $d : \mathscr{G} \times \mathscr{G} \to \mathbb{R}$ is an appropriately defined graph edit distance.

Obviously, by means of this definition we obtain a vector space where each axis is associated with a prototype graph $p_i \in \mathscr{P}$ and the coordinate values of an embedded graph g are the distances of g to the elements in $\mathscr{P}$. In this way, we can transform any graph g from the set $\mathscr{T}$, as well as any other graph from $\mathscr{G}$, into a vector of real numbers. Note that graphs, which have been selected as prototypes before, have a zero entry in their corresponding graph map.

The selection of the n prototypes $\mathscr{P} = \{p_1, \ldots, p_n\}$ is a critical issue in the embedding framework. That is, not only the prototypes p_i themselves but also their number n affect the resulting graph embedding $\varphi_n^{\mathscr{P}}(\cdot)$, and thus the performance of the pattern recognition algorithm in the resulting embedding space. In [32] the selection of prototypes $\mathscr{P} = \{p_1, \ldots, p_n\}$ is addressed by various procedures. Three of them are briefly outlined in the next three paragraphs.

First, a number of *prototype selection methods* have been presented [34–36]. These prototype selection strategies use some heuristics based on the underlying dissimilarities in the original graph domain. Basically, these approaches select prototypes from $\mathcal{T}$ that best possibly reflect the distribution of the graph set $\mathcal{T}$ or that cover a predefined region of $\mathcal{T}$. The rationale of this procedure is that capturing distances to significant prototypes from $\mathcal{T}$ lead to meaningful dissimilarity vectors.

A severe shortcoming of prototype selection strategies is that the dimensionality of the embedding space has to be determined by the user. Thus, a prototype selection method that automatically infers the dimensionality of the resulting embedding space has been proposed in [37]. This scheme is adopted from well-known concepts of *prototype reduction* [38] originally used for the task of condensing training sets in nearest-neighbor classification systems.

Finally, in [39, 40] the problem of prototype selection has been reduced to a feature subset selection problem. That is, for graph embedding, all available elements from the complete set $\mathcal{T}$ are used as prototypes, i.e., $\mathcal{P} = \mathcal{T}$. Next, various *feature selection strategies* [41–44] are applied to the resulting large-scale vectors eliminating redundancies and noise, finding good features, and simultaneously reducing the dimensionality of the graph maps.

References

1. V. Levenshtein, Binary codes capable of correcting deletions, insertions and reversals. Sov. Phys. Dokl. **10**(8), 707–710 (1966)
2. R.A. Wagner, M.J. Fischer, The string-to-string correction problem. J. Assoc. Comput. Mach. **21**(1), 168–173 (1974)
3. S.M. Selkow, The tree-to-tree editing problem. Inf. Process. Lett. **6**(6), 184–186 (1977)
4. M.A. Eshera, K.S. Fu, A graph distance measure for image analysis. IEEE Trans. Syst. Man Cybern. (Part B) **14**(3), 398–408 (1984)
5. W.H. Tsai, K.S. Fu, Error-correcting isomorphism of attributed relational graphs for pattern analysis. IEEE Trans. Syst. Man Cybern. (Part B) **9**(12), 757–768 (1979)
6. W.H. Tsai, K.S. Fu, Subgraph error-correcting isomorphisms for syntactic pattern recognition. IEEE Trans. Syst. Man Cybern. (Part B) **13**, 48–61 (1983)
7. H. Bunke, G. Allermann, Inexact graph matching for structural pattern recognition. Pattern Recognit. Lett. **1**, 245–253 (1983)
8. A. Sanfeliu, K.S. Fu, A distance measure between attributed relational graphs for pattern recognition. IEEE Trans. Syst. Man Cybern. (Part B) **13**(3), 353–363 (1983)
9. X. Gao, B. Xiao, D. Tao, X. Li, A survey of graph edit distance. Pattern Anal. Appl. **13**(1), 113–129 (2010)
10. R. Ambauen, S. Fischer, H. Bunke, Graph edit distance with node splitting and merging and its application to diatom identification, in *Proceedings of the 4th International Workshop on Graph Based Representations in Pattern Recognition*, ed. by E. Hancock, M. Vento. LNCS, vol. 2726 (Springer, New York, 2003), pp. 95–106
11. M. Neuhaus, H. Bunke, *Bridging the Gap Between Graph Edit Distance and Kernel Machines* (World Scientific, Singapore, 2007)
12. F. Serratosa, X. Cortés, A. Solé-Ribalta, On the graph edit distance cost: Properties and applications. Int. J. Pattern Recognit. Artif. Intell. **26**(5) (2012)

13. M. Neuhaus, H. Bunke, A probabilistic approach to learning costs for graph edit distance, in *Proceedings of the 17th International Conference on Pattern Recognition*, ed. by J. Kittler, M. Petrou, M. Nixon, vol. 3 (2004), pp. 389–393

14. M. Neuhaus, H. Bunke, Self-organizing maps for learning the edit costs in graph matching. IEEE Trans. Syst. Man Cybern. (Part B) **35**(3), 503–514 (2005)

15. M. Neuhaus, H. Bunke, Automatic learning of cost functions for graph edit distance. Inf. Sci. **177**(1), 239–247 (2007)

16. X. Cortes, F. Serratosa, Learning graph-matching edit-costs based on the optimality of the oracle's node correspondences. Pattern Recognit. Lett. **56**, 22–29 (2015)

17. F. Serratosa, A. Solé-Ribalta, X. Cortes, Automatic learning of edit costs based on interactive and adaptive graph recognition, in *Proceedings of the 8th International Workshop on Graph Based Representations in Pattern Recognition*, ed. by X. Jiang, M. Ferrer, A. Torsello. LNCS, vol. 6658 (2011), pp. 152–163

18. E. Ristad, P. Yianilos, Learning string edit distance. IEEE Trans. Pattern Anal. Mach. Intell. **20**(5), 522–532 (1998)

19. A.C.M. Dumay, R.J. van der Geest, J.J. Gerbrands, E. Jansen, J.H.C. Reiber, Consistent inexact graph matching applied to labelling coronary segments in arteriograms, in *Proceedings of the 11th IAPR International Conference on Pattern Recognition*, Conference C: Image, Speech and Signal Analysis, vol. III (1992), pp. 439–442

20. L. Gregory, J. Kittler, Using graph search techniques for contextual colour retrieval, in *Proceedings of the Joint IAPR International Workshop on Structural, Syntactic, and Statistical Pattern Recognition*, ed. by T. Caelli, A. Amin, R.P.W. Duin, M. Kamel, D. de Ridder. LNCS, vol. 2396 (2002), pp. 186–194

21. S. Berretti, A. Del Bimbo, E. Vicario, Efficient matching and indexing of graph models in content-based retrieval. IEEE Trans. Pattern Anal. Mach. Intell. **23**(10), 1089–1105 (2001)

22. K. Riesen, S. Fankhauser, H. Bunke, Speeding up graph edit distance computation with a bipartite heuristic, in *Proceedings of the 5th International Workshop on Mining and Learning with Graphs*, ed. by P. Frasconi, K. Kersting, K. Tsuda (2007), pp. 21–24

23. A. Fischer, R. Plamandon, Y. Savaria, K. Riesen, H. Bunke, A hausdorff heuristic for efficient computation of graph edit distance, in *Proceedings of the International Workshop on Structural and Syntactic Pattern Recognition*, ed. by P. Fränti, G. Brown, M. Loog, F. Escolano, M. Pelillo. LNCS, vol. 8621 (2014), pp. 83–92

24. P.E. Hart, N.J. Nilsson, B. Raphael, A formal basis for the heuristic determination of minimum cost paths. IEEE Trans. Syst. Sci. Cybern. **4**(2), 100–107 (1968)

25. R. Duda, P. Hart, D. Stork, *Pattern Classification*, 2nd edn. (Wiley-Interscience, New York, 2000)

26. J. Shawe-Taylor, N. Cristianini, *Kernel Methods for Pattern Analysis* (Cambridge University Press, Cambridge, 2004)

27. B. Schölkopf, A. Smola, *Learning with Kernels* (MIT Press, Cambridge, 2002)

28. B. Schölkopf, K. Tsuda, J.-P. Vert (eds.), *Kernel Methods in Computational Biology* (MIT Press, Cambridge, 2004)

29. C.H. Berg, J. Christensen, P. Ressel, *Harmonic Analysis on Semigroups* (Springer, New York, 1984)

30. M. Neuhaus, H. Bunke, *Bridging the Gap Between Graph Edit Distance and Kernel Machines* (World Scientific, Singapore, 2007)

31. B. Haasdonk, Feature space interpretation of SVMs with indefinite kernels. IEEE Trans. Pattern Anal. Mach. Intell. **27**(4), 482–492 (2005)

32. K. Riesen, H. Bunke, *Graph Classification and Clustering Based on Vector Space Embedding* (World Scientific, Singapore, 2010)

33. E. Pekalska, R. Duin, *The Dissimilarity Representation for Pattern Recognition: Foundations and Applications* (World Scientific, Singapore, 2005)

34. E. Pekalska, R. Duin, P. Paclik, Prototype selection for dissimilarity-based classifiers. Pattern Recognit. **39**(2), 189–208 (2006)

35. B. Spillmann, M. Neuhaus, H. Bunke, E. Pekalska, R. Duin, Transforming strings to vector spaces using prototype selection, in *Proceedings of the 11th International Workshop on Strucural and Syntactic Pattern Recognition*, ed. by D.-Y. Yeung, J.T. Kwok, A. Fred, F. Roli, D. de Ridder. LNCS, vol. 4109 (2006), pp. 287–296
36. K. Riesen, H. Bunke, Graph classification based on vector space embedding. Int. J. Pattern Recognit. Artif. Intell. **23**(6), 1053–1081 (2008)
37. K. Riesen, H. Bunke, Dissimilarity based vector space embedding of graphs using prototype reduction schemes, in *Proceedings of the 6th International Conference Machine Learning and Data Mining in Pattern Recognition*, ed. by P. Perner (2009), pp. 617–631. (Accepted for publication in)
38. J.C. Bezdek, L. Kuncheva, Nearest prototype classifier designs: an experimental study. Int. J. Intell. Syst. **16**(12), 1445–1473 (2001)
39. K. Riesen, V. Kilchherr, H. Bunke, Reducing the dimensionality of vector space embeddings of graphs, in *Proceedings of the 5th International Conference on Machine Learning and Data Mining*, ed. by P. Perner. LNAI, vol. 4571 (Springer, Berlin, 2007), pp. 563–573
40. K. Riesen, H. Bunke, Reducing the dimensionality of dissimilarity space embedding graph kernels. Eng. Appl. Artif. Intell. **22**(1), 48–56 (2008)
41. K. Kira, L.A. Rendell, A practical approach to feature selection, *Ninth International Workshop on Machine Learning* (Morgan Kaufmann, Burlington, 1992), pp. 249–256
42. P. Pudil, J. Novovicova, J. Kittler, Floating search methods in feature-selection. Pattern Recognit. Lett. **15**(11), 1119–1125 (1994)
43. A. Jain, D. Zongker, Feature selection: evaluation, application, and small sample performance. IEEE Trans. Pattern Anal. Mach. Intell. **19**(2), 153–158 (1997)
44. R.A. Fisher, The statistical utilization of multiple measurements. Ann. Eugen. **8**, 376–386 (1938)

Chapter 3
Bipartite Graph Edit Distance

Abstract In this chapter, we reformulate the graph edit distance problem to a quadratic assignment problem. This reformulation actually builds the basis for a recent approximation algorithm, which in turn builds the core algorithm for the second part of the present book. This particular approximation algorithm, which gives rise to an upper and a lower bound of the true edit distance, is thoroughly reviewed in the present chapter (including an empirical evaluation on four standard graph sets). Finally, we give a brief survey of pattern recognition applications that make use of this specific approximation algorithm.

3.1   Graph Edit Distance as Quadratic Assignment Problem

Exact graph edit distance computation based on a tree search algorithm (as described in Sect. 2.2) is exponential in the number of nodes of the involved graphs. Formally, for graphs with m and n nodes, we observe a time complexity of $O(m^n)$. This means that for large graphs, the computation of exact edit distance is intractable. In fact, graph edit distance belongs to the family of *quadratic assignment problems* (QAPs) [1], which in turn belong to the class of NP-complete problems. That is, an exact and efficient algorithm for the graph edit distance problem cannot be developed unless $P = NP$.

Roughly speaking, QAPs deal with the problem of assigning n entities of a first set $S = \{s_1, \ldots, s_n\}$ to n entities of a second set $Q = \{q_1, \ldots, q_n\}$ under some (computationally demanding) side constraints. A common way to formally represent assignments between the entities of S and Q are given by means of permutations $(\varphi_1, \ldots, \varphi_n)$ of the integers $(1, 2, \ldots, n)$. A permutation $(\varphi_1, \ldots, \varphi_n)$ refers to the assignment where the first entity $s_1 \in S$ is mapped to entity $q_{\varphi_1} \in Q$, the second entity $s_2 \in S$ is assigned to entity $q_{\varphi_2} \in Q$, and so on.

By reformulating the graph edit distance problem to an instance of a QAP, two major issues have to be resolved.

- First, QAPs are generally stated on sets with equal cardinality. Yet, in case of graph edit distance, the elements to be assigned to each other are given by the sets of nodes (and edges) with unequal cardinality in general.

© Springer International Publishing Switzerland 2015   45
K. Riesen, *Structural Pattern Recognition with Graph Edit Distance*,
Advances in Computer Vision and Pattern Recognition,
DOI 10.1007/978-3-319-27252-8_3

- Second, solutions to QAPs refer to assignments of elements in which every element of the first set is assigned to exactly one element of the second set and vice versa (i.e., a solution to a QAP corresponds to a bijective assignment of the underlying entities). Yet, graph edit distance is a more general assignment problem as it explicitly allows both deletions and insertions to occur on the basic entities (rather than only substitutions).

These two issues can be simultaneously resolved by adding an appropriate number of empty nodes ε to both graphs g_1 and g_2. Assuming that $|V_1| = n$ and $|V_2| = m$, we extend V_1 and V_2 according to

$$V_1^+ = V_1 \cup \overbrace{\{\varepsilon_1, \ldots, \varepsilon_m\}}^{m \text{ empty nodes}}$$

and

$$V_2^+ = V_2 \cup \underbrace{\{\varepsilon_1, \ldots, \varepsilon_n\}}_{n \text{ empty nodes}}.$$

The graph edit distance computation is eventually carried out on the graphs with extended node sets, i.e., we assume from now on that $g_1 = (V_1^+, E_1, \mu_1, \nu_1)$ and $g_2 = (V_2^+, E_2, \mu_2, \nu_2)$.

Since both graphs g_1 and g_2 have now an equal number of nodes, viz., $(n + m)$, their corresponding adjacency matrices $\mathbf{A}$ and $\mathbf{B}$ also offer equal dimensions. These adjacency matrices of g_1 and g_2 are defined by

$$\mathbf{A} = \begin{array}{c} \\ 1 \\ \vdots \\ n \\ 1 \\ \vdots \\ m \end{array} \overset{\begin{array}{cccc} 1 & \cdots & n & 1 & \cdots & m \end{array}}{\left[\begin{array}{ccc|ccc} a_{11} & \cdots & a_{1n} & \varepsilon & \cdots & \varepsilon \\ \vdots & \ddots & \vdots & \vdots & \ddots & \vdots \\ a_{n1} & \cdots & a_{nn} & \varepsilon & \cdots & \varepsilon \\ \varepsilon & \cdots & \varepsilon & \varepsilon & \cdots & \varepsilon \\ \vdots & \ddots & \vdots & \vdots & \ddots & \vdots \\ \varepsilon & \cdots & \varepsilon & \varepsilon & \cdots & \varepsilon \end{array} \right]} \tag{3.1}$$

and

$$\mathbf{B} = \begin{array}{c} \\ 1 \\ \vdots \\ m \\ 1 \\ \vdots \\ n \end{array} \overset{\begin{array}{cccc} 1 & \cdots & m & 1 & \cdots & n \end{array}}{\left[\begin{array}{ccc|ccc} b_{11} & \cdots & b_{1m} & \varepsilon & \cdots & \varepsilon \\ \vdots & \ddots & \vdots & \vdots & \ddots & \vdots \\ b_{m1} & \cdots & b_{mm} & \varepsilon & \cdots & \varepsilon \\ \varepsilon & \cdots & \varepsilon & \varepsilon & \cdots & \varepsilon \\ \vdots & \ddots & \vdots & \vdots & \ddots & \vdots \\ \varepsilon & \cdots & \varepsilon & \varepsilon & \cdots & \varepsilon \end{array} \right]} \tag{3.2}$$

If there actually is an edge between node $u_i \in V_1$ and $v_j \in V_1$, entry a_{ij} refers to this edge $(u_i, v_j) \in E_1$, and otherwise to the empty edge ε. Note that there cannot be any edge from an existing node in V_1 to an empty node ε and thus the corresponding entries $a_{ij} \in \mathbf{A}$ with $i > n$ and/or $j > n$ are also empty. The same observations account for entries b_{ij} in $\mathbf{B}$.

Based on the extended node sets

$$V_1^+ = \{u_1, \ldots, u_n, \varepsilon_1, \ldots, \varepsilon_m\} \quad \text{and} \quad V_2^+ = \{v_1, \ldots, v_m, \varepsilon_1, \ldots, \varepsilon_n\}$$

of g_1 and g_2, respectively, a *cost matrix* $\mathbf{C}$ can now be established as follows.

$$
\mathbf{C} =
\begin{array}{c}
\\ u_1 \\ u_2 \\ \vdots \\ u_n \\ \varepsilon_1 \\ \varepsilon_2 \\ \vdots \\ \varepsilon_m
\end{array}
\begin{bmatrix}
\begin{array}{cccc|cccc}
v_1 & v_2 & \cdots & v_m & \varepsilon_1 & \varepsilon_2 & \cdots & \varepsilon_n \\
c_{11} & c_{12} & \cdots & c_{1m} & c_{1\varepsilon} & \infty & \cdots & \infty \\
c_{21} & c_{22} & \cdots & c_{2m} & \infty & c_{2\varepsilon} & \ddots & \vdots \\
\vdots & \vdots & \ddots & \vdots & \vdots & \ddots & \ddots & \infty \\
c_{n1} & c_{n2} & \cdots & c_{nm} & \infty & \cdots & \infty & c_{n\varepsilon} \\
c_{\varepsilon 1} & \infty & \cdots & \infty & 0 & 0 & \cdots & 0 \\
\infty & c_{\varepsilon 2} & \ddots & \vdots & 0 & 0 & \ddots & \vdots \\
\vdots & \ddots & \ddots & \infty & \vdots & \ddots & \ddots & 0 \\
\infty & \cdots & \infty & c_{\varepsilon m} & 0 & \cdots & 0 & 0
\end{array}
\end{bmatrix}
\quad (3.3)
$$

Entry c_{ij} thereby denotes the cost $c(u_i \rightarrow v_j)$ of the node substitution $(u_i \rightarrow v_j)$, $c_{i\varepsilon}$ denotes the cost $c(u_i \rightarrow \varepsilon)$ of the node deletion $(u_i \rightarrow \varepsilon)$, and $c_{\varepsilon j}$ denotes the cost $c(\varepsilon \rightarrow v_j)$ of the node insertion $(\varepsilon \rightarrow v_j)$.

Obviously, the left upper part of the cost matrix $\mathbf{C} = (c_{ij})$ represents the costs of all possible node substitutions, the diagonal of the right upper part the costs of all possible node deletions, and the diagonal of the bottom left part the costs of all possible node insertions. Note that every node can be deleted or inserted at most once. Therefore any non-diagonal element of the right-upper and left-lower part can be set to ∞. The bottom right part of the cost matrix is set to zero since substitutions of the form $(\varepsilon \rightarrow \varepsilon)$ should not cause any cost. In [2–4] alternative definitions of a cost matrix $\mathbf{C}$ have been proposed in order to slightly decrease the size of the problem (however, these reformulations are not adequate for the approach pursued in this chapter).

Given the adjacency matrices $\mathbf{A}$ and $\mathbf{B}$ of the extended graphs g_1 and g_2, respectively, as well as the cost matrix $\mathbf{C}$ (Eqs. 3.1–3.3), the following optimization problem can now be stated.

$$(\varphi_1, \ldots, \varphi_{(n+m)}) = \underset{(\varphi_1,\ldots,\varphi_{(n+m)})\in \mathscr{S}_{(n+m)}}{\arg\min} \left[\sum_{i=1}^{n+m} c_{i\varphi_i} + \sum_{i=1}^{n+m}\sum_{j=1}^{n+m} c(a_{ij} \rightarrow b_{\varphi_i \varphi_j}) \right], \quad (3.4)$$

where $\mathscr{S}_{(n+m)}$ refers to the set of all $(n+m)!$ possible permutations of the integers $1, 2, \ldots, (n+m)$.

The optimal permutation $(\varphi_1, \ldots, \varphi_{(n+m)})$ (as well as any other valid permutation) corresponds to a bijective assignment

$$\lambda = \{(u_1 \to v_{\varphi_1}), (u_2 \to v_{\varphi_2}), \ldots, (u_{m+n} \to v_{\varphi_{m+n}})\}$$

of the extended node set V_1^+ of g_1 to the extended node set V_2^+ of g_2. That is, assignment λ includes node edit operations of the form $(u_i \to v_j)$, $(u_i \to \varepsilon)$, $(\varepsilon \to v_j)$, and $(\varepsilon \to \varepsilon)$ (the latter can be dismissed, of course). In other words, an arbitrary permutation $(\varphi_1, \ldots, \varphi_{(n+m)})$ perfectly corresponds to a valid and complete edit path $\lambda \in \Upsilon(g_1, g_2)$ according to Definition 2.2.

The objective function of the optimization problem stated in Eq. 3.4 consists of a linear term and a quadratic term. Hence, this optimization problem exactly corresponds to a standard quadratic assignment problem. The linear term $\sum_{i=1}^{n+m} c_{i\varphi_i}$ refers to the sum of node edit costs which are defined by the permutation $(\varphi_1, \ldots, \varphi_{n+m})$. The quadratic term $\sum_{i=1}^{n+m} \sum_{j=1}^{n+m} c(a_{ij} \to b_{\varphi_i\varphi_j})$ refers to the implied edge edit cost defined by permutation $(\varphi_1, \ldots, \varphi_{(n+m)})$. That is, since node $u_i \in V_1^+$ is assigned to node $v_{\varphi_i} \in V_2^+$ and node $u_j \in V_1^+$ is assigned to node $v_{\varphi_j} \in V_2^+$, the edge $(u_i, u_j) \in E_1 \cup \{\varepsilon\}$ has to be assigned to the edge $(v_{\varphi_i}, v_{\varphi_j}) \in E_2 \cup \{\varepsilon\}$. These two edges, which might be empty, are stored in $a_{ij} \in \mathbf{A}$ and $b_{\varphi_i\varphi_j} \in \mathbf{B}$, respectively.

The result of a QAP optimization consists of a permutation $(\varphi_1, \ldots, \varphi_{n+m})$ of the integers $(1, 2, \ldots, (n+m))$ that minimizes the overall cost of editing the source graph into the target graph. The minimum cost permutation $(\varphi_1, \ldots, \varphi_{n+m})$ and the minimum cost edit path $\lambda_{\min}$ are thus equivalent to each other. That is, the graph edit distance $d_{\lambda_{\min}}$ can be computed via

$$d_{\lambda_{\min}} = \min_{(\varphi_1,\ldots,\varphi_{(n+m)}) \in \mathscr{S}_{(n+m)}} \left[\sum_{i=1}^{n+m} c_{i\varphi_i} + \sum_{i=1}^{n+m} \sum_{j=1}^{n+m} c(a_{ij} \to b_{\varphi_i\varphi_j}) \right].$$

For our further investigations it will be necessary to subdivide any graph distance value $d_\lambda(g_1, g_2)$ corresponding to a (not necessarily minimal) edit path $\lambda \in \Upsilon(g_1, g_2)$ into the sum of costs $C_\lambda^{\langle V \rangle}$ of all node edit operations $e_i \in \lambda$ and the sum of costs $C_\lambda^{\langle E \rangle}$ of all edge edit operations implied by the node operations $e_j \in \lambda$. That is,

$$d_\lambda(g_1, g_2) = C_\lambda^{\langle V \rangle} + C_\lambda^{\langle E \rangle}. \tag{3.5}$$

Assuming that the permutation $(\varphi_1, \ldots, \varphi_{(n+m)})$ is equivalent to the edit path λ, we have

$$C_\lambda^{\langle V \rangle} = \sum_{i=1}^{n+m} c_{i\varphi_i}$$

and

Fig. 3.1 Two graphs g_1 and g_2

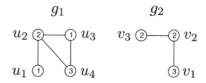

$$C_\lambda^{\langle E \rangle} = \sum_{i=1}^{n+m} \sum_{j=1}^{n+m} c(a_{ij} \to b_{\varphi_i \varphi_j}).$$

Remember that in case of undirected graphs every edge $(u_i, u_j) \in E$ has a reverse counterpart $(u_j, u_i) \in E$ with an identical label. Yet, all of these pairs of edges actually represent only one (undirected) relationship between two nodes. Therefore, in case of undirected edges the quadratic term $C_\lambda^{\langle E \rangle}$ has to be reformulated to

$$\sum_{i=1}^{n+m} \sum_{j=i+1}^{n+m} c(a_{ij} \to b_{\varphi_i \varphi_j})$$

such that every edge of E_1 and E_2 is actually considered only once.[1]

Example 9 Consider, for instance, the two undirected graphs g_1 and g_2 in Fig. 3.1. After extending the node sets V_1 and V_2 we get the following adjacency matrices **A** and **B** for g_1 and g_2, respectively.

$$
\mathbf{A} =
\begin{array}{c}
\begin{array}{ccccccc}
& u_1 & u_2 & u_3 & u_4 & \varepsilon\ \varepsilon\ \varepsilon
\end{array} \\
\begin{array}{c}
u_1 \\ u_2 \\ u_3 \\ u_4 \\ \varepsilon \\ \varepsilon \\ \varepsilon
\end{array}
\left[
\begin{array}{cccc|c}
\varepsilon & (u_1, u_2) & \varepsilon & \varepsilon & \\
(u_2, u_1) & \varepsilon & (u_2, u_3) & (u_2, u_4) & \\
\varepsilon & (u_3, u_2) & \varepsilon & (u_3, u_4) & \varepsilon \\
\varepsilon & (u_4, u_2) & (u_4, u_3) & \varepsilon & \\
\hline
 & & \varepsilon & & \varepsilon
\end{array}
\right]
\end{array}
\tag{3.6}
$$

and

$$
\mathbf{B} =
\begin{array}{c}
\begin{array}{ccccc}
& v_1 & v_2 & v_3 & \varepsilon\ \varepsilon\ \varepsilon\ \varepsilon
\end{array} \\
\begin{array}{c}
v_1 \\ v_2 \\ v_3 \\ \varepsilon \\ \varepsilon \\ \varepsilon \\ \varepsilon
\end{array}
\left[
\begin{array}{ccc|c}
\varepsilon & (v_1, v_2) & \varepsilon & \\
(v_2, v_1) & \varepsilon & (v_2, v_3) & \varepsilon \\
\varepsilon & (v_3, v_2) & \varepsilon & \\
\hline
 & \varepsilon & & \varepsilon
\end{array}
\right]
\end{array}
\tag{3.7}
$$

---

[1] Alternatively, one could use half of the cost. Formally, $\frac{1}{2} \sum_{i=1}^{n+m} \sum_{j=1}^{n+m} c(a_{ij} \to b_{\varphi_i \varphi_j})$.

Defining the cost for node edit operations by $c(u \rightarrow v) = |\mu_1(u) - \mu_2(v)|$ and $c(u \rightarrow \varepsilon) = c(\varepsilon \rightarrow v) = 1$ $(\forall u \in V_1$ and $\forall v \in V_2)$, the following cost matrix $\mathbf{C}$ is obtained.

$$
\mathbf{C} = \begin{array}{c} \\ u_1 \\ u_2 \\ u_3 \\ u_4 \\ \varepsilon \\ \varepsilon \\ \varepsilon \end{array}
\begin{array}{ccc} v_1 & v_2 & v_3 \end{array}
\left[\begin{array}{ccc|cccc}
2 & 1 & 1 & 1 & \infty & \infty & \infty \\
1 & 0 & 0 & \infty & 1 & \infty & \infty \\
2 & 1 & 1 & \infty & \infty & 1 & \infty \\
0 & 1 & 1 & \infty & \infty & \infty & 1 \\ \hline
1 & \infty & \infty & & & & \\
\infty & 1 & \infty & & & 0 & \\
\infty & \infty & 1 & & & & \\
\end{array} \right]
\qquad (3.8)
$$

The following permutation

$$(2, 1, 3, 7, 5, 6, 4)$$

of the integers $(1, \ldots, 7)$ corresponds to the edit path

$$\lambda = \{(u_1 \rightarrow v_2), (u_2 \rightarrow v_1), (u_3 \rightarrow v_3), (u_4 \rightarrow \varepsilon)\}.$$

The linear term of the QAP according to cost matrix $\mathbf{C}$ and with respect to permutation $(2, 1, 3, 7, 5, 6, 4)$ amounts then to

$$C_\lambda^{\langle V \rangle} = \sum_{i=1}^{n+m} c_{i \varphi_i} = 1 + 1 + 1 + 1 + 0 + 0 + 0 = 4.$$

Let us assume that edge substitutions are free of cost while the cost for deletions and insertions of edges is set to 1. Then the quadratic term of the QAP with respect to permutation $(2, 1, 3, 7, 5, 6, 4)$ applied on both adjacency matrices $\mathbf{A}$ and $\mathbf{B}$ amounts to

$$C_\lambda^{\langle E \rangle} = \sum_{i=1}^{n+m} \sum_{j=i+1}^{n+m} c(a_{ij} \rightarrow b_{\varphi_i \varphi_j}) = 4$$

Hence, we have $d_\lambda(g_1, g_2) = 8$.

For the permutation $(4, 3, 2, 1, 5, 6, 7)$, which actually corresponds to one of the optimal edit paths

$$\lambda_{\min} = \{(u_1 \rightarrow \varepsilon), (u_2 \rightarrow v_3), (u_3 \rightarrow v_2), (u_4 \rightarrow v_1)\},$$

we obtain

$$C^{\langle V \rangle}_{\lambda_{\min}} = \sum_{i=1}^{n+m} c_{i\varphi_i} = 2 \quad \text{and} \quad C^{\langle E \rangle}_{\lambda_{\min}} = \sum_{i=1}^{n+m} \sum_{j=i+1}^{n+m} c(a_{ij} \rightarrow b_{\varphi_i\varphi_j}) = 2$$

and thus $d_{\lambda_{\min}}(g_1, g_2) = 4$.

3.2 Bipartite Graph Edit Distance

In recent years, a number of methods addressing the high complexity of graph edit distance computation have been proposed. Local optimization criteria [5–7], for instance, are used to solve the error-tolerant graph matching problem in a more efficient way. Another idea for efficient graph edit distance is to prune the underlying search tree and consequently reduce both the search space and the matching time [8]. Linear programming for computing the edit distance of graphs with unlabeled edges is proposed in [9]. Finding an optimal match between the sets of subgraphs by means of dynamic programming [10, 11] is another possibility for speeding up the computation of graph edit distance.

The author of the present book introduced an algorithmic framework which allows the approximate computation of graph edit distance in a substantially faster way than traditional methods on general graphs [12]. The basic idea of this approach is to reduce the quadratic assignment problem of graph edit distance computation to an instance of a *Linear Sum Assignment Problem (LSAP)*. LSAPs are similar to QAPs in the sense of also formulating an assignment problem of entities. Yet, in contrast with QAPs, LSAPs are able to optimize the permutation $(\varphi_1, \ldots, \varphi_{(n+m)})$ with respect to the linear term $\sum_{i=1}^{n+m} c_{i\varphi_i}$ only. That is, LSAPs consider a single cost matrix $\mathbf{C}$ without any side constraints.

For solving LSAPs a large number of algorithms exist (see [13] for an exhaustive survey). They range from primal-dual combinatorial algorithms [14–16], to simplex-like methods [17, 18] and other approaches [19, 20]. The time complexity of the best performing exact algorithms for LSAPs is cubic in the size of the problem. Hence, LSAPs can be—in contrast with QAPs—quite efficiently solved.

Yet, by omitting the quadratic term $\sum_{i=1}^{n+m} \sum_{j=1}^{n+m} c(a_{ij} \rightarrow b_{\varphi_i\varphi_j})$ during the optimization process, we neglect the structural relationships between the nodes (i.e., the edges between the nodes). In fact, LSAPs are not able to consider these relationships in a global and consistent way. However, in order to integrate knowledge about the graph structure, to each entry $c_{ij} \in \mathbf{C}$, i.e., to each cost of a node edit operation $(u_i \rightarrow v_j)$, the minimum sum of edge edit operation costs, implied by the corresponding node operation, can be added.

Formally, for every entry c_{ij} in the cost matrix $\mathbf{C}$ we solve an LSAP on the in- and outgoing edges of node u_i and v_j and add the resulting cost to c_{ij}. That is, we define

$$c_{ij}^* = c_{ij} + \min_{(\varphi_1, \ldots, \varphi_{(n+m)}) \in \mathcal{S}_{(n+m)}} \sum_{k=1}^{n+m} \left(c(a_{ik} \to b_{j\varphi_k}) + c(a_{ki} \to b_{\varphi_k j}) \right), \qquad (3.9)$$

where $\mathcal{S}_{(n+m)}$ refers to the set of all $(n+m)!$ possible permutations of the integers $1, \ldots, (n+m)$.

For undirected graphs Eq. 3.9 can be slightly simplified as we have to consider only one of the two edges between two nodes (e.g., the outgoing edges). Formally,

$$c_{ij}^* = c_{ij} + \min_{(\varphi_1, \ldots, \varphi_{(n+m)}) \in \mathcal{S}_{(n+m)}} \sum_{k=1}^{n+m} c(a_{ik} \to b_{j\varphi_k}). \qquad (3.10)$$

To entry $c_{i\varepsilon}$, which denotes the cost of a node deletion, the cost of the deletion of all incident edges of u_i can be added, and to the entry $c_{\varepsilon j}$, which denotes the cost of a node insertion, the cost of all insertions of the incident edges of v_j can be added. We denote the cost matrix which is enriched with structural information with $\mathbf{C}^* = (c_{ij}^*)$ from now on.

Example 10 Consider the two graphs g_1 and g_2 in Fig. 3.1, the corresponding extended adjacency matrices $\mathbf{A}$ and $\mathbf{B}$, as well as the cost matrix $\mathbf{C}$ (Eqs. 3.6–3.8). The enriched cost matrix $\mathbf{C}^*$ is then given by

$$\mathbf{C}^* = \begin{array}{c} \\ u_1 \\ u_2 \\ u_3 \\ u_4 \\ \varepsilon \\ \varepsilon \\ \varepsilon \end{array} \begin{array}{ccc} v_1 & v_2 & v_3 \end{array} \begin{array}{cccc} \varepsilon & \varepsilon & \varepsilon & \varepsilon \end{array} \left[\begin{array}{ccc|cccc} 2 & 2 & 1 & 2 & \infty & \infty & \infty \\ 3 & 1 & 2 & \infty & 4 & \infty & \infty \\ 3 & 1 & 2 & \infty & \infty & 3 & \infty \\ 1 & 1 & 2 & \infty & \infty & \infty & 3 \\ \hline 2 & \infty & \infty & & & & \\ \infty & 3 & \infty & & \mathbf{0} & & \\ \infty & \infty & 2 & & & & \end{array} \right]$$

For instance, entry $c_{2\varepsilon}^* = 4$ is composed of $c_{2\varepsilon} = 1$ and the cost of deleting the three incident edges of u_2 $((u_1, u_2), (u_2, u_3),$ and $(u_2, u_4))$. Entry $c_{23}^* = 2$ is composed of $c_{23} = 0$ and the minimal cost of assigning the edges of u_2 to the edges of v_3. Formally,

$$\min_{(\varphi_1, \ldots, \varphi_7) \in \mathcal{S}_7} \sum_{k=1}^{7} c(a_{2k} \to b_{3\varphi_k}) = 2$$

This particular encoding of the minimum matching cost arising from the local edge structure enables the LSAP to consider information about the local, yet not global, edge structure of a graph. Hence, this heuristic procedure partially resolves the issue that LSAP are able to take into account the linear term only. Clearly, a complete solution for this problem would be equivalent to the definition of a QAP (or the exact computation of graph edit distance), which we want to avoid.

In [21, 22] other approaches for encoding the local edge structure into individual entries $c_{ij} \in \mathbf{C}$ have been proposed. The method proposed in [21], for instance, exploits walks centered on each node, while the strategy presented in [22] makes use of small subgraphs defined around each node in order to capture the local edge structure in a more comprehensive way.

In [12] the cost matrix $\mathbf{C}^* = (c_{ij}^*)$ as defined above is employed in order to solve an LSAP. The LSAP optimization consists in finding a permutation $(\varphi_1^*, \ldots, \varphi_{n+m}^*)$ of the integers $(1, 2, \ldots, (n+m))$ that minimizes the overall assignment cost $\sum_{i=1}^{(n+m)} c_{i\varphi_i^*}^*$. Formally, the LSAP solver aims at finding the minimum cost permutation

$$(\varphi_1^*, \ldots, \varphi_{(n+m)}^*) = \underset{(\varphi_1^*, \ldots, \varphi_{(n+m)}^*) \in \mathscr{S}_{(n+m)}}{\arg\min} \sum_{i=1}^{n+m} c_{i\varphi_i^*}^*.$$

Similar to the permutation $(\varphi_1, \ldots, \varphi_{n+m})$ obtained on the QAP, the permutation $(\varphi_1^*, \ldots, \varphi_{n+m}^*)$ corresponds to a bijective assignment of the entities in V_1^+ to the entities in V_2^+ defined by

$$\psi = \{(u_1 \to v_{\varphi_1^*}), (u_2 \to v_{\varphi_2^*}), \ldots, (u_{m+n} \to v_{\varphi_{m+n}^*})\}.$$

Hence, the LSAP optimization finds a permutation $(\varphi_1^*, \ldots, \varphi_{(n+m)}^*)$ which refers to an admissible and complete (yet not necessarily optimal) edit path between the graphs under consideration, i.e., $\psi \in \Upsilon(g_1, g_2)$.[2]

In [12] the algorithm of *Munkres* [14] has been employed in order to solve the basic LSAP stated on $\mathbf{C}^*$, while in [23, 24] the algorithm of *Volgenant-Jonker* [16] is used for the same task. Note that any other algorithm for LSAPs could be employed as well.

Example 11 The permutation

$$(3, 2, 6, 1, 4, 5, 7)$$

is an optimal solution (with a total cost of 6) for the LSAP stated on the enriched cost matrix $\mathbf{C}^*$ in Example 10. This permutation corresponds to the edit path

$$\psi = \{(u_1 \to v_3), (u_2 \to v_2), (u_3 \to \varepsilon), (u_4 \to v_1)\}$$

The total cost of this edit path amounts to 4.

---

[2]Note the change of notation from λ to ψ. From now on we will use ψ for explicitly denoting edit paths, which are found by an LSAP solving algorithm on $\mathbf{C}^*$.

3.2.1   Deriving Upper and Lower Bounds on the Graph Edit Distance

Two different distance values that approximate the exact graph edit distance $d_{\lambda_{\min}}$ (g_1, g_2) can be inferred from the minimum cost permutation $(\varphi_1^*, \ldots, \varphi_{(n+m)}^*)$ derived on $\mathbf{C}^*$, viz., an upper and a lower bound on the true graph edit distance. Let us first consider the upper bound.

Remember that the edge operations are always implied by edit operations on their adjacent nodes. Hence, we can use the node assignment ψ, or more precisely the corresponding permutation $(\varphi_1^*, \ldots, \varphi_{n+m}^*)$, to infer the globally consistent edge edit operations. The sum of costs of the node edit operations and the implied edge costs gives us a first approximation value $d_\psi(g_1, g_2)$, or d_ψ for short, which is defined by

$$d_\psi(g_1, g_2) = \sum_{i=1}^{n+m} c_{i\varphi_i^*} + \sum_{i=1}^{n+m}\sum_{j=1}^{n+m} c(a_{ij} \to b_{\varphi_i^*\varphi_j^*}). \qquad (3.11)$$

The linear term refers to the cost of node edit operations captured in ψ (yet this time applied on $\mathbf{C}$ rather than on $\mathbf{C}^*$). The quadratic term refers to the globally consistent edge edit operations that are implied by the node edit operations in ψ. Remember that in the case of undirected graphs the quadratic term of Eq. 3.11 has to be multiplied by $\frac{1}{2}$ (or the inner sum has to be adapted such that to $j = i + 1, \ldots, n + m$).

Example 12 Applying the permutation

$$(3, 2, 6, 1, 4, 5, 7),$$

which is obtained on $\mathbf{C}^*$ in Example 11, to the original cost matrix $\mathbf{C}$ and the adjacency matrices $\mathbf{A}$ and $\mathbf{B}$ (Eqs. 3.6–3.8), we obtain

$$d_\psi(g_1, g_2) = 2 + 2 = 4$$

Note that in case of $d_{\lambda_{\min}}$ the quadratic term of edge edit cost $\sum_{i=1}^{n+m}\sum_{j=1}^{n+m} c(a_{ij} \to b_{\varphi_i\varphi_j})$ is considered during the QAP optimization for every possible permutation $(\varphi_1, \ldots, \varphi_{(n+m)}) \in \mathscr{S}_{(n+m)}$. Yet, for the approximation $d_\psi(g_1, g_2)$ the sum of edge costs $\sum_{i=1}^{n+m}\sum_{j=1}^{n+m} c(a_{ij} \to b_{\varphi_i^*\varphi_j^*})$ is added to the sum of node edit cost $\sum_{i=1}^{n+m} c_{i\varphi_i^*}$ only after the optimization process has been terminated on $\mathbf{C}^*$ by returning one particular permutation. This is because LSAP solving algorithms are not able to take information about assignments of adjacent nodes into account during run time. In other words, for finding the edit path $\psi \in \varUpsilon(g_1, g_2)$ based on the cost matrix $\mathbf{C}^* = (c_{ij}^*)$ the structural information of the graphs is considered in an isolated way only (single nodes and their adjacent edges). This observation brings us to the following lemma.

Lemma 3.1 *The distance $d_\psi(g_1, g_2)$ derived from the node assignment ψ constitutes an upper bound on the true graph edit distance $d_{\lambda_{\min}}(g_1, g_2)$. That is,*

$$d_\psi(g_1, g_2) \geq d_{\lambda_{\min}}(g_1, g_2)$$

holds for every pair of graphs g_1, g_2.

Proof [25] We distinguish two cases.

1. $\psi = \lambda_{\min}$: That is, the edit path ψ returned by the LSAP approximation framework is identical with the edit path $\lambda_{\min}$ computed by an exact algorithm. In other words, $(\varphi_1, \ldots, \varphi_{(n+m)}) = (\varphi_1^*, \ldots, \varphi_{(n+m)}^*)$. It follows that

$$\sum_{i=1}^{n+m} c_{i\varphi_i} + \sum_{i=1}^{n+m}\sum_{j=1}^{n+m} c(a_{ij} \to b_{\varphi_i\varphi_j}) = \sum_{i=1}^{n+m} c_{i\varphi_i^*} + \sum_{i=1}^{n+m}\sum_{j=1}^{n+m} c(a_{ij} \to b_{\varphi_i^*\varphi_j^*})$$

and thus $d_{\lambda_{\min}} = d_\psi$.
2. $\psi \neq \lambda_{\min}$: In this case $(\varphi_1^*, \ldots, \varphi_{(n+m)}^*) \neq (\varphi_1, \ldots, \varphi_{(n+m)})$ and thus, $d_\psi \neq d_{\lambda_{\min}}$. Note that an exact algorithm for graph edit distance computation optimizes the permutation $(\varphi_1, \ldots, \varphi_{(n+m)})$ with respect to the corresponding edit distance. If we assume that $d_\psi < d_{\lambda_{\min}}$, an exact algorithm for graph edit distance computation, which exhaustively explores $\Upsilon(g_1, g_2)$, would return $(\varphi_1^*, \ldots, \varphi_{(n+m)}^*)$ as optimal permutation with respect to the resulting edit distance. In other words, ψ would refer to the edit path with minimal cost, i.e., $\psi = \lambda_{\min}$. Yet, this is a contradiction to our initial assumption that $\psi \neq \lambda_{\min}$. It follows that $d_\psi > d_{\lambda_{\min}}$.

The distance value $d_\psi(g_1, g_2)$ can be directly used as an approximate graph edit distance between graphs g_1 and g_2. In [25], however, another approximation of the true graph edit distance based on mapping ψ has been defined. As we will see below, this additional approximation builds a lower bound on the true graph edit distance $d_{\lambda_{\min}}(g_1, g_2)$.

The second approximation is based on the minimal sum of assignment costs $\sum_{i=1}^{(n+m)} c_{i\varphi_i^*}^*$ returned by an LSAP solving algorithm. Remember that every entry $c_{i\varphi_i^*}^*$ reflects the cost of the corresponding node edit operation ($u_i \to v_{\varphi_i^*}$) plus the minimal cost of editing the incident edges of u_i to the incident edges of $v_{\varphi_i^*}$. Hence, given an optimal permutation $(\varphi_1^*, \ldots, \varphi_{(n+m)}^*)$, the sum $\sum_{i=1}^{(n+m)} c_{i\varphi_i^*}^*$ can be—similarly to Eq. 3.11—subdivided into costs for node edit operations and costs for edge edit operations.[3] That is,

---

[3]For the sake of convenience we regard the undirected case only. That is, for the computation of $c_{i\varphi_i^*}^*$ the outgoing edges are considered only. Formally, we make use of Eq. 3.10 instead of Eq. 3.9 (yet, the directed case can be defined analogously).

$$\sum_{i=1}^{(n+m)} c_{i\varphi_i^*}^* = \sum_{i=1}^{n+m} \left[c_{i\varphi_i^*} + \min_{(\varphi_1,\dots,\varphi_{(n+m)})\in\mathscr{S}_{(n+m)}} \sum_{k=1}^{n+m} c(a_{ik} \to b_{\varphi_i^*\varphi_k}) \right]$$

$$= \sum_{i=1}^{n+m} c_{i\varphi_i^*} + \sum_{i=1}^{n+m} \left[\min_{(\varphi_1,\dots,\varphi_{(n+m)})\in\mathscr{S}_{(n+m)}} \sum_{k=1}^{n+m} c(a_{ik} \to b_{\varphi_i^*\varphi_k}) \right]. \quad (3.12)$$

Analogously to Eq. 3.11, the first sum corresponds to the sum of costs for node edit operations. Yet, note the difference between

$$\sum_{i=1}^{n+m} \left[\min_{(\varphi_1,\dots,\varphi_{(n+m)})\in\mathscr{S}_{(n+m)}} \sum_{k=1}^{n+m} c(a_{ik} \to b_{\varphi_i^*\varphi_k}) \right] \quad (3.13)$$

and

$$\sum_{i=1}^{n+m} \sum_{j=i+1}^{n+m} c(a_{ij} \to b_{\varphi_i^*\varphi_j^*}). \quad (3.14)$$

The sum in Eq. 3.14 reflects the costs of editing the edge structure from g_1 to the edge structure of g_2 in a globally consistent way. That is, the edge structure is edited with respect to the edit operations $(u_i \to v_{\varphi_i^*})$ and $(u_j \to v_{\varphi_j^*})$ applied on both adjacent nodes of every edge (thus, the edge a_{ij} is edited with the edge $b_{\varphi_i^*\varphi_j^*}$). Yet, the sum in Eq. 3.13 is based on limited, because local, information about the edge structure only. That is, for this particular sum the information about one single node operation is available only, viz., $(u_i \to v_{\varphi_i^*})$. Based on this information, the edge structure of node u_i is then edited with the edge structure of $v_{\varphi_i^*}$ in a minimal cost way.

Every edge (u_i, u_j) is adjacent with two individual nodes u_i and u_j and thus the sum of minimal local edge edit costs (Eq. 3.13) considers every edge twice in two independent edit operations (once in row i and once in row j). In order to derive a suitable approximation $d'_\psi(g_1, g_2)$ for the true edit distance, the sum of Eq. 3.13 has thus to be multiplied by $\frac{1}{2}$. Formally, we define the second approximative graph edit distance $d'_\psi(g_1, g_2)$ by

$$d'_\psi(g_1, g_2) = \min_{(\varphi_1^*,\dots,\varphi_{(n+m)}^*)\in\mathscr{S}_{(n+m)}} \sum_{i=1}^{n+m} c_{i\varphi_i^*}$$

$$+ \frac{1}{2} \sum_{i=1}^{n+m} \left[\min_{(\varphi_1,\dots,\varphi_{(n+m)})\in\mathscr{S}_{(n+m)}} \sum_{k=1}^{n+m} c(a_{ik} \to b_{\varphi_i^*\varphi_k}) \right] \quad (3.15)$$

Note that $d'_\psi(g_1, g_2)$ only depends on the permutation $(\varphi_1^*, \dots, \varphi_{(n+m)}^*)$, which is already computed for d_ψ.

The approximation d_ψ corresponds to an admissible and complete edit path with respect to the nodes and edges of the underlying graphs. Yet, the second approximation d'_ψ is not related to a valid edit path since the edges of both graphs are not uniquely assigned to each other (or deleted/inserted at most once).

Example 13 Given the permutation

$$(3, 2, 6, 1, 4, 5, 7)$$

which is obtained on **C*** in Example 11, we get

$$d'_\psi = 1 + 0 + 1 + 0 + 0 + 0 + 0 + \frac{0 + 1 + 2 + 1 + 0 + 0 + 0}{2} = 4$$

The following lemma shows an ordering relationship between d_ψ and d'_ψ.

Lemma 3.2 *For the graph edit distance approximations $d_\psi(g_1, g_2)$ (Eq. 3.11) and $d'_\psi(g_1, g_2)$ (Eq. 3.15) the inequality*

$$d'_\psi(g_1, g_2) \le d_\psi(g_1, g_2)$$

holds for every pair of graphs g_1, g_2 and every complete node assignment ψ.

Proof For the present proof we regard the undirected case. However, the directed case can be derived analogously.

Let us assume that ψ corresponds to the permutation $(\varphi_1^*, \ldots, \varphi_{(n+m)}^*) \in \mathscr{S}_{(n+m)}$. According to Eqs. 3.11 and 3.15 we have to show that

$$\frac{1}{2} \sum_{i=1}^{n+m} \left[\min_{(\varphi_1, \ldots, \varphi_{(n+m)}) \in \mathscr{S}_{(n+m)}} \sum_{k=1}^{n+m} c(a_{ik} \to b_{\varphi_i^* \varphi_k}) \right] \le \frac{1}{2} \sum_{i=1}^{n+m} \sum_{j=1}^{n+m} c(a_{ij} \to b_{\varphi_i^* \varphi_j^*}).$$

In order to show this inequality, we show that the inequality holds for all $(n + m)$ addends of both outer sums. That is, we show that

$$\min_{(\varphi_1, \ldots, \varphi_{(n+m)}) \in \mathscr{S}_{(n+m)}} \sum_{k=1}^{n+m} c(a_{ik} \to b_{\varphi_i^* \varphi_k}) \le \sum_{j=1}^{n+m} c(a_{ij} \to b_{\varphi_i^* \varphi_j^*}) \qquad (3.16)$$

holds for $i = 1, \ldots, (n + m)$.

In both sums, all $(n + m)$ entries $a_{ij} \in \mathbf{A}$ of row i ($j = 1, \ldots, (n + m)$) are uniquely assigned to the $(n + m)$ entries in row φ_i^* of **B**. The right side of Eq. 3.16 regards only one possible assignment of these entries, viz., the assignment according to permutation $(\varphi_1^*, \ldots, \varphi_{(n+m)}^*) \in \mathscr{S}_{(n+m)}$. Yet, on the left side of Eq. 3.16 we seek for the minimum cost permutation $(\varphi_1, \ldots, \varphi_{(n+m)}) \in \mathscr{S}_{(n+m)}$ for assigning these $(n + m)$ entries to each other. Hence, if $(\varphi_1, \ldots, \varphi_{(n+m)}) = (\varphi_1^*, \ldots, \varphi_{(n+m)}^*)$ both terms in Eq. 3.16 are equal, otherwise, the left side of Eq. 3.16 has to be smaller than the right side due to the minimization process.

We can now show that d'_ψ constitutes a lower bound on $d_{\lambda_{\min}}$.

Lemma 3.3 *The distance $d'_\psi(g_1, g_2)$ derived from the node assignment ψ constitutes a lower bound on the true graph edit distance $d_{\lambda_{\min}}(g_1, g_2)$. That is,*

$$d'_\psi(g_1, g_2) \leq d_{\lambda_{\min}}(g_1, g_2)$$

holds for every pair of graphs g_1, g_2.

Proof [25] We distinguish two cases.

1. $\psi = \lambda_{\min}$: In this case ψ is the optimal edit path and thus $d_\psi = d_{\lambda_{\min}}$. From Lemma 3.2 we know that $d'_\psi \leq d_\psi$ and thus $d'_\psi \leq d_{\lambda_{\min}}$.
2. $\psi \neq \lambda_{\min}$: In this case ψ corresponds to a suboptimal edit path with cost d_ψ greater than (or possibly equal to) $d_{\lambda_{\min}}$. The question remains whether or not $d_{\lambda_{\min}} < d'_\psi$ might hold in this case. According to Lemma 3.2 we know that $d'_{\lambda_{\min}} \leq d_{\lambda_{\min}}$ and thus by assuming that $d_{\lambda_{\min}} < d'_\psi$, it follows that $d'_{\lambda_{\min}} < d'_\psi$. Yet, this is contradictory to the optimality of the LSAP solving algorithm that guarantees to find the assignment ψ with lowest cost d'_ψ.

We can now conclude this section with the following theorem.

Theorem 3.1

$$d'_\psi(g_1, g_2) \leq d_{\lambda_{\min}}(g_1, g_2) \leq d_\psi(g_1, g_2) \quad \forall g_1, g_2$$

Proof See Lemmas 3.1–3.3.

3.2.2 Summary

Algorithm 2 BP-GED(g_1, g_2)

1: Build cost matrix $\mathbf{C}^* = (c_{ij}^*)$ according to the input graphs g_1 and g_2
2: Compute optimal node assignment $\psi = \{u_1 \rightarrow v_{\varphi_1}, \dots, u_{m+n} \rightarrow v_{\varphi_{m+n}}\}$ on $\mathbf{C}^*$
3: Complete edit path according to ψ and **return** $d_\psi(g_1, g_2)$ and/or $d'_\psi(g_1, g_2)$

From a high level perspective, the algorithmic framework presented in [12] consists of three major steps (see Algorithm 2). In a first step the graphs to be matched are subdivided into individual nodes including local structural information. Next, in step 2, an algorithm that solves the LSAP is employed in order to find an optimal assignment of the nodes (plus local structures) of both graphs. Finally, in step 3, an approximate graph edit distance (i.e., both an upper and lower bound) is derived from the assignment of step 2. For the remainder of this book we denote this graph edit distance approximation algorithm with *BP-GED* (*Bipartite Graph Edit Distance*[4]).

---

[4]The assignment problem can also be formulated as finding a matching in a *complete bipartite graph* and is therefore also referred to as *bipartite graph matching problem*.

3.3 Experimental Evaluation

Overall aim of this experimental evaluation (originally published in [26]) is to empirically measure the under- and overestimation of BP-GED. To this end, we compute the mean relative deviation ($\varnothing e$) from the true graph edit distance achieved with the lower and upper bound d'_ψ and d_ψ, respectively. Obviously, the smaller this mean relative deviation is, the better (i.e., nearer to the exact distance) is the approximation.

For experimental evaluations four data sets from the IAM graph database repository for graph-based pattern recognition and machine learning are used [27]. The graph data sets involve graphs that represent molecular compounds (AIDS), fingerprint images (FP), symbols from architectural and electronic drawings (GREC), and letter line drawings (LETTER). For details on the graphs, the graph extraction processes, as well as the definition of the cost model we refer to Chap. 9. From all data sets used in the present experimental evaluation, subsets of 1,000 graphs are randomly selected.

In Table 3.1 the mean relative error $\varnothing e$ and the matching time $\varnothing t$ achieved with BP-GED are shown. First we focus on the exact distances $d_{\lambda_{min}}$ provided by A*. As $d_{\lambda_{min}}$ refers to the exact edit distance values, the mean relative error $\varnothing e$ is zero on all data sets, of course. We observe that the mean run time for the computation of $d_{\lambda_{min}}$ lies between 3.1 and 5.6 s on the first three data sets, while on the rather simple LETTER graphs the exact computation can be conducted in less than 2 ms on average.

Using the approximation framework BP-GED, a massive speed-up of computation time can be observed. That is, on all data sets the graph edit distance approximation framework allows the computation of d_ψ and d'_ψ in less than (or approximately) 0.5 ms on average (note that both distance measures are simultaneously computed and thus offer the same matching time).

Yet, the substantial speed-up is at the expense of loss of distance accuracy. That is, the upper bound d_ψ differs by 15.37 % on average from the exact graph edit distance on the AIDS data set, while on FP and GREC the mean relative error of the approximation amount to 5.76 and 2.89 %, respectively. On the LETTER data set the approximation value d_ψ strongly overestimates the true edit distance by 27.19 % on average. The lower bound d'_ψ leads to better approximation on three out of four data sets (all but GREC). On the FP data set the mean relative error can be dramatically decreased from 5.76 to 0.36 % when employing d'_ψ rather than d_ψ.

Table 3.1 The mean relative error of the approximated graph edit distance ($\varnothing e$) in percentage and the mean run time for one matching in ms ($\varnothing t$) using a specific graph edit distance computation

Distance	Data Set							
	AIDS		FP		GREC		LETTER	
	$\varnothing e$	$\varnothing t$	$\varnothing e$	$\varnothing t$	$\varnothing e$	$\varnothing t$	$\varnothing e$	$\varnothing t$
$d_{\lambda_{min}}$	0.00	5629.53	0.00	5000.85	0.00	3103.76	0.00	1.86
d_ψ	15.37	0.44	5.76	0.56	2.89	0.43	27.19	0.17
d'_ψ	8.41	0.44	0.36	0.56	3.53	0.43	15.67	0.17

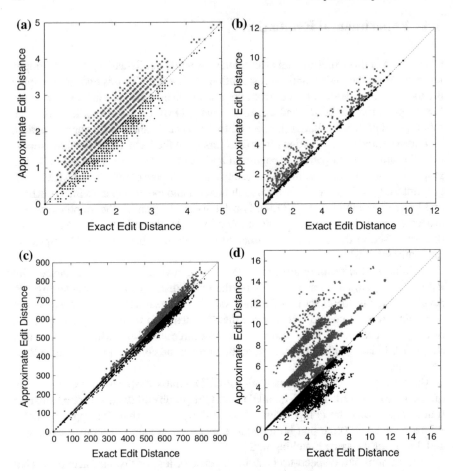

Fig. 3.2 Exact (x-axis) versus approximate (y-axis) graph edit distance computed with BP-GED resulting in d_ψ (*red points*) and d'_ψ (*black points*) on all data sets. **a** AIDS, **b** FP, **c** GREC, **d** LETTER

The over- and underestimation of d_ψ and d'_ψ compared to $d_{\lambda_{\min}}$ can be also observed in the correlation scatter plots in Fig. 3.2 on all data sets. These scatter plots give us a visual representation of the accuracy of the approximations. Every figure shows for each pair of graphs their exact distance $d_{\lambda_{\min}}$ on the x-axis and approximate distance values d_ψ (red dots) and d'_ψ (black dots) on the y-axis. The over- and underestimation of the exact edit distance is clearly observable. In Fig. 3.2b the remarkable result achieved by the lower bound d'_ψ on the FP data is clearly visible.

The algorithm BP-GED might find an optimal node assignment which eventually causes additional edge operations, which are in turn often deletions or insertions. This leads to additional costs of a multiple of the edit cost parameter and explains the accumulation of points in line-like areas parallel to the diagonal in some of the plots.

3.4   Pattern Recognition Applications of Bipartite Graph Edit Distance

The approximation framework BP-GED has been used in various pattern recognition applications during the last decade. In the next five paragraphs some major application areas, which have been (in part) tackled by means of BP-GED, are briefly summarized.

Chemoinformatics

Chemoinformatics has become a well established field of research. Chemoinformatics is mainly concerned with the prediction of molecular properties by means of informational techniques. The assumption that two similar molecules should have similar activities and properties, is one of the major principles in this particular field. Clearly, molecules can be readily described with labeled graphs $G = (V, E, \mu, \nu)$, where the edges encode the structure of the molecule while μ assigns the atoms label to the corresponding nodes and ν typically characterizes the type of bond between two atoms (e.g., *single*, *double*, *triple*, or *aromatic*).

In [28, 29] the approximation of graph edit distance by means of BP-GED is used to build a novel graph kernel for activity predictions of molecular compounds. In [30] various graph embeddings methods and graph kernels, which are in part built upon the BP-GED framework, are evaluated in diverse chemoinformatics applications. Finally, in [31] an algorithm to compute single summary graphs from a collection of molecule graphs has been proposed. The formulation of the cost of a matching, which is actually used in this methodology, is based on BP-GED.

Malware Detection

Anti-virus companies receive huge amounts of samples of potentially harmful executables. This growing amount of data makes robust and automatic detection of malware necessary. The differentiation between malicious and original binary executables is another field where the framework BP-GED has been extensively used. In [32–36], for instance, malware detection based on comparisons of *call graphs* has been proposed. In particular, the authors propose to represent malware samples as call graphs such that certain variations of the malware can be generalized. This approach enables the detection of structural similarities between samples in a robust way. For pairwise comparisons of these call graphs the approximation of BP-GED is employed. In [37] a similar approach has been pursued for the detection of malware by using weighted contextual API dependency graphs in conjunction with an extended version of BP-GED for graph comparison. Finally, in [33] BP-GED has been employed for the development of a polynomial time algorithm for calculating the differences between two binaries.

Biometrics

The approximation framework BP-GED has been also used in various applications for biometric person authentication (e.g., in authentication systems which are based on

the retina [38, 39], hand vein images [40], or fingerprints [41]). Re-identification, that
is recognizing whether an object appearing in a scene is a reoccurrence of an object
seen previously by the system (by the same camera or possibly by a different one) is
a challenging problem in video surveillance. In [42, 43], this problem is addressed
by means of a graph-based representation of the objects of interest. Eventually, the
similarity between the extracted graphs is computed with a method that is based on
BP-GED.

Document Analysis

The graph edit distance framework BP-GED has been also used in the context of
document analysis. In [44, 45], for instance, BP-GED is used for keyword spotting,
which refers to the process of retrieving all instances of a given keyword or a key
phrase from a document. Handwriting recognition, which is in part based on BP-
GED has been proposed in [46–48]. Other document analysis applications that make
use of the approximation framework BP-GED are concerned with the clustering
of historical document images [49], the retrieval of envelope images [50], and the
clarification of the relationships among different online news events [51].

Other Application Fields

The framework BP-GED has also been used for ontology matching [52, 53], shoeprint
recognition [54], petroglyph similarity computation [55], story similarity estimation [56], forecasts of thermal breakthroughs [57], plagiarism detection [58, 59],
software engineering [60], and medical image analysis [61, 62].

References

1. T.C. Koopmans, M.J. Beckmann, Assignment problems and the location of economic activities.
   Econometrica **25**, 53–76 (1975)
2. K. Riesen, M. Neuhaus, H. Bunke, Bipartite graph matching for computing the edit distance
   of graphs, in *Proceedings of 6th International Workshop on Graph Based Representations in
   Pattern Recognition*. LNCS, vol. 4538, ed. by F. Escolano, M. Vento (2007), pp. 1–12
3. F. Serratosa, Fast computation of bipartite graph matching. Pattern Recognit. Lett. **45**, 244–250
   (2014)
4. F. Serratosa, Speeding up fast bipartite graph matching through a new cost matrix. Int. J. Pattern
   Recognit. Art. Intell. **29**(2) (2015)
5. M. Neuhaus, H. Bunke, *Bridging the Gap Between Graph Edit Distance and Kernel Machines*
   (World Scientific, Singapore, 2007)
6. M.C. Boeres, C.C. Ribeiro, I. Bloch, A randomized heuristic for scene recognition by graph
   matching, in *Proceedings of 3rd Workshop on Efficient and Experimental Algorithms*. LNCS,
   vol. 3059, ed. by C.C. Ribeiro, S.L. Martins (Springer, New York, 2004), pp. 100–113
7. S. Sorlin, C. Solnon, Reactive tabu search for measuring graph similarity, in *Proceedings of
   5th International Workshop on Graph-based Representations in Pattern Recognition*. LNCS,
   vol. 3434, ed. by L. Brun, M. Vento (Springer, New York, 2005), pp. 172–182
8. M. Neuhaus, K. Riesen, H. Bunke, Fast suboptimal algorithms for the computation of graph edit
   distance, in *Proceedings of 11th International Workshop on Strucural and Syntactic Pattern
   Recognition*. LNCS, vol. 4109, ed. by D.-Y. Yeung, J.T. Kwok, A. Fred, F. Roli, D. de Ridder
   (2006), pp. 163–172

9. D. Justice, A. Hero, A binary linear programming formulation of the graph edit distance. IEEE Trans. Pattern Anal. Mach. Intell. **28**(8), 1200–1214 (2006)
10. M.A. Eshera, K.S. Fu, A graph distance measure for image analysis. IEEE Trans. Syst. Man Cybern. (Part B) **14**(3), 398–408 (1984)
11. M.A. Eshera, K.S. Fu, A similarity measure between attributed relational graphs for image analysis, *Proceedings of 7th International Confernece on Pattern Recognition* (1984), pp. 75–77
12. K. Riesen, H. Bunke, Approximate graph edit distance computation by means of bipartite graph matching. Image Vis. Comput. **27**(4), 950–959 (2009)
13. R. Burkard, M. Dell'Amico, S. Martello, *Assignment Problems*, Society for Industrial and Applied Mathematics (Philadelphia, 2009)
14. J. Munkres, Algorithms for the assignment and transportation problems. J. Soc. Ind. Appl. Math. **5**(1), 32–38 (1957)
15. H.W. Kuhn, The Hungarian method for the assignment problem. Nav. Res. Logist. Q. **2**, 83–97 (1955)
16. R. Jonker, A. Volgenant, A shortest augmenting path algorithm for dense and sparse linear assignment problems. Computing **38**, 325–340 (1987)
17. J.B. Orlin, On the simplex algorithm for networks and generalized networks. Math. Program. Stud. **24**, 166–178 (1985)
18. R.K. Ahuja, J.B. Orlin, The scaling network simplex algorithm. Oper. Res. **40**(1), 5–13 (1992)
19. V. Srinivasan, G.L. Thompson, Cost operator algorithms for the transportation problem. Math. Program. **12**, 372–391 (1977)
20. H. Achatz, P. Kleinschmidt, K. Paparrizos, Chapter A dual forest algorithm for the assignment problem, *Applied Geometry and Discrete Mathematics* (AMS, Providence, 1991), pp. 1–11
21. B. Gauzere, S. Bougleux, K. Riesen, L. Brun, Approximate graph edit distance guided by bipartite matching of bags of walks, in *Proceedings of International Workshop on Structural and Syntactic Pattern Recognition*. LNCS, vol. 8621, ed. by P. Fränti, G. Brown, M. Loog, F. Escolano, M. Pelillo (2014), pp. 73–82
22. V. Carletti, B. Gauzere, L. Brun, M. Vento, Approximate graph edit distance computation combining bipartite matching and exact neighborhood substructure distance, in *Proceedings of 10th International Workshop on Graph Based Representations in Pattern Recognition*. LNCS, vol. 9069, ed. by C.L. Liu, B. Luo, W. Kropatsch, J. Cheng (2015), pp. 188–197
23. S. Fankhauser, K. Riesen, H. Bunke, Speeding up graph edit distance computation through fast bipartite matching, in *Proceedings of 8th International Workshop on Graph Based Representations in Pattern Recognition*. LNCS, vol. 6658, ed. by X. Jiang, M. Ferrer, A. Torsello (2011), pp. 102–111
24. W. Jones, A. Chawdhary, A. King, Revisiting volgenant-jonker for approximating graph edit distance, in *Proceedings of 10th International Workshop on Graph Based Representations in Pattern Recognition*. LNCS, vol. 9069, ed. by C.L. Liu, B. Luo, W. Kropatsch, J. Cheng (2015), pp. 98–107
25. K. Riesen, A. Fischer, H. Bunke, Computing upper and lower bounds of graph edit distance in cubic time, in *Proceedings of International Workshop on Artificial Neural Networks in Pattern Recognition*. LNAI, vol. 8774, ed. by N.E. Gayar, F. Schwenker, Ch. Suen (2014), pp. 129–140
26. K. Riesen, A. Fischer, H. Bunke, Estimating graph edit distance using lower and upper bounds of bipartite approximations. Int. J. Pattern Recognit. Artif. Intell. **29**(2) (2015)
27. K. Riesen, H. Bunke, IAM graph database repository for graph based pattern recognition and machine learning, in *Structural, Syntactic, and Statistical Pattern Recognition*, vol. 5342, LNCS, ed. by N. da Vitoria Lobo, et al. (a, a, 2008), pp. 287–297
28. B. Gauzere, L. Brun, D. Villemin, Two new graph kernels and applications to chemoinformatics, in *Proceedings 8th International Workshop on Graph Based Representations in Pattern Recognition*, ed. by X. Jiang, M. Ferrer, A. Torsello (2011), pp. 112–121
29. L. Brun, D. Conte, P. Foggia, M. Vento, Symbolic learning vs. graph kernels: An experimental comparison in a chemical application, in *Proceedings of the Fourteenth East-European Conference on Advances in Databases and Information Systems*, ed. by I. Ivanovic, B. Thalheim, B. Catania, Z. Budimac (2010), pp. 31–40

30. B. Gauzere, H. Makoto, L. Brun, S. Tabbone, Implicit and explicit graph embedding: Comparison of both approaches on chemoinformatics applications, in *Proceedings of 14th International Workshop on Structural and Syntactic Pattern Recognition*. LNCS, vol. 7626, ed. by G. Gimel'farb, E.R. Hancock, A. Imiya, A. Kuijper, M. Kudo, S. Omachi, T. Windeatt, K. Yamad (2012), pp. 510–518

31. D. Koop, J. Freire, C.T. Silva, Visual summaries for graph collections, in *Proceedings of IEEE Pacific Visualization Symposium (PacificVis)* (2013), pp. 57–64

32. J. Kinable, O. Kostakis, Malware classification based on call graph clustering. J. Comput. Virol. **7**(4), 233–245 (2011)

33. M. Bourquin, A. King, E. Robbins, Binslayer: Accurate comparison of binary executables, in *Proceedings 2nd ACM SIGPLAN Program Protection and Reverse Engineering Workshop* (2013)

34. A.A.E. Elhadi, M.A. Maarof, A.H. Osman, Malware detection based on hybrid signature behaviour application programming interface call graph. Am. J. Appl. Sci. **9**(3), 283–288 (2012)

35. O. Kostakis, H. Mahmoudi, J. Kinable, K. Mustonen, Improved call graph comparison using simulated annealing, in *Proceedings of 2011 ACM Symposium on Applied Computing* (2011), pp. 1516–1523

36. O. Kostakis, Classy: fast clustering streams of call-graphs. Data Min. Knowl. Discov. **28**(5–6), 1554–1585 (2014)

37. M. Zhang, Y. Duan, H. Yin, Z. Zhao, Semantics-aware android malware classification using weighted contextual api dependency graphs, in *Proceedings of 2014 ACM SIGSAC Conference on Computer and Communications Security* (2014), pp. 1105–1116

38. A. Arakala, S.A. Davis, K.J. Horadam, Retina features based on vessel graph substructures, in *International Joint Conference on Biometrics (IJCB)* (2011), pp. 1–6

39. S. Mehdi, A. Arakala, S.A. Davis, K.J. Horadam, Retina verification system based on biometric graph matching. IEEE Trans. Image Process. **22**(9), 3625–3635 (2013)

40. S. Mehdi Lajevardi, A. Arakala, S.A. Davis, K.J. Horadam, Hand vein authentication using biometric graph matching. IET Biom. **3**(4), 302–313 (2014)

41. Y. Choi, G. Kim, Graph-based fingerpring classification using orientation field in core area. IEICE Electron. Express **7**(17), 1303–1309 (2010)

42. L. Brun, D. Conte, P. Foggia, M. Vento, People re-identification by graph kernels methods, in *Proceedings of 8th Int Workshop on Graph Based Representations in Pattern Recognition*. LNCS, vol. 6658, ed. by X. Jiang, M. Ferrer, A. Torsello (2011), pp. 285–294

43. L. Brun, D. Conte, P. Foggia, M. Vento, A graph-kernel method for re-identification, in *Proceedings of Image Analysis and Recognition*. LNCS, vol. 6753, ed. by M. Kamel, A. Campilho (2011), pp. 173–182

44. P. Wang, V. Eglin, Ch. Largeron, J. Lladós, A. Fornés, A novel learning-free word spotting approach based on graph representation, in *Proceedings of 11th IAPR International Workshop on Document Analysis Systems* (2014), pp. 207–211

45. P. Wang, V. Eglin, Ch. Largeron, J. Lladós, A. Fornés, A coarse-to-fine word spotting approach for historical handwritten documents based on graph embedding and graph edit distance, in *Proceedings of 22nd International Conference on Pattern Recognition (ICPR)* (2014), pp. 3074–3079

46. A. Fischer, K. Riesen, H. Bunke, Graph similarity features for hmm-based handwriting recognition in historical documents, in *Proceedings of International Conference on Frontiers in Handwriting Recognition* (2010), pp. 253–258

47. A. Fischer, C.Y. Suen, V. Frinken, K. Riesen, H. Bunke, A fast matching algorithm for graph-based handwriting recognition, in *Proceedings of 8th International Workshop on Graph Based Representations in Pattern Recognition*. LNCS, vol. 7877, ed. by W. Kropatsch, N. Artner, Y. Haxhimusa, X. Jiang (2013), pp. 194–203

48. A. Fischer, H. Bunke, Character prototype selection for handwriting recognition in historical documents with graph similarity features, in *Proceedings of 19th European Signal Processing Conference* (2011), pp. 1435–1439

49. S. Jouili, M. Coustaty, S. Tabbone, J.-M. Ogier, Navidomass: Structural-based approaches towards handling historical documents, in *Proceedings of 20th International Conference on Pattern Recognition* (2010), pp. 946–949
50. L. Liu, Y. Lu, C.Y. Suen, Retrieval of envelope images using graph matching, in *Proceedings* (2011), pp. 99–103
51. H. Ishii, Q. Ma, M. Yoshikawa, Incremental construction of causal network from news articles. Inf. Media Technol. **7**(1), 110–118 (2012)
52. D. Sanchez, A. Solé-Ribalta, M. Batet, F. Serratosa, Enabling semantic similarity estimation across multiple ontologies: An evaluation in the biomedical domain. J. Biomed. Inform. **45**, 141–155 (2012)
53. A. Solé-Ribalta, D. Sanchez, M. Batet, F. Serratosa, Towards the estimation of feature-based semantic similarity using multiple ontologies. Knowl.-Based Syst. **55**, 101–113 (2014)
54. M. Hasegawa, S. Tabbone, A local adaptation of the histogram radon transform descriptor: an application to a shoe print dataset, in *Proceedings of 14th International Workshop on Structural and Syntactic Pattern Recognition*. LNCS, vol. 7626, ed. by G. Gimel'farb, E.R. Hancock, A. Imiya, A. Kuijper, M. Kudo, S. Omachi, T. Windeatt, K. Yamad (2012), pp. 675–683
55. M. Seidl, E. Wieser, M. Zeppelzauer, A. Pinz, Ch. Breiteneder, Graph-based shape similarity of petroglyphs, in *Computer Vision—ECCV 2014 Workshops*. LNCS, vol. 8925, ed. by L. Agapito, et al. (2015), pp. 133–148
56. S. Paul, Exploring story similairities using graph edit distance algorithms, Master's thesis, University of Delaware (2013)
57. M. Ames, Ph. Brodrick, R. Horne, A framework for comparative inverse modeling of tracers for thermal breakthrough forecasting using fracture network models, *Proceedings of Fourtieth Workshop on Geothermal Reservoir Engineering* (2014)
58. H.D Rokenes, Graph-based natural language processing—graph edit distance applied to the task of detecting plagiarism, Master's thesis, Norwegian University of Science and Technology (2012)
59. M.L. Kammer, Plagiarism detection in haskell programs using call graph matching, Master's thesis, Utrecht University (2011)
60. H. Kpodjedo, Approximate Graph Matching for Software Engineering. Ph.D. thesis, Ecole Polytechnique de Montreal (2011)
61. J.M. Nunez, J. Bernal, M. Ferrer, F. Vilarino, Impact of keypoint detection on graph-based characterization of blood vessels in colonoscopy videos, in *Computer-Assisted and Robotic Endoscopy*. LNCS, vol. 8899, ed. by X. Luo (2014), pp. 22–33
62. E. Ozdemir, C. Gunduz-Demir, A hybrid classification model for digital pathology using structural and statistical pattern recognition. IEEE Trans. Med. Imag. **32**(2), 474–483 (2013)

Part II
Recent Developments and Research on Graph Edit Distance

Chapter 4
Improving the Distance Accuracy of Bipartite Graph Edit Distance

Abstract One of the major problems of the approximation framework BP-GED (presented in the previous chapter) is that it over- or underestimates the true edit distance quite often. This chapter is concerned with two recent extensions of BP-GED that aim at making the distance approximation more accurate. The first idea is based on a post-processing search procedure. That is, rather than directly returning the approximate edit distance $d_\psi(g_1, g_2)$, a search procedure taking the initial assignment ψ as the starting point is carried out. The second strategy for reducing the approximation error of BP-GED is to take more structural information into account when the basic assignment problem is solved on the local substructures of the graphs. To this end, various node centrality measures, originally developed in the context of network analysis, have been adopted by the matching process of BP-GED. These two lines of research are reviewed and evaluated in the present chapter (in Sects. 4.2 and 4.3, respectively).

4.1 Change of Notation

In the present (as well as in the following) chapter we assume that an LSAP solving algorithm has found an optimal permutation $(\varphi_1^*, \ldots, \varphi_{(n+m)}^*)$ on the enriched cost matrix $\mathbf{C}^*$. That is, we make use of BP-GED as thoroughly defined in Sect. 3.2. Yet, for the sake of simplicity and better readability, we conduct the following change of notation, which is used for the remainder of the present book.

- We write $\mathbf{C}$ instead of $\mathbf{C}^*$, and
- $(\varphi_1, \ldots, \varphi_{(n+m)})$ instead of $(\varphi_1^*, \ldots, \varphi_{(n+m)}^*)$.

That is, we omit the asterisk in both the enriched cost matrix and the optimal permutation achieved on $\mathbf{C}^*$. However, for the edit path that corresponds to the permutation as well as the corresponding approximate edit distance, we use the same notation as in Part I of the present book, viz. ψ and d_ψ, respectively.

Moreover, note that in this chapter, we are concerned with the upper bound d_ψ of the exact edit distance $d_{\lambda_{\min}}$ only. In particular, we show how the accuracy of this

© Springer International Publishing Switzerland 2015
K. Riesen, *Structural Pattern Recognition with Graph Edit Distance*,
Advances in Computer Vision and Pattern Recognition,
DOI 10.1007/978-3-319-27252-8_4

upper bound can be substantially improved with respect to the true edit distance. The lower bound d'_ψ is actually not considered for these improvements. Note, however, that all algorithms described in the present chapter could be readily applied for the improvement of d'_ψ as well.

4.2 Improvements via Search Strategies

In the experimental evaluation of [1] it has been empirically confirmed that the suboptimality of BP-GED is very often due to a few incorrectly assigned nodes in ψ. That is, only few incorrect node edit operations from the second step of Algorithm 2 are responsible for the additional, suboptimal edit operations in the third step (and the resulting overestimation of the true edit distance). The work presented in [1] ties in at this observation. In particular, it has been proposed to improve the quality of the distance approximation $d_\psi(g_1, g_2)$ by systematically varying the initial assignment ψ to get improved assignments $\psi_1, \psi_2, \ldots$ with respect to their corresponding distance approximations $d_{\psi_1}(g_1, g_2), d_{\psi_2}(g_1, g_2), \ldots$

Two major challenges have to be dealt by this search procedure. First, the search space contains $(n + m)!$ variations of the assignment ψ. Hence, an exhaustive search on these variations is both unreasonable and intractable. Second, the variations $\psi_1, \psi_2, \ldots$ that are constructed from ψ have to remain bijective—otherwise no valid graph edit distance approximation can be derived from them.

In [1] six different search strategies, which are actually able to meet the given requirements, have been introduced. The basic idea of the first three search procedures is to prevent certain node edit operations in ψ and eventually recompute an optimal assignment. The remaining search procedures aim at finding better approximations by means of pairwise swaps of individual node edit operations. The complete set of search strategies is thoroughly reviewed in the next subsections.

4.2.1 Iterative Search

The first strategy exploits the fact that certain node edit operations lead to higher implied edge costs than others. That is, given the implied edge operations derived from the node assignment ψ, one can determine the node edit operation $(u_i \rightarrow v_{\varphi_i}) \in \psi$ that implies edge operations with highest cost among all node operations in ψ. Remember that optimal procedures for graph edit distance computation dynamically consider the cost of implied edge operations during optimization. Hence, there is at least some evidence that node operations $(u_i \rightarrow v_{\varphi_i}) \in \psi$ with high implied edge costs would not be part of an optimal edit path.

The present strategy prevents these particular node operations to occur in an edit path by updating the cost matrix $\mathbf{C}$ such that $c_{i\varphi_i} = \infty$. Given the updated cost matrix $\mathbf{C}'$ one can repeat step 2 and step 3 of BP-GED in order to find another assignment ψ' (which does not contain $(u_i \rightarrow v_{\varphi_i})$ any more). The variation of assignment ψ to ψ' in turn leads to a variation of the edit path and thus to another approximation $d_{\psi'}(g_1, g_2)$ of the true edit distance.

Note that ψ' corresponds to an optimal solution of the LSAP stated on the altered cost matrix $\mathbf{C}'$. Hence, though some node edit operations in ψ have been prevented and substituted with other edit operations, the assignment ψ' is still bijective. That is, also in ψ' every node of g_1 is assigned to a single node of g_2 (or deleted) and every node of g_2 is assigned to a single node of g_1 (or inserted).

This additional iteration of step 2 and step 3 of Algorithm 2 with modified cost matrix can be repeated q times, each time preventing another node operation through a modification of the last version of $\mathbf{C}$ (i.e., after t iterations t entries in $\mathbf{C}$ are set to ∞). This iterative procedure potentially leads to $(q + 1)$ different approximations of the true graph edit distance. The approximation with smallest cost among all of them can finally be returned as the approximate distance value (note that this value is still guaranteed to be larger than or equal to the optimal edit distance).

Clearly, q can be used as a trade-off parameter between run time and approximation accuracy. That is, the larger q is, the better the approximation but also the higher the run time. Note, however, that parameter q can be defined too large such that too many entries in $\mathbf{C}$ are set to ∞. This might make it impossible to find a bijection between the node sets. In this case, the iterative procedure has to be stopped before the maximum number of iteration has been conducted.

The iterative procedure is summarized in Algorithm 3 taking two graphs g_1 and g_2 to be matched as arguments and the number of iterations q as a meta parameter. Note that the first three lines exactly correspond to the algorithmic framework BP-GED (Algorithm 2). This extension of BP-GED is denoted by *BP-Iterative* from now on.

Algorithm 3 BP-Iterative (g_1, g_2) (Meta Parameter: q)

1: Build cost matrix $\mathbf{C} = (c_{ij})$ according to the input graphs g_1 and g_2
2: Compute optimal node assignment $\psi = \{u_1 \rightarrow v_{\varphi_1}, \ldots, u_{m+n} \rightarrow v_{\varphi_{m+n}}\}$ on $\mathbf{C}$
3: $d_{best} = d_\psi(g_1, g_2)$
4: $i = 0$
5: **while** $i < q$ **do**
6:     $i + +$
7:     Determine node operation $(u_i \rightarrow v_{\varphi_i}) \in \psi$ with highest implied edge edit cost
8:     Modify $\mathbf{C}$ by setting $c_{i\varphi_i} = \infty$ (prevent $(u_i \rightarrow v_{\varphi_i})$ for future solutions)
9:     Compute optimal node assignment ψ' on modified cost matrix $\mathbf{C}$ and set $\psi = \psi'$
10:    **if** $d_{\psi'}(g_1, g_2) < d_{best}$ **then**
11:        $d_{best} = d_{\psi'}(g_1, g_2)$
12:    **end if**
13: **end while**
14: **return** d_{best}

4.2.2 Floating Search

The algorithm BP-Iterative described in the previous section can be interpreted as a greedy forward search. In every iteration, one particular cost entry $c_{i\varphi_i}$ is set to ∞ such that the corresponding node edit operation $(u_i \rightarrow v_{\varphi_i}) \in \psi$ cannot occur in the next assignments to be explored. Yet, once a modification of the form $c_{i\varphi_i} = \infty$ has been conducted, the corresponding node operation $(u_i \rightarrow v_{\varphi_i})$ is lost for the remainder of the search procedure, i.e., the modifications on $\mathbf{C}$ cannot be made undone. The second search strategy presented in [1] resolves this drawback by using a floating rather than a forward search.

Floating search strategies have been originally employed for the task of feature subset selection [2]. The basic idea of floating search is as follows. In every iteration, the best entity (in combination with the already selected entities) is added to the existing solution (known as *forward step*). After every forward step a number of *backward steps*, which potentially remove entities from the current (partial) solution, are applied as long as the resulting solutions can be improved (with respect to the previous solutions).

In the context of the approximation framework, forward steps correspond to preventions of node operations by means of cost entries $c_{i\varphi_i}$ which are set to ∞. Backward steps refer to resets of cost entries $c_{i\varphi_i}$ to their original cost value. The algorithm—denoted by *BP-Floating* from now on—is given in detail in Algorithm 4. Similar to Algorithm 3, the number of iterations q is the sole meta parameter and lines 1, 2, and 4 correspond to the original algorithm BP-GED.

On line 3 of Algorithm 4 an empty array $d[0 \ldots q]$ of size $(q + 1)$ is initialized. This array is used to buffer the individually computed distance approximations when $i = 0, 1, 2, \ldots, q$ node edit operations are prevented. At position 0 of array $d[0 \ldots q]$ the original distance approximation of BP-GED is stored (line 4). On line 5 an empty list f is initialized. The purpose of list f is to buffer pairs of indices (k, φ_k) that correspond to previously prevented node edit operations $(u_k \rightarrow v_{\varphi_k})$.

On line 7, the main loop of the floating search starts. Index i counts the number of forward steps (i.e., the number of node preventions) that have been carried out so far. The main loop is repeated until q entries in $\mathbf{C}$ are set to ∞. From lines 8 to 12 the forward step is carried out. This forward step is identical to the procedure described in BP-Iterative. The distance value $d_{\psi'}(g_1, g_2)$, which corresponds to the approximation when i entries in $\mathbf{C}$ are set to ∞, is stored at position i in the array $d[0 \ldots q]$ (line 11). Moreover, the indices (k, φ_k) of the prevented node operation $(u_k \rightarrow v_{\varphi_k})$ are buffered in f (line 12).

After every forward step, $j \geq 0$ backward steps are carried out (starting on line 14). Formally, as long as node preventions can be successfully removed from the current solution, backward steps are actually conducted (to this end, on line 13 the boolean variable *removed* is initialized with *true*). Index j counts the number of backward steps that have been carried out (initially $j = 0$), and the variables ξ_1 and ξ_2 hold the indices of the cost entry $c_{\xi_1 \xi_2}$ that will be possibly reset from ∞ to the original cost such that the node edit operation $(u_{\xi_1} \rightarrow v_{\xi_2})$ could again be added to ψ in the next iteration.

Algorithm 4 BP-Floating (g_1, g_2) (Meta Parameter: q)

1: Build cost matrix $\mathbf{C} = (c_{ij})$ according to the input graphs g_1 and g_2
2: Compute optimal node assignment $\psi = \{u_1 \to v_{\varphi_1}, \ldots, u_{m+n} \to v_{\varphi_{m+n}}\}$ on $\mathbf{C}$
3: Initialize empty array for buffering $(q+1)$ distance values $d[0 \ldots q]$
4: $d[0] = d_\psi (g_1, g_2)$
5: Initialize empty list for buffering prevented edit operations $f = \{\}$
6: $i = 1$
7: **while** $i \le q$ **do**
8:    Determine node operation $(u_k \to v_{\varphi_k}) \in \psi$ with highest implied edge edit cost
9:    Modify $\mathbf{C}$ by setting $c_{k\varphi_k} = \infty$ (prevent $(u_k \to v_{\varphi_k})$ for future solutions)
10:    Compute optimal node assignment ψ' on modified cost matrix $\mathbf{C}$
11:    $d[i] = d_{\psi'}(g_1, g_2)$ (buffer approximation value with i preventions)
12:    $f = f \cup \{(k, \varphi_k)\}$ (buffer the indices of the prevented node operation)
13:    $removed = true; j=0; \xi_1 = (-), \xi_2 = (-)$
14:    **while** $removed$ **do**
15:       $removed = false; d_r = \infty; j{+}{+}$
16:       **for** all indices pairs $(k, \varphi_k) \in f$ **do**
17:          Modify $\mathbf{C}$ by resetting $c_{k\varphi_k}$ to the original cost entry
18:          Compute optimal node assignment ψ' on modified cost matrix
19:          **if** $d_{\psi'}(g_1, g_2) < d_r$ **then**
20:             $d_r = d_{\psi'}$
21:             $\xi_1 = (k), \xi_2 = (\varphi_k)$
22:          **end if**
23:          Modify $\mathbf{C}$ by setting $c_{k\varphi_k} = \infty$
24:       **end for**
25:       **if** $d_r < d[i - j]$ **then**
26:          $d[i - j] = d_r$
27:          $f = f - \{(\xi_1, \xi_2)\}$
28:          $removed = true;$
29:          Modify $\mathbf{C}$ by resetting $c_{\xi_1 \xi_2}$ to the original cost entry
30:          $\psi =$ optimal node assignment on $\mathbf{C}$
31:       **else**
32:          $j{-}{-}$
33:       **end if**
34:    **end while**
35:    $i = i - j$
36: **end while**
37: **return** $\min_{1,\ldots,q} d[i]$

In the **for**-loop (starting on line 16) all pairs of indices that have been prevented in previous forward steps are individually admitted by means of resetting the corresponding cost entry (which is currently ∞) to its original cost value. By means of the **if**-clause from line 19 to 22 the best performing backward step, i.e., the one with minimal corresponding distance value $d_{\psi'}$, is detected. The minimal distance value that can be achieved with one individual backward step is finally buffered in d_r and the indices of the nodes of the corresponding edit operation are stored in the variables ξ_i and ξ_2 (line 20 and 21). Note that every backward step is individually regarded and thus on line 23 the values of $\mathbf{C}$ are reset to the original specification after every loop.

On line 25 to 31 it is checked whether or not the best performing backward step with distance d_r leads to a solution that is better than the approximation with $(i - j)$ preventions (buffered at position $(i - j)$ in array $d[0 \ldots q]$). If this is the case, the backward step is actually carried out. That is, $d[i - j]$ is replaced by d_r, the indices of the backward step (ξ_1, ξ_2) are removed from f, the cost entry $c_{\xi_1 \xi_2}$ in $\mathbf{C}$ is permanently reset to its original value, and assignment ψ is replaced by the optimal assignment on the reverted cost matrix $\mathbf{C}$.

The complete **while**-loop for the backward step (line 14–34) is repeated until none of the tested backward steps is able to improve the distance quality. Note that when the **while**-loop ends, the variable j has to be decremented by one as j counts the number of backward steps actually carried out.

After j backward steps have been carried out ($j \in \{0, 1, \ldots, i\}$), the number of forward steps i has to be adopted accordingly (line 35). Then, the next forward step, viz. the ith prevention of a node edit operation, is carried out. Finally, the minimal distance in array $d[0 \ldots q]$ is returned as approximate distance value (line 37).

4.2.3 Genetic Search

The next improvement of Algorithm 2, which has been presented in [1], is based on a genetic search. *Genetic algorithms* (GAs) have been proposed in the context of error-tolerant graph matching in various publications (e.g., [3–5]). The basic idea of this approach is to formalize matchings as states (*chromosomes*) with a corresponding performance (*fitness*). An initial pool of these chromosomes, i.e., matchings, evolves iteratively into other generations. To this end, different genetic operations are applied to the current matchings. Though the search space is explored in a random fashion, genetic algorithms can be designed so as to favor promising chromosomes, i.e., well-fitting matchings, and further improve them by specific genetic operations.

The chromosomes in the genetic search procedure presented in [1] are assignments related to the original node assignment ψ. In order to build an initial population $P(0)$ containing chromosomes (assignments), N random variations $\{\psi_1^{(0)}, \ldots, \psi_N^{(0)}\}$ of ψ are computed first.

A single variation $\psi_k^{(0)} \in P(0)$ of ψ is computed similarly to the approach described in the previous sections. That is, in an alternative assignment $\psi_k^{(0)}$ the nodes u_i and v_{φ_i} are enforced to be assigned to other nodes than v_{φ_i} and u_i, respectively. This is again ensured by means of an update of the cost matrix $\mathbf{C}$ such that entry $c_{i\varphi_i}$ (corresponding to the edit operation $(u_i \rightarrow v_{\varphi_i})$) is set to ∞.

Yet, in contrast with the two former procedures, the node operation $(u_i \rightarrow v_{\varphi_i}) \in \psi$ to be prohibited is randomly selected (rather than searching for the node operation that implies highest edge operation costs). More formally, every node edit operation $(u_i \rightarrow v_{\varphi_i}) \in \psi$ is possibly prohibited with *mutation probability* p. Hence, it might be that zero, one, or more than one entry in the cost matrix $\mathbf{C}$ is set to ∞ at once.

Given the updated cost matrix (with zero, one, or more ∞-entries) an optimal node assignment is computed. This results in a new assignment $\psi_k^{(0)}$ possibly containing several altered node edit operations.

The whole mutation procedure as described above can be repeated $N - 1$ times to the original assignment ψ in order to get $N - 1$ (possibly) different assignments

$P(0) = \{\psi_1^{(0)}, \ldots, \psi_{N-1}^{(0)}\}$. Additionally, the original assignment ψ is added to $P(0)$ such that the approximation found by this extension is guaranteed to be at least as accurate as the original approximation $d_\psi(g_1, g_2)$. Note that all of the approximate edit distances, that correspond to the assignments of the population $P(0)$, are still equal to, or larger than, the exact edit distance. Hence, the fitness of every chromosome, i.e., assignment $\psi_k^{(0)} \in P(0)$, can be rated according to its specific distance value $d_{\psi_k^{(0)}}(g_1, g_2)$. Formally, the lower $d_{\psi_k^{(0)}}(g_1, g_2)$ is, the better the fitness of chromosome $\psi_k^{(0)}$.

Given the initial population $P(0)$ the following iterative procedure is carried out. A new population $P(t + 1)$ of assignments is built upon a subset $E \subset P(t)$, often referred to as *parents*. In order to select the parents from a given population $P(t)$, the $(f \cdot N)$ best approximations, i.e., the approximations in $P(t)$ with lowest distance values, are selected first ($f \in]0, 1]$). In the framework presented in [1], all approximations from E are added without any modifications to the next population $P(t + 1)$. This ensures that the best solution found so far will not be lost during the search procedure (known as *survival of the fittest*).

In order to derive the remaining assignments of the new population $P(t + 1)$, the following procedure is repeated $(N - |E|)$-times. Two assignments, ψ' and ψ'', from the pool of parents E are randomly selected and eventually combined to one assignment ψ. To this end, the cost matrices $\mathbf{C}' = (c_{ij}')$ and $\mathbf{C}'' = (c_{ij}'')$ corresponding to assignments ψ' and ψ'', respectively, are merged by means of

$$\mathbf{C}_m = (\max\{c_{ij}', c_{ij}''\}).$$

Based on $\mathbf{C}_m$ an optimal assignment ψ is computed and eventually added to $P(t + 1)$. Due to the definition of $\mathbf{C}_m$ (and in particular due to the max function) the node edit operations, which are forbidden in at least one of the assignments ψ' and ψ'', will also be prevented in the merged assignment ψ.

The two main steps of the genetic algorithm (selection of parents $E \subseteq P(t)$ and computation of a new generation of assignments $P(t + 1)$ based on E) are repeated until the best distance approximation has not been improved during the last δ iterations (clearly, other termination criteria could be employed as well).

It is well known that genetic algorithms are not deterministic. Therefore, one might repeat the complete search procedure s times from scratch and return the overall best approximation found in these s runs (which makes the algorithmic procedure more stable and reduces the risk of finding a poor approximation due to a poor random initialization).

Given that the genetic search procedure stops after t iterations on average, the two main steps of the original approximation framework BP-GED, namely the computation of an optimal assignment ψ based on a cost matrix and the derivation of the corresponding edit distance, have to be carried out $(s \cdot t \cdot N)$-times. Hence, one can expect that this extended framework increases the run time by the magnitude of $(s \cdot t \cdot N)$ compared to BP-GED.

The complete algorithmic procedure is given in Algorithm 5. We denote this variant of BP-GED with *BP-GA* from now on. Note that BP-GA has five meta parameters to be defined by the user, viz. the population size N, the mutation probability p, the termination threshold δ, the ratio f of chromosomes selected as parents, and the number of runs s.

Algorithm 5 BP-GA (g_1, g_2) (Meta Parameters: N, p, δ, f, s)

1: Build cost matrix $\mathbf{C} = (c_{ij})$ according to the input graphs g_1 and g_2
2: Compute optimal node assignment $\psi = \{u_1 \rightarrow v_{\varphi_1}, \ldots, u_{m+n} \rightarrow v_{\varphi_{m+n}}\}$ on $\mathbf{C}$
3: $d_{best} = d_\psi(g_1, g_2)$
4: **for** $i = 1, \ldots, s$ **do**
5:     build $P(0) = \{\psi, \psi_1^{(0)}, \ldots, \psi_{N-1}^{(0)}\}$ based on ψ using mutation probability p
6:     $t = 0; l = 0$
7:     **while** $t - l < \delta$ **do**
8:         select a subset $E \subseteq P(t)$ of parents ($|E| = f \cdot N$)
9:         build a new population $P(t+1) = E \cup \{\psi_1^{(t+1)}, \ldots, \psi_{N-|E|}^{(t+1)}\}$ from E
10:        $d = \min_{i=1,\ldots,N} \{d_{\psi_i^{(t+1)}}(g_1, g_2)\}$
11:        $t = t + 1$
12:        **if** $d < d_{best}$ **then**
13:            $d_{best} = d; l = t$
14:        **end if**
15:    **end while**
16: **end for**
17: **return** d_{best}

4.2.4 Greedy Search

The basic idea of the first three search procedures described so far is to systematically manipulate the underlying matching costs $c_{ij} \in \mathbf{C}$. Eventually, optimal assignments based on these cost variations are recomputed (Step 2 of BP-GED). The detour via an optimal assignment on a modified cost matrix $\mathbf{C}'$ ensures that altered assignments ψ' are still consistent with the underlying graphs (nodes of both graphs are uniquely assigned to nodes of the other graph or deleted/inserted at most once). Yet, this particular computation of optimal assignments based on altered cost matrices is evidently a computational bottleneck.

This bottleneck is eliminated by means of the fourth strategy that has been presented in [1]. Rather than altering the approximation via cost manipulation in $\mathbf{C}$, the original assignment ψ is varied by means of pairwise swaps of node assignments. Hence, in contrast with the previous search methods the time consuming recomputation of optimal node assignments based on slightly varied cost models can be omitted. Moreover, given that the assignment swaps are independently carried out, it can still be guaranteed that the assignments remain consistent with the underlying graphs.

An algorithmic procedure, which uses this particular swap strategy, is given in Algorithm 6. Note that the first three lines of Algorithm 6 again correspond to the original framework BP-GED, resulting in a (first) approximation value d_{best}, while line 4–26 describe the proposed extension, denoted by *BP-Greedy-Swap* from now on.

Algorithm 6 BP-Greedy-Swap (g_1, g_2) (Meta Parameter: θ)

1: Build cost matrix $\mathbf{C} = (c_{ij})$ according to the input graphs g_1 and g_2
2: Compute optimal node assignment $\psi = \{u_1 \to v_{\varphi_1}, \ldots, u_{m+n} \to v_{\varphi_{m+n}}\}$ on $\mathbf{C}$
3: $d_{best} = d_{\psi}(g_1, g_2)$
4: *swapped* = *true*
5: **while** *swapped* **do**
6:    *swapped* = *false*
7:    **for** $i = 1, \ldots, (m+n-1)$ **do**
8:        **for** $j = i + 1, \ldots, (m+n)$ **do**
9:            $cost_{orig} = c_{i\varphi_i} + c_{j\varphi_j}$
10:           $cost_{swap} = c_{i\varphi_j} + c_{j\varphi_i}$
11:           **if** $|cost_{orig} - cost_{swap}| \leq \theta \cdot cost_{orig}$ **then**
12:               $\psi' = \psi \setminus \{u_i \to v_{\varphi_i}, u_j \to v_{\varphi_j}\} \cup \{u_i \to v_{\varphi_j}, u_j \to v_{\varphi_i}\}$
13:               Derive approximate edit distance $d_{\psi'}(g_1, g_2)$
14:               **if** $d_{\psi'}(g_1, g_2) < d_{best}$ **then**
15:                   $d_{best} = d_{\psi'}(g_1, g_2)$
16:                   *best-swap* = $\{i, \varphi_j, j, \varphi_i\}$
17:                   *swapped* = *true*
18:               **end if**
19:           **end if**
20:        **end for**
21:    **end for**
22:    **if** *swapped* **then**
23:        update ψ according to *best-swap*
24:    **end if**
25: **end while**
26: **return** d_{best}

By means of two **for**-loops all pairs of node assignments $(u_i \to v_{\varphi_i}, u_j \to v_{\varphi_j})$ are systematically considered $(i = 1, \ldots, (m+n-1)$ and $j = (i+1), \ldots, (m+n))$. For each pair one can compute its total assignment cost $cost_{orig} = c_{i\varphi_i} + c_{j\varphi_j}$. Furthermore, the cost $c_{i\varphi_j} + c_{j\varphi_i}$ of the swapped edit operations $(u_i \to v_{\varphi_j}, u_j \to v_{\varphi_i})$ can also be computed and buffered in $cost_{swap}$ (line 7–10). In order to decide whether or not the swap is further investigated, it is verified whether the absolute value of difference between $cost_{orig}$ and $cost_{swap}$ lies below a certain threshold.

In the procedure of [1] a threshold that depends on the cost of the original assignment is used, viz. $\theta \cdot cost_{orig}$, where θ is a user defined parameter (line 11).[1] The intuition behind this procedure is that two node edit operations with similar cost values might have been mixed up in the second step of BP-GED. Thus, it is possibly beneficial to change the respective node operation for further investigations. Clearly, the greater θ is defined, the more swaps are considered. That is, small values of θ help in focusing on the most promising node swaps only. On the other hand, defining θ large (or in the extreme case omitting the complete **if** statement) one considers a

---

[1]For instance, defining $\theta = 0.1$ implies that the cost of a swap can differ at most 10 % from the original cost to be further considered.

large number (or even all) possible swaps in the procedure which in turn increases the probability of finding a better approximation.

Next, one can integrate the swapped edit operation in the original assignment ψ. That is, one derives a novel assignment

$$\psi' = \psi \setminus \{u_i \rightarrow v_{\varphi_i}, u_j \rightarrow v_{\varphi_j}\} \cup \{u_i \rightarrow v_{\varphi_j}, u_j \rightarrow v_{\varphi_i}\}$$

and one can compute the corresponding edit distance $d_{\psi'}(g_1, g_2)$ (line 12–13). If this distance value constitutes a better approximation than the currently best approximation value d_{best}, d_{best} is replaced by $d_{\psi'}(g_1, g_2)$ and the swap actually carried out is buffered in a list named *best-swap* (line 14–17).

After testing all pairs of node edit operations (i.e., the two **for**-loops from line 7–21 have been completely executed), the best individual swap *best-swap* (if any) is actually carried out on assignment ψ (line 23).

This procedure is repeated as long as in each complete iteration through all possible swaps at least one beneficial swap constellation can be found. This is handled by means of a **while**-loop (line 5–25) and the boolean variable *swapped* which turns *true* if the swap under consideration leads to an overall better approximation value than the currently best distance approximation (line 17).

Note that this procedure carries out at most one single swap in every iteration through the **while**-loop. This restriction prevents the computation of inconsistent node edit operations (which assign, for instance, two different nodes u_i and u_j from V_1 to the same node v_k from V_2). In other words, the procedure guarantees that the modified assignment ψ remains bijective at any given time.

Note that BP-Greedy-Swap resembles the algorithm BP-Iterative in terms of its greedy behavior. Yet, in contrast with BP-Iterative this search variant cannot be generalized using a floating search strategy. This is because two forward steps with pairwise swaps might not necessarily be independent from each other. Consider, for instance, a swap $(u_i \rightarrow v_{\varphi_j}, u_j \rightarrow v_{\varphi_i})$ that has been performed in one of the last iterations (forward step). Possibly, this swap cannot be undone in a backward step as in the meantime u_i and/or u_j may have become part of another swap. However, the idea of a genetic search can also be applied in combination with the present swap strategy (discussed in the next section).

4.2.5 Genetic Search with Swap Strategy

This search method is a variation of BP-GA discussed in Sect. 4.2.3. The two major differences to BP-GA are how the subroutines on line 5 and line 9 are actually carried out. That is, both the building of the initial population $P(0)$ and the building of a new population $P(t + 1)$ from a subset of an existing population $P(t)$ crucially differ to the corresponding subroutines of BP-GA.

The initial pool $P(0)$ is built using pairwise swaps rather than recomputations of optimal assignments on altered cost matrices (as carried out with BP-GA). That is, in order to build an initial population $P(0)$, part of the two **for**-loops of Algorithm 6 (BP-Greedy-Swap) are carried out N times. The subroutine for building the initial pool $P(0)$ of assignment variations of ψ is given in Algorithm 7 (the subroutine needs to access the original cost matrix $\mathbf{C} = (c_{ij})$, the size of the population N, and the mutation probability p). Additionally, parameter θ, defined in Algorithm 6, is needed to decide whether or not a swap is further considered.

First, the original assignment ψ is added to $P(0)$ (line 1). Next, the absolute value of difference between $cost_{orig} = c_{i\varphi i} + c_{j\varphi_j}$ and $cost_{swap} = c_{i\varphi_j} + c_{j\varphi_i}$ is computed for every pair of node edit operation $(u_i \rightarrow v_{\varphi_i}, u_j \rightarrow v_{\varphi_j})$ in ψ (analogous to Algorithm 6). If this difference lies below a ratio of the original cost, we derive a novel assignment

$$\psi' = \psi \setminus \{u_i \rightarrow v_{\varphi_i}, u_j \rightarrow v_{\varphi_j}\} \cup \{u_i \rightarrow v_{\varphi_j}, u_j \rightarrow v_{\varphi_i}\}$$

which is in turn added to $P(0)$ with mutation probability p, otherwise assignment ψ' is dismissed (line 9 and 10).

Note that every assignment ψ' added to $P(0)$ contains only one swap operation since every variation ψ' is computed on the original assignment ψ (which remains unaltered during the complete process). Furthermore, the control variables i and j are set to $(m + n)$ and $(m + n + 1)$ in case of adding ψ' to $P(0)$. This disables further iterations through the **for**-loop after a swap has been carried out (i.e., exactly one swap is carried out only). This procedure also guarantees that $P(0)$ contains exactly N (and not more than N) assignments.

Algorithm 7 Build-Initial-Pool (ψ) (Meta Parameter: $\mathbf{C} = (c_{ij})$, N, p)

1: Initialize $P(0) = \{\psi\}$
2: **while** $P(0) < N$ **do**
3:    **for** $i = 1, \ldots, (m + n - 1)$ **do**
4:       **for** $j = i + 1, \ldots, (m + n)$ **do**
5:          $cost_{orig} = c_{i\varphi_i} + c_{j\varphi_j}$
6:          $cost_{swap} = c_{i\varphi_j} + c_{j\varphi_i}$
7:          **if** $|cost_{orig} - cost_{swap}| \leq \theta \cdot cost_{orig}$ **then**
8:             Generate random number $r \in [0, 1]$
9:             **if** $r < p$ **then**
10:                $\psi' = \psi \setminus \{u_i \rightarrow v_{\varphi_i}, u_j \rightarrow v_{\varphi_j}\} \cup \{u_i \rightarrow v_{\varphi_j}, u_j \rightarrow v_{\varphi_i}\}$
11:                $P(0) = P(0) \cup \{\psi'\}$
12:                $i = (m + n); j = (m + n + 1)$
13:             **end if**
14:          **end if**
15:       **end for**
16:    **end for**
17: **end while**
18: **return** $P(0)$

In contrast with BP-GA, where the next population $P(t + 1)$ is built by means of merging two cost matrices $\mathbf{C}'$ and $\mathbf{C}''$ into $\mathbf{C}_m$ and recomputing an optimal assignment on the merged matrix $\mathbf{C}_m$, the present approach makes use of mutations of one single assignment from the previous population. Similar to BP-GA, all approximations from the set of parents E are added without any modification to the next population $P(t + 1)$. Next, the following procedure is repeated $(N - |E|)$ times in order to derive the remaining assignments of the new population $P(t + 1)$. First, one single assignment $\psi \in E$ is randomly selected. Using ψ, the subroutine Build-Initial-Pool(ψ) (Algorithm 7) with $N = 1$ is carried out.[2] That is, the node assignment ψ is altered by at most one additional swap. This mutated assignment is added to $P(t + 1)$.

The remaining parts of the genetic search are equal to BP-GA, and therefore, this search procedure needs the same meta parameters, viz. the population size N, the mutation probability p, the termination threshold δ, the ratio f of chromosomes selected as parents, and the number of runs s. We denote this search method by *BP-GA-Swap* from now on.

4.2.6 Beam Search

For the last search procedure presented in [1] the original node assignment ψ is also systematically varied by swapping the target nodes v_{φ_i} and v_{φ_j} of two node edit operations $(u_i \rightarrow v_{\varphi_i}) \in \psi$ and $(u_j \rightarrow v_{\varphi_j}) \in \psi$. Yet, rather than a greedy forward search or a genetic search procedure, this strategy makes use of tree search.

The tree nodes in this particular search procedure correspond to triples (ψ, q, d_ψ) where ψ is a certain node assignment, q denotes the depth of the tree node in the search tree, and d_ψ is the approximate edit distance corresponding to ψ. The root node of the search tree refers to the optimal node assignment

$$\psi = \{u_1 \rightarrow v_{\varphi_1}, u_2 \rightarrow v_{\varphi_2}, \ldots, u_{m+n} \rightarrow v_{\varphi_{m+n}}\}$$

found by BP-GED. Hence, the root node (with depth $= 0$) is given by the triple $(\psi, 0, d_\psi)$.

As usual in tree search-based methods, a set *open* is employed that holds the unprocessed tree nodes. As proposed in [1], we keep the tree nodes in *open* sorted in ascending order according to their depth in the search tree (known as *breadth-first search*). Thus, at position 1 of *open* the tree node with smallest depth among all unprocessed tree nodes can be found. As a second-order criterion, the approximate edit distance d_ψ is used. That is, if two tree nodes have same depth in the search tree, they are queued in *open* according to ascending edit distances.

In some preliminary experiments it turned out that a pure best-first search algorithm, where *open* is sorted in ascending order according to the cost of the respective solution, is not suitable for the present task (high run times and no substantial improvements of the distance accuracy have been observed in [1]). In fact, best-first search algorithms expect that the cost of a solution monotonically increases with the increase of the depth in the search tree. Obviously, this is not the case in this particular

---

[2]Note that the first line of Algorithm 7 has to be omitted here, of course.

scenario since for two tree nodes $(\psi', q', d_{\psi'})$ and $(\psi'', q'', d_{\psi''})$, where the first tree node is a (direct) predecessor of the second tree node, it must not necessarily hold that $d_{\psi'} < d_{\psi''}$. This is due to the fact that each tree node in the search tree represents a complete node assignment.

Algorithm 8 BP-Beam (g_1, g_2) (Meta Parameter: b)

1: Build cost matrix $\mathbf{C} = (c_{ij})$ according to the input graphs g_1 and g_2
2: Compute optimal node assignment $\psi = \{u_1 \to v_{\varphi_1}, \ldots, u_{m+n} \to v_{\varphi_{m+n}}\}$ on $\mathbf{C}$
3: $d_{best} = d_\psi(g_1, g_2)$
4: Initialize $open = \{(\psi, 0, d_\psi(g_1, g_2))\}$
5: **while** $open$ is not empty **do**
6:     Remove first tree node in $open$: $(\psi, q, d_\psi(g_1, g_2))$
7:     **for** $j = (q + 1), \ldots, (m + n)$ **do**
8:         $\psi' = \psi \setminus \{u_{q+1} \to v_{\varphi_{q+1}}, u_j \to v_{\varphi_j}\} \cup \{u_{q+1} \to v_{\varphi_j}, u_j \to v_{\varphi_{q+1}}\}$
9:         Derive approximate edit distance $d_{\psi'}(g_1, g_2)$
10:        $open = open \cup \{(\psi', q + 1, d_{\psi'}(g_1, g_2))\}$
11:        **if** $d_{\psi'}(g_1, g_2) < d_{best}$ **then**
12:           $d_{best} = d_{\psi'}(g_1, g_2)$
13:        **end if**
14:     **end for**
15:     **while** size of $open > b$ **do**
16:        Remove tree node with highest approximation value d_ψ from $open$
17:     **end while**
18: **end while**
19: **return** d_{best}

The extended framework BP-GED with the tree search-based improvement is given in Algorithm 8. Before the main loop of the search procedure starts, $open$ is initialized with the root node (line 4). As long as $open$ is not empty, we retrieve (and remove) the triple (ψ, q, d_ψ) at the first position in $open$ (the one with minimal depth and minimal distance value), generate the successors of this specific tree node and add them to $open$ (line 6–10). Therefore, similarly to exact computation of the graph edit distance (see for instance Algorithm 1), the search tree is dynamically built at run time.

The successors of tree node (ψ, q, d_ψ) are generated as follows. The node edit operations of the original node assignment ψ are processed according to the depth q of the current search tree node. Thus, at depth q the edit operation $(u_q \to v_{\varphi_q})$ is processed and swapped with other edit operations. Formally, in order to build the set of successors of node (ψ, q, d_ψ) all pairs of node edit operations $(u_{q+1} \to v_{\varphi_{q+1}})$, $(u_j \to v_{\varphi_j})$ with $j = (q + 1), \ldots, (n + m)$ are individually regarded. For each of these pairs, the target nodes $v_{\varphi_{q+1}}$ and v_{φ_j} are swapped resulting in two new edit operations $(u_{q+1} \to v_{\varphi_j})$ and $(u_j \to v_{\varphi_{q+1}})$. In order to derive node assignment ψ' from ψ, the original pair of node edit operations is removed from ψ and the swapped node operation is added to ψ (see line 8). On line 9 the corresponding distance value $d_{\psi'}$ is derived and finally, the triple $(\psi', q + 1, d_{\psi'})$ is added to $open$ (line 10). Since index j starts at $(q + 1)$ we also allow that a node edit operation $(u_{q+1} \to v_{\varphi_{q+1}})$ remains unaltered at depth $(q + 1)$ in the search tree.

Note that the algorithmic procedure described so far exactly corresponds to an exhaustive search. That is, with the procedure described above, one would explore the space of all possible variations of ψ through pairwise swaps and finally return the best possible approximation among all possible variations (which corresponds to the exact edit distance, of course). However, such an exhaustive search is both unreasonable and intractable.

In order to make the tree search procedure applicable for the present task, in [1] the breadth-first-search described above is manipulated such that not the complete search tree is expanded but only part of it. Formally, it has been proposed to make use of *beam search*—a variant of a tree search algorithm—for dynamically pruning the search tree. The basic idea of beam search is that only a fixed number b of (partial) solutions to be processed are kept in *open* at any time.

The idea of beam search can be easily integrated in the search procedure as outlined in Algorithm 8. Whenever the **for**-loop on lines 7–14 has added altered node edit operations to *open*, only the b assignments with the lowest approximate distance values are kept in *open*, and the remaining tree nodes are removed. This means that not the full search space is explored, but only those nodes are expanded that belong to the most promising assignments (line 15–17). Clearly, by pruning parts of the search tree, it might be that the optimal solution is lost during the search process.

Note that parameter b can be used for trading-off between run time and approximation quality. That is, it can be expected that larger values of b lead to both better approximations and increased run time (and vice versa). From now on, we refer to this variant of the framework as *BP-Beam*.

4.2.6.1 Improving the Beam Search Strategy

Remember that in Algorithm 8 the tree nodes with depth $q = 1, \ldots, (m + n)$ process the target node v_{φ_q} of the node edit operation $(u_q \to v_{\varphi_q})$ (i.e., v_{φ_q} is substituted with other target nodes at depth q). Hence, the order in which the individual node edit operations $(u_q \to v_{\varphi_q})$ of an edit path ψ are processed is uniquely determined by the node order $u_1, u_2, \ldots$ of the first graph g_1. However, the nodes of a graph offer no natural order in general. In other words, the order of the nodes in V_1 is arbitrarily defined and thus, the successors of the tree node (ψ, q, d_ψ) are also generated in an arbitrary order.

Algorithm 9 SBP-Beam (g_1, g_2) (Meta Parameter: b)

1: $d_\psi(g_1, g_2) = BP - GED(g_1, g_2)$
2: $\psi' = Sort(\psi)$
3: $d_{SortedBeam}(g_1, g_2) = BP\text{-}Beam(g_1, g_2, d_\psi, \psi', b)$
4: **return** $d_{SortedBeam}(g_1, g_2)$

In [6] it has been proposed to reorder the nodes in V_1 such that the resulting beam search procedure might possibly be improved. The proposed algorithm, referred to as SBP-Beam (the initial S stands for *Sorted*), is given in Algorithm 9. Note that SBP-Beam is a direct extension of BP-Beam. That is, the sole, yet crucial, difference to BP-Beam is that the original assignment ψ is first reordered according to a specific sorting strategy (line 2) before BP-Beam is carried out using assignment ψ' (rather than ψ). Note that for this version we have to skip the first two lines of BP-Beam and directly use ψ' instead.

The reordered assignment ψ' contains the same node edit operations as ψ but in a different order. That is, the subroutine $Sort(\psi)$ (line 2 in Algorithm 9) only varies the order of the node operations in ψ but not the nodes in the individual edit operations $(u_i \rightarrow v_{\varphi_i}) \in \psi$.

In [6] six different order criteria for node edit operations $(u_i \rightarrow v_{\varphi_i}) \in \psi$ have been proposed. All of these criteria can be used to sort the edit operations $(u_i \rightarrow v_{\varphi_i})$ in both ascending or descending order (resulting in 12 differently sorted node assignments). More formally, each criterion defines a weight (or rank) for the source nodes u_i of the edit operations in ψ. Then, the order of the individual node operations $(u_i \rightarrow v_{\varphi i}) \in \psi'$ is set either in ascending or descending order according to the corresponding weight of u_i. All sorting criteria presented in [6] can be used to put evident edit operations (i.e., those to be supposed to be correct with respect to the exact edit path) at the beginning or at the end of ψ' such that they are processed first or last in the tree search, respectively.

In Chap. 8 all sorting criteria are thoroughly reviewed. Moreover, in the same chapter an exhaustive experimental evaluation is given that empirically confirms the benefit of this reordering in the context of BP-Beam. Note, however, that in the following experimental evaluation the basic beam search algorithm is evaluated only.

4.2.7 *Experimental Evaluation*

The aim of the following experimental evaluation (originally presented in [1]) is to empirically demonstrate the gain of distance accuracy through the post-processing procedures introduced in the previous sections. Hence, we address the question to what extent the proposed search methodologies are able to reduce the overestimation of graph edit distance approximation returned by BP-GED. The overestimation is measured by the relative difference between the distance computed by the exact algorithm and the distance that is returned by a particular approximation algorithm. More formally, on each data set and for each graph edit distance algorithm proposed in the present chapter, the mean relative overestimation of the exact graph edit distance $(\varnothing o)$ is computed. Obviously, the smaller the mean relative overestimation of a specific graph edit distance approximation is, the better (i.e., nearer to the exact distance) is the approximation.

One can expect that the improvement of the distance accuracy is at the expense of a run time increase. Hence, we also aim at investigating how the different search strategies (with their different parametrizations) increase the mean run time $\varnothing t$ compared to the original framework BP-GED.

The second aim of the experiments is to verify the impact of reducing the overestimation of edit distances in a pattern recognition scenario. To this end, a comprehensive comparison of clusterings based on the original and the improved graph edit distances is given.

4.2.7.1 Data Sets

For experimental evaluations, five data sets from the IAM graph database repository for graph-based pattern recognition and machine learning are used [7]. Two data sets consist of graphs representing molecular compounds from different applications, viz. AIDS and MUTA. The third data set (FP) consists of graphs representing fingerprint images coming from the NIST-4 reference database of fingerprints [8]. The LETTER data set involves graphs that represent distorted letter drawings and finally, the GREC data set consists of graphs representing symbols from architectural and electronic drawings. For details on the graph extraction methods and the graph characteristics, we refer to Chap. 9.

From all data sets, subsets of 1,000 graphs are randomly selected on which 1,000,000 pairwise graph edit distance computations are conducted.

4.2.7.2 Overestimation and Computation Time

In Table 4.1 the overestimation $\varnothing o$ and matching time $\varnothing t$ achieved with two reference systems, viz. A* and BP-GED, and the various extensions of the approximation framework BP-GED are shown.

First of all, we observe that the overestimation can be substantially reduced with all of the present search methods on all data sets. Yet, there are distinctive differences between the individual algorithms (and their respective parametrizations) with respect to both run time and distance accuracy. In the following paragraphs the main findings are summarized.

Reference Systems

First, we focus on the two reference systems. As A* computes the exact edit distance, the mean relative overestimation $\varnothing o$ is zero on all data sets. Note that on the last data set (MUTA) exact computations of the graph edit distance using an A* algorithm lead to a computation failure due to lack of memory.

The original framework (BP-GED) overestimates the graph distance by 12.68 % on average on the AIDS data, while on FP and GREC the overestimations of the true distances amount to 6.38 and 2.98 %, respectively. On the LETTER data set, BP-GED leads to a strong overestimation of the true edit distance of 37.70 %.

Table 4.1 The mean relative overestimation of the exact graph edit distance ($\varnothing o$) and the mean run time for one matching in ms ($\varnothing t$) using a specific graph edit distance algorithm

Algorithm	Data Set									
	AIDS		FP		GREC		LETTER		MUTA	
	$\varnothing o$	$\varnothing t$	$\varnothing o$	$\varnothing t$	$\varnothing o$	$\varnothing t$	$\varnothing o$	$\varnothing t$	$\varnothing o$	$\varnothing t$
A* (Exact)	0.00	5629.53	0.00	5000.85	0.00	3103.76	0.00	1.86	–	–
BP-GED	12.68	0.44	6.38	0.56	2.98	0.43	37.70	0.17	0.00	1.51
BP-Iterative(1)	9.64	0.53	1.75	0.64	2.14	0.55	23.38	0.22	−2.94	1.92
BP-Iterative(3)	7.38	0.72	0.82	0.80	1.52	0.77	13.06	0.27	−5.88	2.74
BP-Iterative(5)	6.31	0.92	0.63	0.97	1.28	0.99	10.00	0.34	−7.34	3.54
BP-Iterative(7)	5.71	1.13	0.55	1.14	1.20	1.21	8.81	0.41	−8.26	4.31
BP-Iterative(9)	5.39	1.35	0.52	1.32	1.16	1.47	8.39	0.45	−8.88	5.13
BP-Iterative(11)	5.18	1.52	0.51	1.51	1.13	1.68	8.23	0.51	−9.34	5.94
BP-Iterative(13)	5.07	1.72	0.50	1.65	1.11	1.93	8.14	0.56	−9.68	6.76
BP-Iterative(15)	5.00	1.98	0.49	1.84	1.10	2.13	8.10	0.66	−9.90	7.66
BP-Floating(1)	9.64	0.71	1.75	0.80	2.14	0.76	23.38	0.27	−2.94	2.75
BP-Floating(3)	7.01	2.24	0.76	2.07	1.41	2.56	12.04	0.80	−6.18	9.21
BP-Floating(5)	5.54	5.22	0.50	4.34	1.04	6.08	7.78	1.77	−7.88	21.51
BP-Floating(7)	4.57	10.18	0.38	7.73	0.82	12.69	–	–	−9.08	41.46
BP-Floating(9)	3.92	17.41	0.31	12.16	0.67	21.24	–	–	−10.02	71.52
BP-Floating($n+m$)	2.74	64.10	0.24	97.17	0.45	62.64	–	–	–	–
BP-GA(50, 0.1)	2.96	114.67	0.20	100.96	1.00	80.29	–	–	−13.63	494.48
BP-GA(50, 0.3)	2.18		0.13		0.83		–	–	−14.59	
BP-GA(50, 0.5)	2.01		0.14		0.83		–	–	−14.53	
BP-GA(50, 0.7)	2.12		0.15		0.89		–	–	−14.15	
BP-GA(100, 0.1)	2.33	227.95	0.14	202.24	0.82	166.78	–	–	−14.99	1052.17

(continued)

Table 4.1 (continued)

Algorithm	Data Set									
	AIDS		FP		GREC		LETTER		MUTA	
	∅o	∅t	∅o	∅t	∅o	∅t	∅o	∅t	∅o	∅t
BP-GA(100, 0.3)	1.53		0.09		0.66		–	–	–16.04	
BP-GA(100, 0.5)	1.42		0.09		0.68		–	–	–15.93	
BP-GA(100, 0.7)	1.54		0.11		0.74		–	–	–15.52	
BP-GA-Swap(100, 0.01)	3.76	15.88	0.74	8.88	1.16	24.00	–	–	–11.48	37.12
BP-GA-Swap(100, 0.05)	2.61		0.48		0.71		–		–9.47	
BP-GA-Swap(100, 0.1)	2.77		0.35		0.76		–		–8.37	
BP-GA-Swap(100, 0.3)	4.18		0.35		1.17		–		–7.51	
BP-GA-Swap(200, 0.01)	3.17	30.94	0.63	16.80	1.04	47.35	–	–	–12.77	76.20
BP-GA-Swap(200, 0.05)	2.18		0.38		0.70		–		–10.60	
BP-GA-Swap(200, 0.1)	2.24		0.30		0.61		–		–9.47	
BP-GA-Swap(200, 0.3)	3.43		0.28		0.94		–		–8.44	
BP-Greedy-Swap(0.1)	4.72	0.88	1.91	0.84	1.22	0.99	30.56	0.26	–15.73	6.39
BP-Greedy-Swap(0.3)	3.97		1.24		1.17		20.67		–15.93	
BP-Greedy-Swap(0.5)	3.97		0.94		1.17		16.91		–16.04	
BP-Greedy-Swap(0.7)	3.95		0.82		1.17		15.45		–16.04	
BP-Greedy-Swap(0.9)	3.95		0.80		1.17		14.82		–16.04	
BP-Greedy-Swap(−)	2.04	1.84	0.35	2.06	0.41	2.45	3.0	0.57	–20.89	20.36
BP-Beam(5)	1.93	3.98	0.61	2.91	0.49	5.83	3.19	1.31	–20.10	31.15
BP-Beam(10)	1.79	7.27	0.56	5.17	0.47	10.97	–	–	–20.65	53.89
BP-Beam(15)	1.68	10.51	0.51	7.32	0.41	15.90	–	–	–20.67	77.45
BP-Beam(20)	1.28	13.48	0.46	9.41	0.33	20.71	–	–	–20.78	102.86
BP-Beam(50)	0.95	31.39	0.35	21.58	0.29	46.49	–	–	–22.62	248.35
BP-Beam(100)	0.87	60.40	0.32	41.87	0.27	86.00	–	–	–23.07	484.96

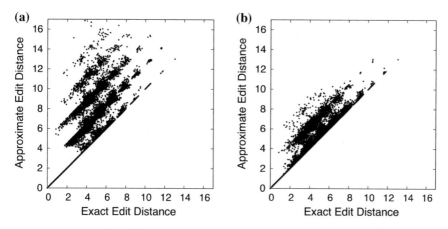

Fig. 4.1 Exact (x-axis) versus approximate (y-axis) graph edit distance on the LETTER data computed with **a** original framework BP-GED and **b** BP-Iterative(15)

On the MUTA graphs only the second reference system (BP-GED) is available, and therefore, $\varnothing o$ refers to the relative reduction of the mean overestimation compared to BP-GED (i.e., on the MUTA data $\varnothing o$ is set to zero for BP-GED which serves as reference point for the extensions).

We observe that the mean run time of A* lies between 3.1 and 5.5 s on the first three data sets, while on the rather small LETTER graphs the exact computation can be conducted in less than 2 ms on average. Using the approximation framework BP-GED, a substantial decrease of the computation time can be observed. That is, on four out of five data sets, BP-GED allows the computation of pairwise graph edit distances in less than or approximately 0.5 ms on average. On the MUTA data set, where exact computation fails, BP-GED needs 1.51 ms per matching on average.

BP-Iterative

We now focus on algorithm BP-Iterative and the mean relative overestimation. On the AIDS data, for instance, the mean relative overestimation $\varnothing o$ can be reduced from 12.68 to 9.64 % with one additional iteration. After 15 iterations the mean relative overestimation of the exact graph edit distance amounts to only 5.00 %. Hence, the mean overestimation of BP-GED can be reduced by more than 50 % on this data set. On the other data sets similar or even better results are achieved.

The substantial improvement of the approximation accuracy can be also observed in the scatter plots in Fig. 4.1 (on the LETTER data set[3]). These scatter plots give us a visual representation of the accuracy of the approximations. We plot for each pair of graphs its exact (horizontal axis) and approximate (vertical axis) distance value. The reduction of the overestimation using the proposed extension is clearly observable.

---

[3]On the other data sets similar results can be observed.

The amount of reduction observable in one iteration monotonically decreases when parameter q is increased. For instance, increasing q from 1 to 3 iterations on the AIDS data results in a decrease of 2.26% (from 9.64 to 7.38%)—from 13 to 15 iterations the reduction merely amounts to 0.07%. We conclude that on all data sets the first 3 to 5 iterations are sufficient to provide a relative high reduction of the overestimation.

As expected, the run time of BP-Iterative is clearly affected by parameter q. On all data sets a linear increase of the run time with respect to the number of iterations can be observed. The average run time per matching on the AIDS data, for instance, is increased from 0.44 ms per matching (original framework) to 1.98 ms (15 iterations).

BP-Floating

With algorithm BP-Floating very similar results to BP-Iterative can be observed. Yet, compared to BP-Iterative the overall reduction of the overestimation can be further increased. On the AIDS data set, for instance, the minimal relative overestimation amounts to 5.00% with BP-Iterative ($q = 15$), while BP-Floating($n + m$) reduces the overestimation of the approximation framework to 2.74% (the parametrization $q = (n + m)$ dynamically adapts the number of iterations to the size of the actual cost matrix **C**.) Yet, this improvement of distance quality is at the expense of a clear run time increase. For instance, on the AIDS data set the run time is increased from 1.98 (BP-Iterative(15)) to 64.10 ms (BP-Floating($n + m$)).

Moreover, we see that BP-Iterative is able to return similar results as BP-Floating (by using some more iterations in general). For instance, on the AIDS data set BP-Floating(5) achieves a result of $\varnothing o = 5.54$ in 5.22 ms on average. Approximately, the same distance quality (i.e., $\varnothing o = 5.39$) can be achieved with BP-Iterative(9) in 1.35 ms on average (four times faster). On the other data sets very similar observations can be made.

Note that on the LETTER data set BP-Floating with $q \in \{7, 9, (n + m)\}$ leads to run times higher than exact computation of graph edit distance, which makes the approximation framework useless, of course. Moreover, on the MUTA data set, the parametrization of $q = (n + m)$ leads to computational problems. Therefore, on these two data sets and the respective parametrizations no results are indicated.

We conclude that BP-Floating is beneficial compared to BP-Iterative when the overestimation of the approximation has to be reduced as much as possible, while run time behavior is of secondary interest only. Yet, if run time is crucial, BP-Iterative is clearly preferable over BP-Floating.

BP-GA

The procedure BP-GA has five meta parameters to be defined by the user. In the present evaluations only two of them are systematically varied in order to evaluate their impact on the approximation quality, viz. the population size N as well as the mutation probability p. It turns out that the remaining parameters—given that they do not fall below a certain threshold—do nearly not affect the resulting approximations.

The genetic algorithm (BP-GA) improves the best possible results from the methods discussed so far on the AIDS, FP, and MUTA data set, while on the GREC data the best result of BP-Floating cannot be further improved. On the FP data set, for

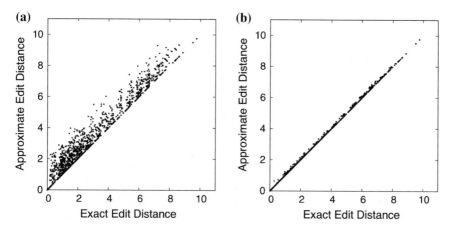

Fig. 4.2 Exact (x-axis) versus approximate (y-axis) graph edit distance on the FP data computed with **a** original framework BP-GED and **b** BP-GA(100, 0.3)

instance, the overestimation can be reduced from 0.24 % (BP-Floating) to 0.09 % with BP-GA ($N = 100$ and $p = 0.3$). On the AIDS and MUTA data significant reductions can be observed as well. Note that BP-GA (and also BP-GA-Swap discussed next) has a run time higher than exact computation of graph edit distance on the LETTER data set (for all tested parametrizations), and thus, no results are shown for this data set.

The substantial improvement of the approximation accuracy can again be seen in the scatter plots in Fig. 4.2 (on the FP data set[4]). The observable reduction of the overestimation using the proposed extension illustrates the power of BP-GA.

The run time shown for differently parametrized BP-GA procedures corresponds to the mean run time measured over all parameter values of the mutation probability p (in fact, p has only marginal influence on the run time). Comparing the mean run time of the novel procedure with the original framework, we observe that BP-GA takes approximately 180 to 300 times longer for one matching on average with $N = 50$ (depending on which data set actually considered). That is, BP-GA provides us with the highest run time of all tested algorithms.

Increasing the population size N from 50 and 100 allows a further decrease of the overestimation on all data sets. Yet, this improvement is accompanied by doubling the mean run time.

BP-GA-Swap

BP-GA-Swap avoids the bottleneck of re-optimizing node assignments by merely swapping pairwise node assignments. In fact, compared to BP-GA a clear speed-up can be observed on all data sets. Yet, we also see that BP-GA-Swap does not reach the same level of distance accuracy as BP-GA. That is, on none of the data sets the result of BP-GA is outperformed by BP-GA-Swap.

---

[4]On the other data sets similar results can be observed.

BP-Greedy-Swap

We first focus on the parametrized version of this method (using parameter θ). Comparing the mean run time of BP-Greedy-Swap with the original framework, we observe that this extension approximately doubles the average runtime for one matching on all data sets but the MUTA graph set (where the run time is approximately increased by a factor of 4).[5] Yet, the average run time still lies below 1 ms per matching on all data sets (except MUTA). We conclude that a greedy search in combination with the swap strategy (rather than the strategy of recomputing optimal assignments) leads to an algorithm with remarkable low run times.

At the same time the mean relative overestimation can be substantially reduced with this extension. We observe that the larger parameter θ is set, the better is the resulting approximation (as expected). In fact, the nonparametrized version of BP-Greedy-Swap, which swaps and tests all pairs of edit operations, achieves the best results among all versions of this algorithm on all data sets (note especially the heavy decrease on the LETTER data). Yet, this result is at the expense of another moderate run time increase compared to the parametrized version (which is clearly due to the increased amount of swap tests that have to be carried out).

BP-Beam

BP-Beam is the last of the six extensions presented in [1]. One can observe that already with the smallest tested value for b (which performs a heavy pruning on the tree) substantial reductions of the overestimation are possible on all data sets. For instance on the AIDS data, the mean relative overestimation can be reduced to 1.93 % with $b = 5$. Increasing the values of parameter b allows to further decrease the relative overestimation. That is, with $b = 100$ the mean relative overestimation amounts to only 0.87 % on the AIDS data set.

As expected, the run time of BP-Beam is clearly affected by parameter b. That is, doubling the values for parameter b (from 5 to 10, 10 to 20, or 50 to 100) approximately doubles the run time of this procedure. Yet, the overall run time remains remarkable low (a few milliseconds per matching on average only).

Summary

On three out of five data sets (AIDS, GREC, and MUTA) BP-Beam achieves the overall best reduction of the overestimation. Yet, these results are achieved with $b = 100$ which requires a relatively high mean matching time. On the other data sets the nonparametrized versions of BP-Greedy-Swap (LETTER) and BP-GA (FP) achieve the overall best results. BP-iterative(1) is the fastest algorithm among all extensions on all data sets. Yet, with this simple variant only a relatively moderate reduction of the overestimation is observed. BP-Greedy-Swap seems to be a good trade-off between distance accuracy and matching time. That is, with this specific extension a relatively high reduction of the overestimation can be achieved on all data sets while the run time remains remarkable low.

---

[5]The run time shown for differently parametrized BP-Greedy-Swap procedures corresponds to the mean run time measured over all five parameter values of θ.

Table 4.2 AIDS data set: 32 improvements and 17 deteriorations of the clustering quality

Index	k						
	2	3	4	5	6	7	8
Dunn	−	−	−	−	−	+	−
C	+	−	+	+	+	+	+
Davies–Bouldin	−	+	−	−	+	−	+
Calinski–Harabasz	−	+	+	−	+	+	+
McClain–Rao	+	+	+	+	+	+	+
Xie–Beni	−	+	−	+	+	+	−
Goodman–Kruskal	+	−	+	+	+	+	+

4.2.7.3 Applications of Improved Distances

The results reported in [9] suggest that the classification accuracy of a distance-based classifier is not negatively affected by using approximate distances of BP-GED rather than the exact ones. This is due to the fact that most of the overestimated distances belong to inter-class pairs of graphs (which have a relatively large distance anyway), while intra-class distances (which are relatively small) are not strongly affected by BP-GED. In fact, for a nearest-neighbor classifier to succeed, small distances are the ones that have the most impact. Consequently, the performance of a nearest-neighbor classifier cannot be significantly improved when more accurate distance values are used. However, as it has been shown in [1], more accurate graph edit distance can be beneficial for clustering tasks.

Using the original distances from BP-GED as well as the best performing extensions for each data set, two clusterings using k-medians algorithm [10] are carried out ($k \in \{2, 3, 4, 5, 6, 7, 8\}$). In order to compare the clusterings based on the original and the improved distances, we use seven well-known cluster validation indices, viz. Dunn [11], C [12], Davies–Bouldin [13], Calinski–Harabasz [14], McClain–Rao [15], Xie–Beni [16], and Goodman–Kruskal [17].

A table is provided for each data set, showing for each of the seven quality criteria and for every number of clusters a plus sign (+) or a minus sign (−). Plus signs indicate improvements of the clustering quality when the more accurate distances rather than the original distances are employed, while minus signs indicate deteriorations of the clustering quality[6].

In Table 4.2 the clustering results on the AIDS data set are summarized. On this data set we notice that for all numbers of k, but $k = 2$, the majority of the seven quality criteria indicate better cluster qualities when the improved rather than the original distances are employed. More precisely, for $k \in \{3, 4, 5\}$ we observe that 4 out of 7 validation criteria indicate improved clusterings using the novel distances,

---

[6]Note that more accurate distance values cannot guarantee more compact and better separable clusters in any case as, for instance, reductions of the overestimation might lead to more overlapping clusterings.

Table 4.3 FP data set: 36 improvements and 13 deteriorations of the clustering quality

Index	k						
	2	3	4	5	6	7	8
Dunn	−	−	−	+	+	+	+
C	−	−	−	+	+	+	+
Davies–Bouldin	+	+	+	+	+	−	+
Calinski–Harabasz	+	+	+	+	+	+	+
McClain–Rao	+	+	+	+	+	+	+
Xie–Beni	−	−	−	+	+	+	+
Goodman–Kruskal	−	−	−	+	+	+	+

Table 4.4 GREC data set: 37 improvements and 11 deteriorations of the clustering quality

Index	k						
	2	3	4	5	6	7	8
Dunn	−	−	−	−	+	+	+
C	+	+	+	+	+	+	−
Davies–Bouldin	+	+	+	+	+	−	−
Calinski–Harabasz	+	+	+	+	+	+	+
McClain–Rao	+	+	+	+	+	+	−
Xie–Beni	−	−	−	−	+	+	+
Goodman–Kruskal	+	+	+	+	+	+	+

while for $k \in \{6, 7\}$ and $k \in \{8\}$, 6 out of 7 and 5 out of 7 criteria measure improved clusterings, respectively. Overall there are 32 improvements versus 17 deteriorations of the clustering quality on this specific data set. This corresponds to a statistically significant improvement of the clustering quality according to a sign-test with $\alpha = 0.02$.

On the other data sets, quite similar results can be observed. That is, on the FP data set (Table 4.3), the more accurate distance values lead to clearly improved clusterings for $k \geq 5$. In total 36 improvements are observed, which are accompanied by 13 deteriorations on this data set (statistically significant improvement, $\alpha = 0.02$). On the GREC data set, a clear majority of the validation criteria indicate improved clustering qualities for every k (see Table 4.4). Overall there are 37 improvements versus 11 deteriorations of the clustering quality on this data set (statistically significant improvement, $\alpha = 0.02$). Finally, we observe that the clustering quality is improved for every tested k but one on the LETTER and MUTA data sets (Tables 4.5 and 4.6). That is, with the exception of $k = 2$ and $k = 3$ on the LETTER and MUTA data sets, respectively, the majority of the cluster validation indices indicate improvements of the clusterings when improved rather than the raw approximation distances of BP-GED are used. In total 40 and 31 improvements of the clustering quality can be observed on these two data sets (statistically significant improvement with $\alpha = 0.02$ and $\alpha = 0.05$, respectively).

Table 4.5 LETTER data set: 40 improvements and 9 deteriorations of the clustering quality

Index	k						
	2	3	4	5	6	7	8
Dunn	−	+	+	+	+	+	+
C	−	+	+	+	+	+	+
Davies–Bouldin	−	−	+	+	+	+	−
Calinski–Harabasz	−	+	+	+	+	+	+
McClain–Rao	−	+	+	+	+	+	+
Xie–Beni	−	+	+	+	+	+	+
Goodman–Kruskal	−	+	+	+	+	+	+

Table 4.6 MUTA data set: 31 improvements and 18 deteriorations of the clustering quality

Index	k						
	2	3	4	5	6	7	8
Dunn	+	+	−	+	−	−	−
C	+	−	+	+	+	+	+
Davies–Bouldin	−	−	+	−	+	−	+
Calinski–Harabasz	+	−	+	−	+	+	−
McClain–Rao	+	−	+	+	+	+	+
Xie–Beni	+	+	−	+	−	−	−
Goodman–Kruskal	+	−	+	+	+	+	+

4.3   Improvements via Integration of Node Centrality Information

Rather than applying a post-processing search procedure to the assignment ψ as proposed in [1] and thoroughly reviewed in the previous section, in [18] the topological information of individual nodes is exploited in order to achieve a better approximation of the true edit distance. In particular, the topological information of the nodes are used in the initial assignment step of the approximation framework BP-GED.

4.3.1   Node Centrality Measures

There exist several standard measures and metrics for quantifying graph structures [19, 20]. Many of them are global measures describing the entire graph structure with a numerical index. Yet, there exist several structure measurements which describe the structural features of a single node. These measures address the question "Which are the most important or central nodes in a graph?". So called *centrality measures* assign a measure of importance to nodes $u \in V$ according to the topology of their surrounding nodes.

An important family of node centrality measures assign high centrality scores to a node $u \in V$ either because u has many neighbors or because it has neighbors with a high centrality. The *degree centrality* [19], the *eigenvector centrality* [21] or *Google's PageRank* algorithm [22] are prominent examples from this family. In [18] these three measurements have been adopted for improving the distance accuracy obtained by BP-GED.

Definition 4.1 (*Degree Centrality*) The *degree centrality* $\lambda_i^{\langle deg \rangle}$ of a node $u_i \in V$ is set to k_i, where k_i refers to the number of edges connected to u_i.

The degree centrality is possibly the simplest centrality measure for nodes. That is, according to the degree centrality a node u_i is regarded as more central than node v_j if u_i has more adjacent nodes than v_j.

An extension of the degree centrality is the *eigenvector centrality* $\lambda_i^{\langle eig \rangle}$ [21]. This centrality measure takes into account that not all neighboring nodes of u_i have the same importance. Hence, instead of giving a centrality score proportional to the number of neighbors, the eigenvector centrality gives each node a score proportional to the sum of centrality scores of its neighbors.

Definition 4.2 (*Eigenvector Centrality*) The *eigenvector centrality* is defined by

$$\lambda_i^{\langle eig \rangle} = \kappa_1^{-1} \sum_j a_{ij} \lambda_j$$

where a_{ij} is an element of the adjacency matrix $\mathbf{A}$ of the graph and κ_1 is the largest eigenvalue of $\mathbf{A}$.

The eigenvector centrality offers the property that it can be large either because a node has many neighbors, or because it has important neighbors, or both [19]. *Google's PageRank* [22] is a variant of the eigenvector centrality measure.

Definition 4.3 (*PageRank Centrality*) The PageRank centrality of node u_i is defined by

$$\lambda_i^{\langle pr \rangle} = \alpha \sum_j a_{ij} \frac{\lambda_j}{\hat{k}_j} + \delta$$

where $\hat{k}_j$ is a slight variant of the node's degree k_j defined by $\hat{k}_j = \max(1, k_j)$.

The variation $\hat{k}_j$ is necessary due to computational problems arising with nodes without edges (divisions by zero). It turns out that δ is an unimportant overall additive constant for this specific centrality and is thus often defined by $\delta = 1$ [19]. Compared to eigenvector centrality, the major differences are the division by the degree and the free parameter α. In the experimental evaluations of [18], the same value for α as used in the *Google* search engine has been employed, viz. $\alpha = 0.85$ (Although it is not known whether or not any rigorous theory can be found behind this choice [19]).

4.3.2 Integrating Node Centrality in the Assignment

Given a particular centrality measure λ_i assigning a real value to each node $u_i \in V$, the original cost matrix $\mathbf{C}$ used in BP-GED is extended by

$$\mathbf{C}' = (\beta \cdot c_{ij} + (1 - \beta) \cdot |\lambda_i - \lambda_j|),$$

where $\beta \in\,]0, 1[$ corresponds to a weighting parameter that balances the influence of the original cost c_{ij} and the absolute value of the difference between the centrality measure values of u_i and v_j (the smaller β, the larger the influence of the node centrality value).

Note that the proposed modification of $\mathbf{C}$ is only conducted for $i \in \{1, \ldots, n\}$ and $j \in \{1, \ldots, m\}$. That is, the left upper part of the cost matrix $\mathbf{C}$ is modified only and the remaining parts of $\mathbf{C}$ are not altered since in these cases centrality information of at most one node is available (for the empty node ε no centrality measure can be computed). Moreover, the altered cost matrix $\mathbf{C}'$ is exclusively used for finding an optimal assignment ψ' of the nodes—the derived graph edit distance $d_{\psi'}(g_1, g_2)$ still makes use of the original cost function (without centrality information), of course (otherwise the exact and approximate distance values would not be comparable).

In the experimental evaluation presented in [18] it turns out that using the enriched cost matrix $\mathbf{C}'$ rather than the original matrix $\mathbf{C}$ for distance approximation does not decrease the overall overestimation in general. On the contrary, we observe for quite a number of pairs of graphs (g_i, g_j) that $d_{\psi'}(g_i, g_j) > d_{\psi}(g_i, g_j)$ holds. That is, for such graph pairs the additional topological information considered in $\mathbf{C}'$ leads to an alternative node assignment ψ' which in turns lead to a worse approximation value than the one based on ψ.

Due to this observation the modification of the original framework presented in [18] takes both assignments ψ and ψ'—computed on $\mathbf{C}$ and $\mathbf{C}'$, respectively— into account. Given ψ and ψ' two graph edit distance approximations are eventually computed and the minimum value of both approximations is finally returned as graph edit distance approximation. Formally, we take

$$\min\{d_{\psi'}(g_i, g_j), d_{\psi}(g_i, g_j)\}$$

as distance approximation.

This procedure ensures that the additional information about node topology is only used in cases when the resulting assignment ψ' reflects the true edit path better than the original assignment ψ.

The idea of taking two assignments into account for deriving a final distance approximation can be generalized. Formally, given the original cost matrix $\mathbf{C}$, t altered cost matrices $\mathbf{C}^{(1)}, \ldots, \mathbf{C}^{(t)}$ can be defined by means of t different topology algorithms. Next, we can obtain the corresponding assignments $\psi, \psi^{(1)}, \ldots, \psi^{(t)}$ and the minimum value of all t distance approximations can finally be returned as approximation value.

For the remainder of this chapter, we denote the extended version of the basic algorithm with BP-$Degree(\beta)$, BP-$Eigen(\beta)$ or BP-$PageRank(\beta)$, depending on which centrality measure is actually employed. The combination of—for instance—degree and eigenvector centralities is denoted with BP-$Degree$-$Eigen$ (the other combinations are analogously denoted).

4.3.3 Experimental Evaluation

For experimental evaluations, three data sets from the IAM graph database repository for graph-based pattern recognition and machine learning are used [7]. The first graph data set involves graphs that represent molecular compounds (AIDS), the second graph data set consists of graphs representing fingerprint images (FP), and the third data set consists of graphs representing symbols from architectural and electronic drawings (GREC). For details about the underlying data and/or the graph extraction processes on all data sets, we refer to Chap. 9.

In Table 4.7 the results (originally presented in [18]) are shown. On each data set and for each graph edit distance algorithm two characteristic numbers are computed, viz. the mean relative overestimation of the exact graph edit distance in percent ($\varnothing o$) and the mean run time to carry out one graph matching in ms ($\varnothing t$). The algorithms employed are A* and BP-GED (reference systems) and BP-Degree(β), BP-Eigen(β) and BP-PageRank(β) with $\beta \in \{0.1, 0.3, 0.5, 0.7, 0.9\}$. The last four lines of the table show results of the four possible combinations of the three centrality measure (for these combinations each centrality measure employs the best particular value for β).

First we focus on the run time of the novel procedure. The run time shown for each centrality measure correspond to the mean run time measured over all five parameter values of β. We aggregate the run times because parameter β has negligible influence on the run time behavior (the variance of the run times with different values of β is close to zero). We observe on all data sets that for both algorithms BP-Degree and BP-Eigen the run time is approximately doubled when compared to the original framework BP-GED (e.g., from 0.44 ms using BP-GED to 0.85 ms using BP-Degree on the AIDS data set). Employing the most elaborated method for centrality computations on nodes described in this paper (PageRank), the run time is approximately multiplied by factor 3 (on FP data) and 7 (on AIDS and GREC data).

Though the relative increase of the run time compared to the original framework BP-GED is clearly observable, the absolute values of the run time are still very low (a few milliseconds for each matching on average). The same accounts for the four possible combinations of the centrality measures where the run time also remains below 5 ms per matching in the worst case on all data sets. Comparing the run time with the run time of the exact algorithm, where the mean matching time amounts to several seconds, the increase seems moderate and quite acceptable.

The original framework (BP-GED) overestimates the graph distance by 12.7 % on average on the AIDS data. On the Fingerprint and GREC data the overestimations of the true distances amount to 6.4 and 3.0 %, respectively. These values can be reduced

Table 4.7 The mean relative overestimation of the exact graph edit distance ($\varnothing o$) and the mean run time for one matching ($\varnothing t$) using a specific graph edit distance algorithm (time measured in ms)

Algorithm	Data Set					
	AIDS		FP		GREC	
	$\varnothing o$	$\varnothing t$	$\varnothing o$	$\varnothing t$	$\varnothing o$	$\varnothing t$
A* (Exact)	–	5629.53	–	5000.85	–	3103.76
BP-GED	12.7	0.44	6.4	0.56	3.0	0.43
BP-Degree(0.1)	12.4	0.85	4.1	1.09	2.5	0.83
BP-Degree(0.3)	12.1		4.0		2.4	
BP-Degree(0.5)	12.1		3.9		2.4	
BP-Degree(0.7)	12.0		3.9		2.7	
BP-Degree(0.9)	12.1		4.7		2.8	
BP-Eigen(0.1)	11.2	0.84	4.5	1.09	2.5	0.82
BP-Eigen(0.3)	11.0		4.4		2.4	
BP-Eigen(0.5)	11.2		4.8		2.4	
BP-Eigen(0.7)	11.4		5.2		2.8	
BP-Eigen(0.9)	11.5		5.7		2.8	
BP-PageRank(0.1)	10.8	3.19	3.8	1.62	2.5	2.83
BP-PageRank(0.3)	10.1		4.0		2.4	
BP-PageRank(0.5)	10.0		4.2		2.4	
BP-PageRank(0.7)	10.1		4.6		2.5	
BP-PageRank(0.9)	10.0		5.4		2.5	
BP-Degree-Eigen	10.6	1.25	3.4	1.61	2.4	1.19
BP-Degree-PageRank	9.7	3.73	3.2	2.15	2.3	3.18
BP-Eigen-PageRank	9.2	3.64	3.8	2.14	2.3	3.15
BP-Degree-Eigen-PageRank	9.0	4.02	3.0	2.61	2.2	3.61

with the extended framework on all data sets. For instance on the AIDS data, the mean relative overestimation can be reduced to 10.0 % using BP-PageRank(0.5). On the FP data set, the mean relative overestimation is almost halved from 6.4 to 3.8 % in the best case (BP-PageRank (0.1)) and on the GREC data the overestimation can be reduced from 3.0 to 2.4 % (observable for all three centrality measures). We furthermore note that on all data sets the PageRank centrality measure leads to the best result (at the expense of the highest run time).

With the combination of the three centrality measures the mean relative overestimation can be further decreased. As one can expect, the best results are achieved when all three centrality measures are combined. In this case the relative overestimation can be reduced from 12.7 to 9.0 % on the AIDS data set. On the other two data sets the reduction amount to 3.4 % (from 6.4 to 3.0 %) on the FP data and 0.8 % (from 3.0 to 2.2 %) on the GREC data.

References

1. K. Riesen, H. Bunke, Improving bipartite graph edit distance approximation using various search strategies. Pattern Recognit. **48**(4), 1349–1363 (2015)
2. P. Pudil, J. Novovicova, J. Kittler, Floating search methods in feature-selection. Pattern Recognit. Lett. **15**(11), 1119–1125 (1994)
3. A. Cross, R. Wilson, E. Hancock, Inexact graph matching using genetic search. Pattern Recognit. **30**(6), 953–970 (1997)
4. I. Wang, K.-C. Fan, J.-T. Horng, Genetic-based search for error-correcting graph isomorphism. IEEE Trans. Syst., Man, Cybern. (Part B) **27**(4), 588–597 (1997)
5. P.N. Suganthan, Structural pattern recognition using genetic algorithms. Patt. Recognit. **35**(9), 1883–1893 (2002)
6. M. Ferrer, F. Serratosa, K. Riesen, Improving bipartite graph matching by assessing the assignment confidence. Accepted for publication in Pattern Recognition Letters
7. K. Riesen, H. Bunke, IAM graph database repository for graph based pattern recognition and machine learning, in *Structural, Syntactic, and Statistical Pattern Recognition*, LNCS 5342, ed. by N. da Vitoria Lobo, et al. (Springer, Berlin, 2008), pp. 287–297
8. C.I. Watson, C.L. Wilson, *NIST Special Database 4, Fingerprint Database* (National Institute of Standards and Technology, 1992)
9. K. Riesen, H. Bunke, Approximate graph edit distance computation by means of bipartite graph matching. Image Vis. Comput. **27**(4), 950–959 (2009)
10. A.K. Jain, R.C. Dubes, *Algorithms For Clustering Data* (Prentice-Hall, Englewood Cliffs, 1988)
11. J. Dunn, Well-separated clusters and optimal fuzzy partitions. J. Cybern. **4**, 95–104 (1974)
12. L. Hubert, J. Schultz, Quadratic assignment as a general data analysis strategy. Br. J. Math. Stat. Psychol. **29**, 190–241 (1976)
13. D.L. Davies, D.W. Bouldin, A cluster separation measure. IEEE Trans. Patt. Anal. Mach. Intell. **1**(2), 224–227 (1979)
14. T. Calinski, J. Harabasz, A dendrite method for cluster analysis. Commun. Stat. **3**(1), 1–27 (1974)
15. J.O. McClain, V.R. Rao, Clustisz: a program to test for the quality of clustering of a set of objects. J. Mark. Res. **12**, 456–460 (1975)
16. X.L. Xie, G. Beni, A validity measure for fuzzy clustering. IEEE Trans. Patt. Anal. Mach. Intell. **13**(4), 841–846 (1991)

17. L.A. Goodman, W.H. Kruskal, *Measures of Association for Cross Classification* (Springer, New York, 1979)
18. K. Riesen, A. Fischer, H. Bunke, Improving graph edit distance approximation by centrality measures, in *Proceedings of the 22nd International Conference on Pattern Recognition* (2014), pp. 3910–3914
19. M.E.J. Newman, *Networks—An Introduction* (Oxford University Press, Oxford, 2010)
20. L.F. da Costa, F.A. Rodrigues, G. Travieso, P.R. Villas Boas, Characterization of complex networks: a survey of measurements. Adv. Phys. **56**(1), 167–242 (2007)
21. P.F. Bonacich, Power and centrality: a family of measures. Am. J. Sociol. **92**(5), 1170–1182 (1987)
22. S. Brin, L. Page, The anatomy of large-scale hypertextual web search engine. Comput. Netw. ISDN Syst. **30**(1–7), 107–117 (1998)

Chapter 5
Learning Exact Graph Edit Distance

Abstract In the previous chapter, two different strategies have been proposed for improving the general distance quality of the approximation framework BP-GED. In the present chapter, two additional approaches are pursued for reducing the approximation error. First, in Sect. 5.1 we introduce a method that aims at estimating the exact edit distance $d_{\lambda_{\min}}(g_1, g_2)$ based on both distance bounds $d_\psi(g_1, g_2)$ and $d'_\psi(g_1, g_2)$ derived from BP-GED. This method is based on regression analysis. Second, in Sect. 5.2 a novel methodology, which is able to predict the incorrect node operations, is introduced. More precisely, a comprehensive set of features—which numerically characterizes individual node edit operations—is defined and extracted from the underlying graphs. These features are in turn used for the development of a classification model for node edit operations.

5.1 Predicting Exact Graph Edit Distance from Lower and Upper Bounds

In Sect. 3.2.1 it has been shown that the approximation framework BP-GED can be used to instantly derive an upper and a lower bound ($d_\psi(g_1, g_2)$ and $d'_\psi(g_1, g_2)$) of the exact graph edit distance $d_{\lambda_{\min}}$. Major aim of the method presented in this chapter is to exploit these two bounds in order to derive a more accurate approximation of the graph edit distance. In particular, we use both the lower and upper bounds in order to predict the true graph edit distance using regression analysis. Note that the present methodology and the corresponding experimental evaluation have been originally presented in [1].

5.1.1 Linear Support Vector Regression

For distance estimations based on both bounds $d_\psi(g_1, g_2)$ and $d'_\psi(g_1, g_2)$ *support vector regression (SVR)* [2] is employed in [1]. Of course, any other regression method could be used for this purpose as well. As pointed out in [1], however,

© Springer International Publishing Switzerland 2015   101
K. Riesen, *Structural Pattern Recognition with Graph Edit Distance*,
Advances in Computer Vision and Pattern Recognition,
DOI 10.1007/978-3-319-27252-8_5

SVR is particularly suitable because of its theoretical advantages and its superior performance that has been empirically confirmed in many practical regression problems [3–6].

SVR has been developed in the course of support vector machines [7], which has become one of the most widely used classifiers in the last decade. SVR is based on the so-called *VC theory* [8] that characterizes how learning machines can be enabled to generalize well on unseen data. That is, while traditional regression procedures are often stated as a process of deriving a function that has the least deviation between predicted and experimentally observed responses for all training examples, SVR attempts to minimize the generalized error bound so as to achieve generalized performance [9].

Formally, assuming a training set of M patterns

$$\{(\mathbf{x}_1, y_1), \ldots, (\mathbf{x}_M, y_M)\} \subset \mathcal{X} \times \mathbb{R}, \tag{5.1}$$

where $\mathcal{X}$ denotes the space of the underlying patterns (e.g., $\mathcal{X} = \mathbb{R}^n$), SVR aims at finding a function $f(\mathbf{x}_i)$ that has at most $\varepsilon \geq 0$ deviation from the given target values y_i for all training data [10]. In other words, we accept errors as long as they are less than, or equal to, ϵ.

We start with a linear function f, taking the form

$$f(\mathbf{x}) = \langle \mathbf{w}, \mathbf{x} \rangle + b \text{ with } \mathbf{w} \in \mathcal{X}, b \in \mathbb{R}, \tag{5.2}$$

where $\langle \cdot, \cdot \rangle$ denotes the dot product in $\mathcal{X}$. Besides the requirement that no deviation from the target values larger than ϵ is accepted, the function f should be as *flat* as possible. This means that we are seeking for a small $\mathbf{w} \in \mathcal{X}$. This can be ensured by minimizing the norm $||\mathbf{w}||^2 = \langle \mathbf{w}, \mathbf{w} \rangle$, and thus this problem can be stated as the following convex optimization problem.

$$\text{minimize} \quad \frac{1}{2}||\mathbf{w}||^2 \tag{5.3}$$

$$\text{subject to} \quad \begin{cases} y_i - \langle \mathbf{w}, \mathbf{x}_i \rangle - b \leq \epsilon \\ -\langle \mathbf{w}, \mathbf{x}_i \rangle + b - y_i \leq \epsilon \end{cases} \tag{5.4}$$

In general one cannot assume that a function $f : \mathcal{X} \to \mathbb{R}$ actually exists that approximates all pairs $(\mathbf{x}_i, y_i)$ from a training set with ϵ precision. Moreover, we also may want to allow for some errors to occur in f. Therefore, analogously to the soft margin loss function used in support vector machines [11], slack variables $\xi_i, \xi_i^* \geq 0$ are introduced and integrated in the optimization problem as follows:

$$\text{minimize} \quad \frac{1}{2}||\mathbf{w}||^2 + C \sum_{i=1}^{M} (\xi_i + \xi_i^*) \tag{5.5}$$

$$\text{subject to} \quad \begin{cases} y_i - \langle \mathbf{w}, \mathbf{x}_i \rangle - b \leq \epsilon + \xi_i \\ -\langle \mathbf{w}, \mathbf{x}_i \rangle + b - y_i \leq \epsilon + \xi_i^* \end{cases} \tag{5.6}$$

The slack variables ξ_i, ξ_i^* enable us to cope with possibly infeasible constraints in an optimization problem, and moreover, allow deviations $|f(\mathbf{x}_i) - y_i| > \epsilon$ for some training objects $(\mathbf{x}_i, y_i)$. The constant C in Eq. 5.5 determines the trade-off between the flatness of function f and the amount up to which deviations larger than ϵ are accepted.

It turns out that $\mathbf{w}$ can be entirely described as a linear combination of the training patterns $\mathbf{x}_i$, and moreover, the complete SVR optimization can be described in terms of dot products between the data [10]. That is, for evaluating $f(\mathbf{x})$, the vector $\mathbf{w}$ needs not to be explicitly computed. We will exploit this fact in the next section for extending the SVR to nonlinear functions.

5.1.2 Nonlinear Support Vector Regression

With the rise of kernel methods a universal solution to the problem of nonlinear data has found its way into pattern recognition (see also Sect. 2.3.2). The basic idea of the kernel approach is to modify the problem domain such that nonlinear regularities are turned into linear ones. Particularly, in order to extend the SVR algorithm to nonlinear functions f, one could preprocess the training patterns $\mathbf{x} \in \mathcal{X}$ by mapping them into some (typically higher dimensional) feature space $\mathcal{F}$ via function $\Phi : \mathcal{X} \to \mathcal{F}$. Eventually, the standard support vector regression algorithm can be applied in $\mathcal{F}$ rather than in the original domain $\mathcal{X}$.

The difficult problem to be solved in the context of mapping data into a higher dimensional feature space is the definition of the mapping function Φ and its corresponding feature space $\mathcal{F}$. Moreover, applying a (nonlinear) mapping $\Phi : \mathcal{X} \to \mathcal{F}$ to the original pattern space $\mathcal{X}$ is often costly. In particular, when the dimensionality of the resulting feature space $\mathcal{F}$ is high, such mappings turn out to be computationally demanding and are often not feasible. Kernel functions offer an elegant solution to this severe problem (see Table 5.1 for three prominent examples of kernel functions applicable on feature vectors $\mathbf{x}, \mathbf{x}' \in \mathbb{R}^n$).

Kernel functions κ constitute a shortcut for computing the dot product in some feature space $\mathcal{F}$. Formally, let $\kappa : \mathcal{X} \times \mathcal{X} \to \mathbb{R}$ be a kernel on a pattern space

Table 5.1 Sample kernel functions defined on patterns $\mathbf{x}, \mathbf{x}' \in \mathbb{R}^n$

Kernel	Definition	Parameter
Linear kernel	$\kappa_{\langle\rangle}(\mathbf{x}, \mathbf{x}') = \langle \mathbf{x}, \mathbf{x}' \rangle$	–
RBF kernel	$\kappa_{rbf}(\mathbf{x}, \mathbf{x}') = \exp\left(-\gamma \|\mathbf{x} - \mathbf{x}'\|^2\right)$	$\gamma > 0$
Polynomial kernel	$\kappa_{poly}(\mathbf{x}, \mathbf{x}') = (\langle \mathbf{x}, \mathbf{x}' \rangle + c)^d$	$d \in \mathbb{N}$ and $c \geq 0$

$\mathcal{X}$. There exists a possibly infinite-dimensional feature space $\mathcal{F}$ and a mapping $\Phi : \mathcal{X} \to \mathcal{F}$ such that

$$\kappa(\mathbf{x}, \mathbf{x}') = \langle \Phi(\mathbf{x}), \Phi(\mathbf{x}') \rangle,$$

for all $\mathbf{x}, \mathbf{x}' \in \mathcal{X}$, where $\langle \cdot, \cdot \rangle$ denotes the dot product in $\mathcal{F}$ (for proofs see [10, 12]). In other words, instead of mapping patterns from $\mathcal{X}$ to the feature space $\mathcal{F}$ and computing their dot product there, one can simply evaluate the value of the kernel function in $\mathcal{X}$ [13].

Kernel functions are particularly interesting for algorithms which can be entirely formulated in terms of dot products (known as *kernel machines*). Clearly, any kernel machine can be turned into an alternative algorithm by merely replacing the dot product $\langle \cdot, \cdot \rangle$ by a kernel function $\kappa(\cdot, \cdot)$. This procedure is commonly referred to as *kernel trick* [10, 12]. From a higher level perspective, the kernel trick allows one to run algorithms in implicitly existing feature spaces $\mathcal{F}$ without computing the mapping $\Phi : \mathcal{X} \to \mathcal{F}$.

Since SVR optimization as well as estimations of novel data via SVR can be reformulated such that only pairwise dot products are needed, the kernel trick is applicable to SVR. Hence, the SVR optimization problem can be restated such that $\mathbf{w}$ is no longer given explicitly and corresponds to finding the flattest function in the implicit feature space $\mathcal{F}$ rather than in $\mathcal{X}$. Note that the linear function f found in $\mathcal{F}$ via SVR might correspond to a nonlinear function f' in the original space $\mathcal{X}$.

5.1.3   Predicting $d_{\lambda_{\min}}$ from d_ψ and d'_ψ

Major goal of the method presented in [1] is to predict the exact graph edit distance $d_{\lambda_{\min}}(g_1, g_2)$ from the upper- and lower bounds of graph edit distance $d_\psi(g_1, g_2)$ and $d'_\psi(g_1, g_2)$, respectively. Formally, for every pair of training graphs (g_i, g_j) the triple

$$(d_\psi(g_i, g_j), d'_\psi(g_i, g_j), d_{\lambda_{\min}}(g_i, g_j)) \in \mathbb{R}^3$$

is computed first. Based on these three distance quantities, a (nonlinear) function $f(d_\psi, d'_\psi)$ for the estimation of $d_{\lambda_{\min}}$ is obtained by means of SVR. From now on, we denote the estimated distances using SVR and a specific kernel function κ with $d_\kappa(g_i, g_j)$, or d_κ for short. Note that in contrast with d_ψ and d'_ψ the estimated distance d_κ is neither an upper nor a lower bound of the exact edit distance (see Fig. 5.1).

Obviously, finding a function f via SVR that is able to predict the exact edit distance by means of both bounds requires the exact graph edit distance values for every pair of training graphs. This might become a drawback of the proposed procedure due to the exponential time complexity of exact graph edit distance. Yet, note that the time consuming computation of exact distances between training graphs can be computed in an offline procedure where high run times might be acceptable.

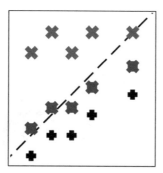

Fig. 5.1 Estimating the exact graph edit distance $d_{\lambda_{\min}}$ (*dashed line*) from the upper bound d_ψ (shown with *red crosses*) and the lower bound d'_ψ (shown with *black crosses*). In the best case, the estimations d_κ (shown with *blue crosses*) reduce the overall approximation error made by both bounds

In particular, the run time of the online SVR estimation is independent of the size of the underlying graphs. Thus, the time complexity of the complete method remains $O((n + m)^3)$.

5.1.4 Experimental Evaluation

The goal of the experimental evaluation (originally presented in [1]) is to empirically demonstrate the gain of distance accuracy through the SVR prediction procedure summarized above. To this end, the mean relative deviation ($\varnothing\ e$) from the true graph edit distance achieved with the individual approximations and predictions is computed. Obviously, the smaller this mean relative deviation is, the better (i.e., nearer to the exact distance) is the approximation. Clearly, the post-processing support vector regression is at the expense of a run time increase. Hence, we also aim at investigating how the regression analysis increases the mean run time ($\varnothing\ t$) compared to the original approximation framework.

For experimental evaluations, four data sets from the IAM graph database repository for graph-based pattern recognition and machine learning are used [14]. The graph data sets involve graphs that represent molecular compounds (AIDS), fingerprint images (FP), symbols from architectural and electronic drawings (GREC), and letter line drawings (LETTER). For details on the graphs and the graph extraction processes we refer to Chap. 9. From all data sets used in the present experimental evaluation, subsets of 1,000 graphs are randomly selected which are in turn subdivided into a training- and test set of equal size.

5.1.4.1 Validation of Meta Parameter

We make use of an SVR with the kernel functions summarized in Table 5.1. Note that other kernel functions are available (e.g., the Sigmoid kernel). In order to define the

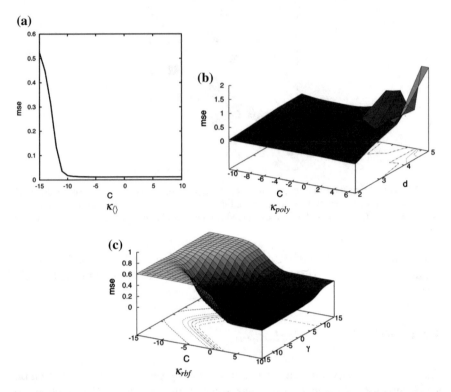

Fig. 5.2 SVR validation on the AIDS data set with **a** linear kernel $\kappa_{()}$, **b** polynomial kernel κ_{poly}, and **c** rbf kernel κ_{rbf} with respect to the mean squared error of the regression function (mse). The parameter values C and γ are on a logarithmic scale to the basis 2

parameters we apply fivefold cross validation on the training set. For every parameter configuration the mean squared error of the regression function (mse) is measured. In Fig. 5.2 the optimization procedure is visualized on the AIDS data set (similar plots are obtained on the other data sets). For the validation with the linear kernel we plot the error as a function of the sole SVR parameter C, while for the polynomial and RBF kernel the error is plotted as a function of C and d and C and γ, respectively.

In Table 5.2 the optimal parameter values found on the training set are summarized for all kernel functions and data sets. In summary, we note that in case of linear kernels small values of parameter C lead to good results on all data sets, while the

Table 5.2 Optimal parameter values for the linear, polynomial, and RBF kernel on all data sets

Data set	$\kappa_{()}$	κ_{poly}		κ_{rbf}	
	C	C	d	C	γ
AIDS	2^{-4}	2^{6}	2	2^{7}	2^{-6}
FP	2^{-7}	2^{-9}	2	2^{5}	2^{-5}
GREC	2^{-1}	2^{-10}	2	2^{9}	2^{-11}
LETTER	2^{-11}	2^{1}	2	2^{4}	2^{-5}

Table 5.3 The mean relative error of the approximated graph edit distance ($\varnothing$ e) in percentage and the mean run time for one matching in ms ($\varnothing$ t) using a specific graph edit distance computation

Distance	Data set							
	AIDS		FP		GREC		LETTER	
	$\varnothing$ e	$\varnothing$ t	$\varnothing$ e	$\varnothing$ t	$\varnothing$ e	$\varnothing$ t	$\varnothing$ e	$\varnothing$ t
$d_{\lambda_{min}}$	0.00	5629.53	0.00	5000.85	0.00	3103.76	0.00	1.86
d_{ψ}	15.37	0.44	5.76	0.56	2.89	0.43	27.19	0.17
d'_{ψ}	8.41	0.44	0.36	0.56	3.53	0.43	15.67	0.17
$d_{\kappa_{()}}$	4.11	0.45	5.87	0.57	5.14	0.46	15.64	0.21
$d_{\kappa_{poly}}$	10.72	0.46	25.54	0.57	8.64	0.46	24.02	0.21
$d_{\kappa_{rbf}}$	3.59	0.48	2.11	0.57	2.12	0.57	10.66	0.23

same parameter should be defined rather large when the RBF kernel is employed (in case of the polynomial kernel no clear tendency is observable). Using the RBF kernel we note that the best performance is obtained with small values for parameter γ on all data sets. Note that the SVR prediction is quite sensitive to parameter γ in case of RBF kernel. The same accounts for the degree d of the polynomial kernel. That is, on all data sets degrees larger than 2 deteriorate the quality of the results in general.

In Table 5.3 the mean relative error $\varnothing$ e and the matching time $\varnothing$ t achieved with various distance computations are shown. Note that the discussion on $d_{\lambda_{min}}$ as well as the two approximations d_{ψ} and d'_{ψ} has been already conducted in Sect. 3.3. Thus in the following we focus on the estimated distances using regression analysis only.

Let us first consider the linear kernel $\kappa_{()}$. On the AIDS data set, for instance, an SVR distance estimation using $\kappa_{()}$ allows a reduction of the mean relative error to 4.11 %. Compared to the 8.41 % achieved by d'_{ψ} the error is more than halved by the regression procedure. Yet, on the other data sets the linear kernel is not able to improve the distance accuracy compared to d_{ψ} and d'_{ψ}. On the contrary, on the FP and GREC data $d_{\kappa_{()}}$ provides a worse distance accuracy than both bounds.

Note that once a function f has been defined via SVR, the prediction based on d_{ψ} and d'_{ψ} is very fast. That is, the prediction of one particular distance value $d_{\kappa_{()}}$ is conducted in 0.01 ms on average on the AIDS data. A similar run time increase is measured on the other data sets (between 0.01 and 0.04 ms on average per matching). In general, the nonlinear kernels κ_{poly} and κ_{rbf} have a slightly higher run time for distance estimation than the linear kernel. Yet, the run time is increased by at most 0.06 ms on average (measured on the LETTER graphs). Compared to the huge run time for exact computation (3 or more seconds per matching), the increase of the run time in the range of a split millisecond is insignificant.

The distance accuracy provided by $d_{\kappa_{poly}}$ is worse than $d_{\kappa_{()}}$ on all data sets. Moreover, using the polynomial kernel in the estimation scheme we are not able to improve the distance accuracy when compared to the original bounds d'_{ψ} and d_{ψ}. In Fig. 5.3 we show the estimated distances obtained by SVR prediction on all data sets using the polynomial kernel κ_{poly}. In these plots we show for each pair of graphs their exact

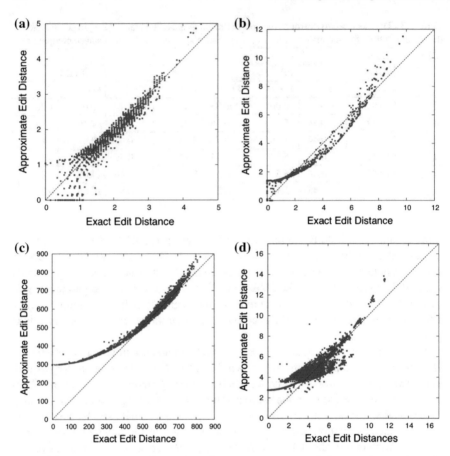

Fig. 5.3 Exact (x-axis) versus SVR estimated distances (y-axis) on all data set using a polynomial kernel. **a** AIDS. **b** FP. **c** GREC. **d** LETTERS

distance $d_{\lambda_{\min}}$ and the estimated distance values $d_{\kappa_{poly}}$. It is clearly observable that this particular kernel is not able to produce accurate distance estimations for small graph edit distances. That is, the large error of $d_{\kappa_{poly}}$ reported in Table 5.3 is mainly due to this handicap.

The overall best distance accuracy can be achieved by means of the RBF kernel. That is, on the AIDS, FP, and GREC data, $d_{\kappa_{rbf}}$ is evidently better than the other SVR estimations. Note that the distance estimation $d_{\kappa_{rbf}}$ achieves better approximations than the original bounds d_ψ and d'_ψ on three out of four data sets (the outstanding result of d'_ψ on the FP data is not reached). In Fig. 5.4 we show the estimated distances obtained by SVR prediction on all data sets using the overall best performing kernel κ_{rbf}. Comparing these scatter plots with the results obtained in the evaluation in Sect. 3.3 (Fig. 3.2) the gain of distance accuracy compared to both bounds is clearly observable (with the exception of the FP data set).

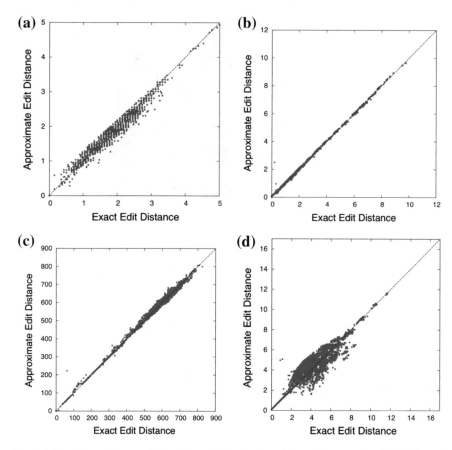

Fig. 5.4 Exact (*x*-axis) versus SVR estimated distances (*y*-axis) on all data set using an RBF kernel.
a AIDS. **b** FP. **c** GREC. **d** LETTERS

In the experimental evaluation of [1] a training and test set of equal size have been
used. Additionally, in order to investigate the impact of the size of the training set in
the procedure, the size of the training set is iteratively increased from 50 to 60 and
70 % of all available graphs (the remaining graphs are eventually used for testing).
We repeat the SVR estimation using the best performing kernel only (RBF kernel).

In Fig. 5.5 we show the mean square error for the three different ratios on all
data sets. The error in case of equal size sets is assumed to be 1.0 and we show the
relative error reduction when the size of the training set is increased. As expected,
the mean error can be further reduced with larger training sets. For instance, using
a ratio of 60/40 rather than 50/50 a moderate reduction of the error is observable on
the AIDS and LETTER data sets, while on FP and GREC quite strong reductions of
the estimation error can be reported. On all data sets but GREC the estimation error
is relatively stable when the size of the training set is further increased from 60 to
70 % (on the GREC data set we observe an overfitting phenomenon in case of 70/30
ratio).

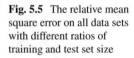

Fig. 5.5 The relative mean square error on all data sets with different ratios of training and test set size

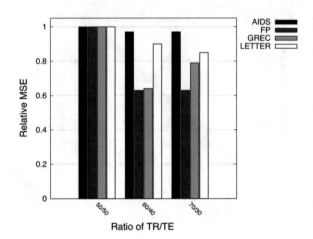

5.2   Predicting the Correctness of Node Edit Operations

As stated in the previous chapters, the node edit operations derived by BP-GED partially differ to the edit operations actually carried out by means of an exact edit distance algorithm. The work presented in [15] pursues the questions whether one can learn which of the node edit operations, delivered by the bipartite algorithm, are incorrect. To this end, a novel set of features that numerically describe a particular node edit operation has been defined.

5.2.1   Features for Node Edit Operations

Major aim of the method, originally presented in [15], is the development of a general procedure to predict whether a particular node edit operation $(u_i \rightarrow v_{\varphi i}) \in \psi$ is correct or not with respect to the node edit operations stored in the optimal edit path $\lambda_{\min}$. Clearly, the intersection $\Theta = \{\lambda_{\min} \cap \psi\}$ refers to the set of correct node edit operations, while $\Delta = \{\psi \setminus (\psi \cap \lambda_{\min})\}$ consists of incorrect node edit operations returned by BP-GED.

The first step for classifying node edit operations as correct or incorrect is to represent them in an appropriate form that can be used as input to any statistical classification algorithm. In [15] a set of 24 features extracted from the cost matrix **C** has been proposed. The aim of these features is to characterize a given edit operation $(u_i \rightarrow v_j) \in \psi$, such that a classifier can learn to discriminate between correct and incorrect node edit operations. That is, to predict whether an edit operation belongs to Θ or Δ, respectively. Note that the features have to be defined for any kind of edit operation $(u_i \rightarrow v_j) \in \psi$ regardless whether it is an insertion ($u_i = \varepsilon$), a substitution ($u_i, v_j \neq \varepsilon$), or a deletion ($v_j = \varepsilon$). In the following we summarize the 24 features.

- **(1–4) Max, Min, Average, and Deviation of C**: The first four features are the maximum, the minimum, the average, and the standard deviation extracted from the left upper part of cost matrix $\mathbf{C}$ (i.e., we regard $c_{ij} \in \mathbf{C}$ with $1 \le i \le n$ and $1 \le j \le m$ only). Thus we avoid dealing with ∞ values when computing the four statistics. Note that these four features are independent of the actual edit operation $(u_i \rightarrow v_j)$ and thus for a pair of graphs g_1 and g_2 these features are identical for all node edit operations in ψ. In other words, these first features characterize the global set up of the complete graph matching process rather than the individual characteristics of the underlying edit operations.
- **(5–6) Assignment and edge cost**: The next two features are the assignment cost c_{ij} and the implied edge cost associated to the node edit operation $(u_i \rightarrow v_j) \in \psi$. Clearly, both values correspond to important characteristics of a given edit operation.
- **(7–10) Max, Min, Average, and Deviation of ith row**: Features 7–10 characterize node edit operations $(u_i \rightarrow v_j) \in \psi$ by means of the maximum, the minimum, the average, and the standard deviation of the entries in row i of the cost matrix $\mathbf{C}$:

$$[c_{i1} \ldots c_{ij} \ldots c_{im} | \infty \ldots c_{i\varepsilon} \ldots \infty] \tag{5.7}$$

Note that the ∞ entries in the row are not considered for computing the four statistics. If the edit operation $(u_i \rightarrow v_j) \in \psi$ is an insertion, all four features are set to 0, since the corresponding row is located in the lower part of the cost matrix $\mathbf{C}$ with one nontrivial cost entry only (i.e., $i > n$ and thus $u_i = \varepsilon$):

$$[\infty \ldots c_{\varepsilon j} \ldots \infty | 0 \ldots 0 \ldots 0] \tag{5.8}$$

These four features describe the overall situation that is met in a particular row by the assignment algorithm. The subsequent features aim at quantifying the level of difficulty for the assignment of the ith node $u_i \in V_1$ to one of the nodes of V_2.
- **(11) Uniqueness of ith row**: The unique feature of edit operation $(u_i \rightarrow v_j) \in \psi$ is defined as

$$\max_{\forall k = 1, \ldots, m} |c_{ij} - c_{ik}|.$$

That is, this feature corresponds to the maximum difference between the cost c_{ij} of the actual edit operation $(u_i \rightarrow v_j) \in \psi$ and the cost of a possible alternative target node v_k for node u_i. (Note that this alternative is forced to be a substitution as we regard $k = 1, \ldots, m$ only.) If the edit operation under consideration is an insertion (i.e., $u_i = \varepsilon$), we explore a row as defined in Eq. 5.8 and we thus set this feature to 0.
- **(12) Divergence of ith row**: The divergence feature of edit operation $(u_i \rightarrow v_j) \in \psi$ is defined as

$$\frac{\sum_{k=1}^{m} |c_{ij} - c_{ik}|}{m(c_{ij} - \overline{c})},$$

where $\bar{c} = \frac{1}{m} \sum_{k=1}^{m} c_{ik}$ (mean value of costs in row i). That is, for this feature we sum up the absolute values of differences between the assignment cost c_{ij} and the other assignment costs in the corresponding row. The denominator is a normalization factor. If the edit operation $(u_i \to v_j) \in \psi$ corresponds to an insertion, this feature is set to 0.

- **(13) Leader of ith row**: The leader feature of edit operation $(u_i \to v_j) \in \psi$ is computed as the difference between the minimum cost assignment of node u_i and the second minimum cost assignment of u_i. Formally, assume we have

$$\min 1_i = \min_{j=1,\dots,m} c_{ij} \quad \text{and} \quad \min 2_i = \min_{j=1,\dots,m, j \neq k} c_{ij},$$

where k refers to the column index of the minimum cost entry $\min 1_i$ ($k = \arg \min_{j=1,\dots,m} c_{ij}$). The feature value for the edit operation amounts then to

$$\frac{\min 1_i - \min 2_i}{\min 2_i},$$

where the denominator normalizes the feature. If the edit operation $(u_i \to v_j) \in \psi$ corresponds to an insertion, this feature is set to 0.

- **(14) Interval of ith row**: Given the row i corresponding to edit operation $(u_i \to v_j) \in \psi$, the interval feature is defined as

$$\frac{\delta_{r_i}}{\delta_r}.$$

The value δ_{r_i} refers to the difference between the maximum and the minimum entry in row i, i.e., $\delta_{r_i} = \max - \min$, where max and min refer to feature 7 and 8, respectively. The value $\bar{\delta}_r$ is the mean of all row intervals δ_{r_i} of the upper part of cost matrix $\mathbf{C}$, i.e., $\bar{\delta}_r = \frac{1}{n} \sum_{i=1}^{n} \delta_{r_i}$. If the edit operation $(u_i \to v_j) \in \psi$ is an insertion, this feature is set to 0.

- **(15) Outlierness of ith row**: Given an edit operation $(u_i \to v_j) \in \psi$, we compute the average $\bar{c}$ and the deviation σ of all cost entries c_{ik} in the corresponding row i (see features 9 and 10 above). The outlierness feature is then defined as

$$\frac{c_{ij}}{\bar{c} - \sigma}.$$

If the edit operation under consideration is an insertion, this feature is set to 0.

- **(16–24) Column features**: The next nine features to describe an edit operation $(u_i \to v_j) \in \psi$ are the same features we defined so far for the ith row, but applied to the corresponding column j. That is, the maximum, the minimum, the average, the standard deviation, the uniqueness, the divergence, the leader, the interval, and the outlierness are computed for the jth column (rather than for row i). Hence, given an edit operation $(u_i \to v_j) \in \psi$, these features characterize the level of difficulty from node v_j's point of view rather than from u_i's perspective.

For all nine column features, the feature value is set to 0 if the edit operation $(u_i \rightarrow v_j) \in \psi$ is a deletion (i.e., $j > m$ and thus $v_j = \varepsilon$). In this particular case we are in the right part of the cost matrix $\mathbf{C}$ and the column has the form

$$[\infty \ldots c_{i\varepsilon} \ldots \infty | 0 \ldots 0 \ldots 0]'$$

with one valid entry only.

5.2.2 Experimental Evaluation

Major goal of the experimental evaluation presented in [15] is to verify if we are able to determine whether a node edit operation $(u_i \rightarrow v_j) \in \psi$ given by BP-GED belongs to Δ or Θ (i.e., whether $(u_i \rightarrow v_j) \in \psi$ is correct or not with respect to the true edit path). The evaluation is carried out on eight different data sets. Four data sets from the IAM graph database repository and four data sets from GREYCs Chemistry data set repository are used [14, 16]. Five out of eight data sets consist of graphs representing molecular compounds from different applications, viz., AIDS, Acyclic, Alkane, MAO, and PAH. A sixth data set consists of graphs representing fingerprint images (FP). The LETTER data set involves graphs that represent distorted letter line drawings, while the GREC data set consists of graphs representing symbols from architectural and electronic drawings. For details on the data sets we refer to Chap. 9.

5.2.2.1 Data Preparation and Experimental Setup

The following evaluation is based on a supervised classification approach, and thus a ground truth is required. For a given set of N graphs $D = \{g_1, g_2, \ldots, g_N\}$, we compute the optimal edit path $\lambda_{min}(g_i, g_j)$ by means of an exact graph edit distance procedure for every pair $(g_i, g_j) \in D \times D$. Consequently, for every pair (g_i, g_j), the ground truth is given by the set of optimal node edit operations $\lambda_{min} = \{e_1, e_2, \ldots, e_k\}$.

Next, we compute pairwise approximate distances between all graph pairs in D using the approximate algorithm BP-GED. Hence, for every graph pair $(g_i, g_j) \in D \times D$ we obtain a (suboptimal) edit path ψ. Clearly, every individual node edit operation $(u_i \rightarrow v_j) \in \psi$ either belongs to Θ (i.e., to the set of correct node edit operations), or to Δ (i.e., to the set of incorrect node edit operations). We label every edit operation $(u_i \rightarrow v_j) \in \psi$ as correct or incorrect depending on whether it belongs to Θ or Δ, respectively.

For the experimental evaluation, we subdivide the complete set of labeled node edit operations into three disjoint data sets, namely the training, the validation, and the test set, $(T_r, T_v,$ and $T_e)$. T_r and T_v are used to train the classifier and to optimize its parameters, respectively. T_e is used to evaluate the quality of the final classifier. On all data sets, 50 % of the node edit operations are used for T_r, and 25 % for T_v and

Table 5.4 Number of graphs
N, the total number of
individual node edit
operations #ψ, and the
relative amount of correct
individual node edit
operations with respect to all
node edit operations $\frac{\#\Theta}{\#\psi}$

	N	#ψ	$\frac{\#\Theta}{\#\psi}$ %
Acyclic	183	40,398	36.4
AIDS	100	12,746	49.3
Alkane	150	6,973	52.3
FP	100	14,825	72.8
GREC	100	46,395	59.6
LETTER	150	71,595	76.5
MAO	68	3,254	77.2
PAH	94	3,751	59.5

T_e, respectively. Table 5.4 shows the number of graphs N in the data set, the total
number of individual node edit operations generated by the pairwise graph distance
computations #ψ, and the relative amount of correct individual node edit operations
with respect to all edit operations $\frac{\#\Theta}{\#\psi}$.

5.2.2.2 Validation of Parameters

As base classifier we employ a *support vector machine* (SVM) in conjunction with
a *Gaussian* kernel (also known as *RBF* kernel) [8, 17]. Note, however, that the
features defined above are independent from the classification methodology actually
employed. That is, any other statistical classifier could have been employed for the
evaluation as well. Two meta parameters have to be tuned when training an SVM
with RBF kernel, namely γ and C. The optimal values for γ and C have to be
empirically determined on every data set. Both parameters are systematically varied
from 0.001 to 10, 000 following a logarithmic scale (i.e., 0.001, 0.01, . . .). For each
pair of (γ, C) an SVM is trained using T_r and the classification accuracy assessed
using T_v. Figure 5.6 plots the classification accuracy on T_v on the AIDS and MAO
data set as a function of parameters γ and C (similar plots are obtained on the other
data sets).

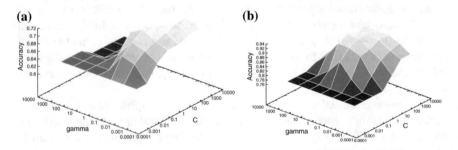

Fig. 5.6 Visualization of the optimization of γ and C on the **a** AIDS and **b** MAO data set

Table 5.5 Best values of γ and C on every data set

	γ	C
Acyclic	1	10
AIDS	0.1	10
Alkane	1	1
FP	0.01	100
GREC	1	10
LETTER	0.1	1
MAO	1	10
PAH	100	1,000

The values of γ and C leading to the best accuracy on the validation set are shown in Table 5.5. We observe that optimal values of γ lie between 0.1 and 1 in the majority of the data sets, while optimal values of C are between 1 and 10. The optimized parameter values are used for the evaluation in the next sections.

5.2.2.3 Experimental Evaluation

For each data set four evaluation metrics are computed on the test set T_e, viz., the base rate accuracy B, the classification accuracy A, the precision P, and the recall R. The base rate accuracy B shows the percentage of the majority class in each test set and represents the classification accuracy of a dummy classifier that always predicts the most frequent class. The base rate accuracy is shown here because we have rather *unbalanced* data sets, i.e., data sets where the proportion of correct versus incorrect classes is highly skewed. In such cases, even a base rate classifier achieves a good (but useless) accuracy.

Accuracy A represents the relative amount of true positives and true negatives with respect to the total number of node edit operations. In this particular setting, we define wrong edit operations as *positive* and correct edit operations as *negative*.[1] Hence, correct node edit operations classified as correct refer to true negatives and incorrect node edit operations classified as incorrect refer to true positives.

Precision P is defined as the percentage of true positives (i.e., true incorrect node edit operations) with respect to all node edit operations classified as positive (i.e., incorrect). The lower this magnitude the higher the number of correct node edit operations classified as incorrect. Likewise, R is defined as the proportion of positive examples classified as positive. The lower this magnitude the more true incorrect node edit operations are actually classified as correct.

---

[1]The assignment of *positive* and *negative* is arbitrary and may depend on the application being evaluated, but in general the label *positive* is assigned to the class one wants to detect, which is not necessarily the correct class. For instance, in a medical setting, a test for a disease giving a positive answer usually means that the disease is present.

Table 5.6 Base rate accuracy
B, the classification accuracy
A, and precision P and recall
R measured on each data set

	B [%]	A [%]	P [%]	R [%]
Acyclic	50.5	61.5	61.9	62.1
AIDS	63.6	71.3	72.7	87.9
Alkane	51.6	57.2	56.1	52.4
FP	72.2	80.3	72.7	46.6
GREC	59.6	83.2	80.9	76.4
LETTER	76.8	79.8	64.8	27.3
MAO	76.8	92.3	92.9	73.6
PAH	61.8	90.6	82.4	95.7

Regarding the results in Table 5.6 we observe that three out of eight data sets
(FP, LETTER and MAO), are quite unbalanced. Their base rate accuracies are above
72 %, and nearly 77 % in two cases. However, the accuracy A shows that the novel
methodology is able to outperform the base rate classifier on all data sets. The difference between B and A ranges from 7 % in case of Alkane to remarkable 28 % in case
of PAH. Moreover, the overall classification accuracy is about 80 % (or higher) in five
out of eight data sets. Precision and recall also indicate that the novel methodology
is beneficial. For instance on PAH we observe a precision of 82.4 % and a recall of
95.7 %. This means that only about 20 % of the node edit operations predicted as
incorrect are actually correct, while only about 5 % of the incorrect node edit operations are classified as correct. On three more data sets (AIDS, GREC, and MAO),
precision is about, or greater than, 72 %, while recall is about, or greater than 73 %.

5.2.2.4 Feature Selection

The results from the evaluation above verify that a remarkable classification accuracy
can be achieved using the feature vector described in Sect. 5.2.1. In this section we aim
at investigating whether all of the novel features have the same degree of importance
for predicting the node assignment correctness.

To this end in [15] a feature ranking using the *Minimum Redundancy and Maximum Relevance* (mRMR) algorithm [18] has been performed. Then, for every feature
the corresponding rank according to mRMR on all data sets is summed up. Finally,
the 24 features are sorted according to their sum of ranks S. The lower the sum
of ranks S for a particular feature is, the better suited is the feature for predicting
the node assignment's correctness. Figure 5.7 shows the sum of ranks S (y-axis) for
the 24 features (x-axis). We observe a nonuniform distribution among all features,
which demonstrates that there are some features more discriminative than others.
The range of S is quite large, starting with $S = 33$ (feature 24) and ending with
$S = 149$ (feature 10).

Table 5.7 shows the five features with lowest and the three features with highest
sum of ranks. Two main observations can be made. First, the difference of the sum
of ranks between the two best features and the three remaining ones is remarkably

Fig. 5.7 Sum of ranks for
each of the 24 features

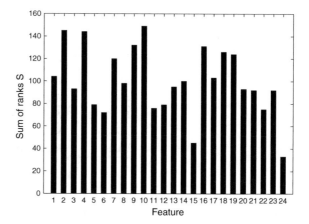

Table 5.7 Five best and three
worst features together with
the corresponding sum of
ranks S

	S
Outlierness column	33
Oulierness row	45
Edge cost	72
Leader column	75
Unique row	76
Deviation of **C**	144
Min of **C**	145
Deviation row	149

large. Second, the two best features correspond to the *Outlierness* feature applied to
the column or row, respectively. This clearly implies that the *Outlierness* (either in
the row or column) is particularly well suited for predicting the node assignment's
correctness. Yet, also the implied edge cost of $(u_i \rightarrow v_j) \in \psi$, the difference between
the minimum and second minimum cost assignment in column j (Leader Column),
as well as the maximum difference between the cost of the actual assignment and a
possible alternative in row i (Unique Row) seem to be appropriate characterizations
for predicting the correctness of individual node edit operations. On the other hand,
the deviation and the minimum of **C**, as well as the deviation of row i, are not well
suited for predicting the assignment's correctness.

Finally, in [15] the classification accuracy using the k best features according to
mRMR on every data set are recomputed (with $k = 2, 3, 4, 5, 7, 10$). The results
are shown in Table 5.8. First of all, we observe that on all data sets but Alkane
the accuracy monotonically increases by increasing k from 2 to 10. Actually, this
applies also for $k = 10, 11, \ldots, 24$ (not shown in Table 5.8). That is, on all data sets
the overall best classification result is achieved using all available features. Second,
it is remarkable that using only two features the base rate classification rate B can
be outperformed in six out of eight cases. This can be particularly observed on the

Table 5.8 Classification
accuracy for each data set and
for different number of
features k used

k	2	3	4	5	7	10
Acyclic	53.4	54.1	54.6	55.1	58.6	59.3
AIDS	63.6	65.6	66.2	67.3	68.3	68.9
Alkane	52.1	52.8	52.4	52.2	52.2	55.7
FP	72.2	72.2	72.5	72.5	73.3	74.1
GREC	76.6	76.7	77.4	78.1	79.9	81.6
LETTER	76.9	76.9	77.4	78.2	78.4	79.1
MAO	86.3	85.9	89.7	89.7	90.5	90.8
PAH	89.9	90.1	90.1	90.4	90.4	90.6

GREC, MAO, and PAH data sets, where B is outperformed by 17, 10, and 22%, respectively. Third, with about half of the number of original features (i.e., when $k = 10$), a similar accuracy as using the complete set of features can be achieved. This is well observable on the last four data sets, where the accuracy differs only about 1–3% with respect to the accuracy obtained using all features.

References

1. K. Riesen, A. Fischer, H. Bunke, Estimating graph edit distance using lower and upper bounds of bipartite approximations. Int. J. Pattern Recognit. Art. Intell. **29**(2), 1550011 (2015)
2. A. Smola, B. Schölkopf, A tutorial on support vector regression. Stat. Comput. **14**, 199–222 (2004)
3. M. Song, C.M. Breneman, J. Bi, N. Sukumar, K.P. Bennett, S. Cramer, N. Tugcu, Prediction of protein retention times in anion-exchange chromatography systems using support vector machine regression. J. Chem. Inf. Comput. Sci. **42**(6), 1347–1357 (2002)
4. C.H. Wu, C.C. Wei, D.C. Su, M.H. Chang, J.M. Ho, Travel-time prediction with support vector regression. IEEE Trans. Intell. Trans. Syst. **5**(4), 276–281 (2004)
5. H. Yang, L. Chan, Laiwan, I. King, Support vector machine regression for volatile stock market prediction, in *Proceedings of the IDEAL 2002, LNCS 2412* (2002), pp. 391–396
6. Y. Wang, R.T. Schultz, R.T. Constable, L.H. Staib, Nonlinear estimation and modeling of fMRI data using spatio-temporal support vector regression, in *Information Processing in Medical Imaging Proceedings* (2003), pp. 647–659
7. C. Burges, A tutorial on support vector machines for pattern recognition. Data Min. Knowl. Discov. **2**(2), 121–167 (1998)
8. V. Vapnik, Statistical Learning Theory (Wiley, 1998)
9. D. Basak, S. Pal, D.C. Patranabis, Support vector regression. Neural Inf. Proc. Lett. Rev. **11**(10), 203–224 (2007)
10. B. Schölkopf, A. Smola, Learning with Kernels (MIT Press, Massachusetts, 2002)
11. C. Cortes, V. Vapnik, Support vector networks. Mach. Learn. **20**, 273–297 (1995)
12. J. Shawe-Taylor, N. Cristianini, Kernel Methods for Pattern Analysis (Cambridge University Press, Cambridge, 2004)
13. M. Neuhaus, H. Bunke, Bridging the Gap Between Graph Edit Distance and Kernel Machines (World Scientific, Singapore, 2007)
14. K. Riesen, H. Bunke, IAM graph database repository for graph based pattern recognition and machine learning, in *Structural, Syntactic, and Statistical Pattern Recognition, LNCS 5342*, ed. by N. da Vitoria Lobo et al. (2008), pp. 287–297

15. K. Riesen, M. Ferrer. Predicting the correctness of node assignments in bipartite graph matching. Accepted for Publication in Pattern Recognition Letters
16. L. Brun, https://brunl01.users.greyc.fr/chemistry/
17. C-C. Chang, C-J. Lin, LIBSVM: a library for support vector machines (2001). Software available at http://www.csie.ntu.edu.tw/cjlin/libsvm
18. H. Peng, F. Long, C. Ding, Feature selection based on mutual information: Criteria of max-dependency, max-relevance, and min-redundancy. IEEE Trans. Pattern Anal. Mach. Intell. **27**(8), 1226–1238 (2005)

Chapter 6
Speeding Up Bipartite Graph Edit Distance

Abstract Major goal of the present chapter is to introduce methods for speeding up the approximation framework BP-GED. In particular, we aim at substantially speeding up the second step of BP-GED, viz., the assignment of local substructures in the LSAP. In BP-GED a state-of-the-art algorithm with cubic time complexity is employed in order to optimally solve the underlying LSAP. In this chapter, we aim at replacing this optimal algorithm with suboptimal greedy algorithms which run in quadratic time. That is, we aim at approximating the basic LSAP which in turn approximates the underlying graph edit distance problem. Due to the lower complexity of a suboptimal assignment process, a substantial speedup of the complete approximation procedure can be expected. Yet, the overall question to be answered is whether this double approximation is able to keep up with the existing framework with respect to distance accuracy.

6.1 Suboptimal Assignment Algorithms

In the second step of BP-GED, an assignment of the nodes (plus local structures) of both graphs has to be found. For this task Munkres' algorithm [1], also referred to as Kuhn–Munkres, or Hungarian algorithm, is deployed in the BP-GED framework [2]. The time complexity of this particular algorithm (as well as the best performing other known algorithms for LSAPs) is cubic in the size of the problem, i.e., $O((n + m)^3)$ in this particular case.

Major contribution of the present chapter is to solve the assignment of local graph structures, viz., the second step of Algorithm 2, with an approximation rather than an exact algorithm. In particular, the present chapter introduces and compares five different strategies for fast suboptimal assignment in the context of graph edit distance approximation. Note that these algorithms have been individually presented in three preliminary papers [3–5] and consolidated in [6]. All of these algorithms are greedy algorithms using some specific heuristics in order to improve the resulting distance approximation.

© Springer International Publishing Switzerland 2015
K. Riesen, *Structural Pattern Recognition with Graph Edit Distance*,
Advances in Computer Vision and Pattern Recognition,
DOI 10.1007/978-3-319-27252-8_6

6.1.1 Basic Greedy Assignment

A basic greedy algorithm that suboptimally solves the LSAP stated on cost matrix $\mathbf{C}$ is formalized in Algorithm 10. This algorithm iterates through $\mathbf{C}$ from top to bottom through all rows and assigns every element to the minimum unused element in a greedy manner. More formally, for each row i in the cost matrix $\mathbf{C} = (c_{ij})$ the minimum cost entry $\varphi_i = \arg\min_{\forall j} c_{ij}$ is determined and the corresponding node edit operation $(u_i \rightarrow v_{\varphi_i})$ is added to ψ. By removing column φ_i in $\mathbf{C}$, it is ensured that every column of the cost matrix is considered exactly once (i.e., $\forall j$ refers to available columns in $\mathbf{C}$). Clearly, the complexity of this suboptimal assignment algorithm is $O((n + m)^2)$. For the remainder of this chapter we denote the graph edit distance approximation where the basic node assignment (i.e., step 2 of BP-GED) is computed by means of this greedy procedure with *Greedy-GED*.

Algorithm 10 Greedy-Assignment ($\mathbf{C} = (c_{ij})$)

1: $\psi = \{\}$
2: **for** $i = 1, \ldots, (m + n)$ **do**
3:    $\varphi_i = \arg\min_{\forall j} c_{ij}$
4:    Remove column φ_i from $\mathbf{C}$
5:    $\psi = \psi \cup \{(u_i \rightarrow v_{\varphi_i})\}$
6: **end for**
7: **return** ψ

6.1.2 Tie Break Strategy

A crucial question in Algorithm 10 is how possible ties between two (or more) cost entries in the same row are resolved. In the basic version of Algorithm 10, a certain row is always assigned to the first minimum column that occurs from left to right. As a refinement of this coarse heuristic in [6], the following procedure has been proposed (denoted by *Greedy-Tie-GED* from now on).

Assume that in the ith row the following $t > 1$ cost entries $\{c_{ij_1}, \ldots, c_{ij_t}\}$ offer minimal cost among all available columns. For each of the corresponding columns $\{j_1, \ldots, j_t\}$, we search the minimum cost row that has not yet been assigned. Eventually, row i is assigned to column $\varphi_i \in \{j_1, \ldots, j_t\}$ that holds the highest minimum entry. Formally, column

$$\varphi_i = \arg\max_{j \in \{j_1, \ldots, j_t\}} \left(\min_{\forall k} c_{kj} \right)$$

is assigned to row i.

The intuition behind this strategy is as follows. The minimum cost

$$\min_{\forall k} c_{kj}$$

refers to the best available alternative for column j besides row i ($\forall k$ refers to all unprocessed rows of matrix $\mathbf{C}$). With other words, if we do not select $(u_i \rightarrow v_j)$ as an assignment, the alternative assignment costs at least $\min_{\forall k} c_{kj}$. Hence, we should select the assignment among $\{u_i \rightarrow v_{j_1}, \ldots, u_i \rightarrow v_{j_t}\}$ where the best possible alternative would lead to the highest cost. The complexity of Greedy-Tie-GED remains in $O((n+m)^2)$.

6.1.3 Refined Greedy Assignment

A next refinement of the basic greedy algorithm presented in [6] is given in Algorithm 11. Similar to Algorithm 10 for every row i, we search for the minimum cost column φ_i (in case of ties the strategy described in the previous section is applied). In addition to Algorithm 10 we also seek for the minimum cost row k for column φ_i.

Algorithm 11 Greedy-Refined-Assignment $(\mathbf{C} = (c_{ij}))$

1: $\psi = \{\}$
2: **while** row i in $\mathbf{C}$ is available **do**
3:    $\varphi_i = \arg \min_{\forall j} c_{ij}$ and $k = \arg \min_{\forall i} c_{i\varphi_i}$
4:    **if** $c_{i\varphi_i} \leq c_{k\varphi_i}$ **then**
5:       $\psi = \psi \cup \{(u_i \rightarrow v_{\varphi_i})\}$
6:       Remove row i and column φ_i from $\mathbf{C}$
7:    **else**
8:       $\psi = \psi \cup \{(u_k \rightarrow v_{\varphi_i})\}$
9:       Remove row k and column φ_i from $\mathbf{C}$
10:   **end if**
11: **end while**
12: **return** ψ

That is, for row i column φ_i is the best assignment. Yet, by considering the assignment process from column φ_i's point of view, row k would be the best choice. We select the assignment which leads to lower cost. That is, if $c_{i\varphi_i} \leq c_{k\varphi_i}$, the assignment $(u_i \rightarrow v_{\varphi_i})$ is added to ψ. This includes the special situation where $i = k$, i.e., column φ_i corresponds to the optimal assignment for row i and vice versa. Otherwise, if $c_{i\varphi_i} > c_{k\varphi_i}$, the assignment $(u_k \rightarrow v_{\varphi_i})$ is selected. Regardless of the assignment actually added to ψ, the corresponding row and column are removed from $\mathbf{C}$.

Note that in contrast with Algorithm 10 where the ith assignment added to ψ always considers row i, this algorithm processes the rows of $\mathbf{C}$ not necessarily from top to bottom. However, the time complexity of this assignment algorithm remains

$O((n+m)^2)$. We denote the graph edit distance approximation where the LSAP is solved by means of Algorithm 11 with *Greedy-Refined-GED*.

6.1.4 Greedy Assignment Regarding Loss

A further refinement of the greedy assignment presented in [6] is given in Algorithm 12. Similar to Algorithm 11, this particular method first finds both the minimum cost column φ_i for row i and the minimum cost row k for column φ_i (again the tie break strategy of Sect. 6.1.2 is applied). Now three cases have to be considered.

Algorithm 12 Greedy-Loss-Assignment ($\mathbf{C} = (c_{ij})$)

1: $\psi = \{\}$
2: **while** row i in $\mathbf{C}$ is available **do**
3:     $\varphi_i = \arg\min\limits_{\forall j} c_{ij}$ and $k = \arg\min\limits_{\forall i} c_{i\varphi_i}$
4:     **if** $i == k$ **then**
5:         $\psi = \psi \cup \{(u_i \to v_{\varphi_i})\}$
6:         Remove row i and column φ_i from $\mathbf{C}$
7:     **else**
8:         $\varphi'_i = \arg\min\limits_{\forall j \neq \varphi_i} c_{ij}$ and $\varphi_k = \arg\min\limits_{\forall j \neq \varphi_i} c_{kj}$
9:         **if** $(c_{i\varphi_i} + c_{k\varphi_k}) < (c_{i\varphi'_i} + c_{k\varphi_i})$ **then**
10:             $\psi = \psi \cup \{(u_i \to v_{\varphi_i}), (u_k \to v_{\varphi_k})\}$
11:             Remove rows i, k and columns φ_i, φ_k from $\mathbf{C}$
12:         **else**
13:             $\psi = \psi \cup \{(u_i \to v_{\varphi'_i}), (u_k \to v_{\varphi_i})\}$
14:             Remove rows i, k and columns φ_i, φ'_i from $\mathbf{C}$
15:         **end if**
16:     **end if**
17: **end while**
18: **return** ψ

---

1. If i equals k, column φ_i is the best available assignment for row i and vice versa (and thus assignment $(u_i \to v_{\varphi_i})$ can safely be added to ψ).
2. If $i \neq k$, the two scenarios have to be distinguished. For both scenarios, the second best assignment φ'_i for row i, as well as the best available assignment φ_k for row k (distinct from φ_i), are determined.

   a. In the first scenario, row i is assigned to its best column φ_i and thus row k has eventually to be assigned to the best alternative φ_k. The sum of cost of this scenario amounts to $(c_{i\varphi_i} + c_{k\varphi_k})$.
   b. In the other scenario, row k is assigned to column φ_i and thus row i has to be assigned to its best possible alternative which is column φ'_i. The sum of cost of this scenario amounts to $(c_{i\varphi'_i} + c_{k\varphi_i})$.

We choose the scenario from 2.a or 2.b which offers a lower sum of cost and remove the corresponding rows and columns from $\mathbf{C}$. We denote the graph edit distance approximation using this greedy approach with *Greedy-Loss-GED* (the complexity of this assignment algorithm remains $O((n+m)^2)$.

6.1.5 Order of Node Processing

Note that the nodes of a graph are generally unordered and thus, the first n rows (and m columns) in $\mathbf{C}$ are arbitrarily ordered. Note, however, that the suboptimal assignment methods operate in a greedy manner, i.e., they are not able to undo a certain node assignment once it has been added to ψ. Hence, all of these methods crucially depend on the order in which the nodes are processed.

Intuitively, one would start the greedy assignment in rows which are somehow easier to cope with than others. To this end, we define three criteria for rows in $\mathbf{C}$ that indicate the level of difficulty with respect to finding an assignment φ_i in a certain row i. Note that for the following criteria the left upper $n \times m$ part of $\mathbf{C}$ is regarded only. Note furthermore that the features defined in Sect. 5.2.1 could also be adopted for the present task.

The first criterion measures the ratio between the cost of the best and second best assignment $\text{min}1_i$ and $\text{min}2_i$, respectively, and is defined as

$$Min1\text{-}Min2\text{-}Ratio(i) = \left(\frac{\text{min}1_i + 1}{\text{min}2_i + 1} \right),$$

where $\text{min}1_i = \min\limits_{j=1,\dots,m} c_{ij}$ and $\text{min}2_i = \min\limits_{j=1,\dots,m, j \neq k} c_{ij}$ (k is the column index in which the minimum cost entry $\text{min}1_i$ of the ith row is found). Note that we add one to both numerator and denominator in order to avoid divisions by zero.

Clearly, the values of the $Min1\text{-}Min2\text{-}Ratio(i)$ criterion lie in the range $]0, 1]$. If both entries $\text{min}2_i$ and $\text{min}1_i$ are equal, this criterion becomes 1 which indicates a maximum level of difficulty for determining an assignment (in particular when the assignment cannot be changed any more). Contrariwise, a ratio near to zero indicates that the difference between the best and second best assignment in row i is large and thus an assignment in row i can be rather easily scheduled.

The second criterion measures the difference between the minimal entry of row i and the mean value of all entries in the respective row. That is,

$$Min\text{-}Mean\text{-}Difference(i) = (\text{min}1_i - \text{mean}_i),$$

where $\text{mean}_i = \frac{1}{m} \sum_{j=1,\dots,m} c_{ij}$.

Clearly, as the minimum of a row is smaller than, or equal to, the mean of the same row, the values of these criterion lie in the range $]-\infty, 0]$. If the minimum is much smaller than the mean (i.e., we receive large negative values), the assignment in the respective row can be regarded as rather evident. Likewise, if the mean and the minimum of a row are near to each other (i.e., we receive negative values near to zero), an assignment, especially when it has to be done in a greedy manner, is rather difficult in this row.

The third criterion takes the information of the columns in $\mathbf{C}$ into account. Let k be the column in which the minimum cost entry $\min 1_i$ of the ith row is found, i.e., $k = \arg\min_{j=1,\ldots,m} c_{ij}$. The third criterion counts the number of entries in column k which are smaller than $\min 1_i$. That is,

$$Min\text{-}Col\text{-}Position(i) = |\{c_{ik} | i = 1, \ldots, n; c_{ik} < \min 1_i\}|$$

Obviously, the values of this criterion lie in the range $[0, n]$ (n is the number of rows considered). If $Min\text{-}Col\text{-}Position(i)$ is zero, the assignment of row i to column k is minimal regarded from both row i and column k. Hence, this assignment can be safely carried out. Contrariwise, if the value of this criterion gets large (i.e., regarded from the column there are many better assignment options), the determination of minimal assignment in this row is somehow risky.

For all of the criteria, we observe that the smaller the value for a certain row i is, the easier is the assignment in the ith row. That is, we can sort the first n rows of matrix $\mathbf{C}$ in ascending order with respect to these criteria such that rows with a low level of assignment difficulty are covered first in the greedy assignment process. Note that the sorting criteria can be used as a preprocessing step for any of the greedy assignment algorithms described so far.

6.1.6 Greedy Sort Assignment

The prime reason for building a square cost matrix $\mathbf{C} = (c_{ij})$ in [2] is to formulate a standard LSAP that takes the peculiarities of graph edit distance into account. In contrast with [2] as well as the above-described greedy methods, the following procedure (originally presented in [6]) is based on a list of costs (rather than a square cost matrix $\mathbf{C}$):

$$\mathbf{l} = \{\underbrace{c_{11}, c_{12}, \ldots c_{ij}, \ldots, c_{nm}}_{\text{substitutions}}, \underbrace{c_{1\varepsilon}, c_{2\varepsilon}, \ldots, c_{n\varepsilon}}_{\text{deletions}}, \underbrace{c_{\varepsilon 1}, c_{\varepsilon 2}, \ldots, c_{\varepsilon m}}_{\text{insertions}}\} \tag{6.1}$$

Obviously, list $\mathbf{l}$ buffers the $n \times m$ elements that represent the costs of all possible node substitutions (left upper corner of $\mathbf{C}$), as well as n and m elements that represent the costs of all possible node deletions and insertions, respectively (diagonals of the right upper and left lower corner of $\mathbf{C}$). Although list $\mathbf{l}$ contains less entries than $\mathbf{C}$, it essentially contains the same information as $\mathbf{C}$ as the omitted elements are ∞ and 0 elements only. The suboptimal assignment algorithm, which takes $\mathbf{l}$ rather than $\mathbf{C}$ as input, is outlined in Algorithm 13.

First, list $\mathbf{l}$ is sorted in ascending order using an optimized merge sort in $O(n \log n)$ time [7]. Next, as long as not all nodes of g_1 and g_2 are processed, the individual cost entries $c_{ij} \in \mathbf{l}$ are visited from head to tail. For the currently visited entry c_{ij}, it is verified whether the pair of indices (i, j) is admissible. Remember that every element c_{ij} uniquely corresponds to a certain node edit operation $(u_i \rightarrow v_j)$. A pair of indices (i, j) is admissible if one of the following three cases is true:

1. both nodes $u_i \in V_1, v_j \in V_2$ are available (substitution of unprocessed nodes u_i, v_j)
2. $i == \varepsilon$ and $v_j \in V_2$ is available (insertion of unprocessed node v_j)
3. $j == \varepsilon$ and $u_i \in V_1$ is available (deletion of unprocessed node u_i)

If (i, j) is admissible, the node edit operation $(u_i \rightarrow v_j)$ is added to the set of assignments ψ. Eventually, the corresponding nodes u_i and v_j are marked as unavailable.[1]

Algorithm 13 Greedy-Sort-Assignment (**l**)

1: Sort elements $c_{ij} \in \mathbf{l}$ in ascending order: $\mathbf{l} = (c^{(1)}, \ldots, c^{(nm+n+m)})$
2: $\psi = \{\}$
3: $k = 1$; mark all nodes in g_1 and g_2 as available
4: **while** nodes in g_1 are available **or** nodes in g_2 are available **do**
5:     Let c_{ij} be the kth element $c^{(k)}$ in list **l**
6:     **if** (i, j) is *admissible* **then**
7:         $\psi = \psi \cup \{(u_i \rightarrow v_j)\}$
8:         Mark u_i and v_j as unavailable
9:     **end if**
10:     $k = k + 1$
11: **end while**
12: **return** ψ

The time critical part of this assignment algorithm is the sorting of list **l** which can be accomplished in linearithmic time with respect to the number of elements in **l**. Assuming $n \approx m$, we have approximately $n^2 + 2n$ elements in **l** and thus the overall complexity of this graph edit distance approximation, denoted by *Greedy-Sort-GED* from now on, amounts to $O(n^2 \log(n^2))$.

6.2 Relations to Exact Graph Edit Distance

Note that in contrast with the optimal permutation $(\varphi_1, \ldots, \varphi_{n+m})$ returned by BP-GED, the permutations $(\varphi_1', \ldots, \varphi_{n+m}')$ of the proposed greedy algorithms are sub-optimal. That is, the sum of assignments costs of all greedy approaches is greater than, or equal to, the minimal sum of assignment cost provided by optimal LSAP solving algorithms. Formally, we have

---

[1]The ith node $u_i \in V_1$ is marked as unavailable only, if the corresponding index i is not equal to ε, of course. The same accounts for index j and node $v_j \in V_2$.

$$\sum_{i=1}^{(n+m)} c_{i\varphi_i'} \geq \sum_{i=1}^{(n+m)} c_{i\varphi_i}.$$

However, for the approximate graph distance values derived by BP-GED and any greedy approach, no globally valid order relation exists. That is, the approximate graph edit distance $d_{\psi'}$ derived from a certain greedy assignment can be greater than, equal to, or smaller than a distance value d_{ψ} returned by BP-GED. However, distance approximations derived from both optimal and suboptimal local assignments constitute upper bounds of the true graph edit distance. Hence, the smaller the approximated distance value is, the nearer it is to the exact graph edit distance.

6.3   Experimental Evaluation

For experimental evaluations, four data sets from the IAM graph database repository [8] and two data sets from GREYC's Chemistry dataset repository[2] are used. Four data sets consist of graphs representing molecular compounds from different applications, viz., AIDS, MUTA, MAO, and PAH (all of these data sets represent two class problems). One data set consists of graphs that represent proteins stemming from six different classes (PROT) and one data set (FP) consists of graphs representing fingerprint images coming from four different classes. For details on the graph extraction methods and the graph characteristics, we refer to Chap. 9.

In Table 6.1, we show different characteristic numbers for BP-GED and all greedy variants for graph edit distance approximation (note that we do not yet employ any of the node reordering strategies described in Sect. 6.1.5 for these evaluations). First, we focus on the mean run time for one matching in ms ($\varnothing t$). On the relatively small graphs (FP, MAO, and PAH), we observe moderate speedups of Greedy-GED compared to BP-GED. Yet, remember that we show the mean computation time for one single matching. Thus, assuming one million of matchings to be completed in a particular application, even a decrease of, say, 0.5 ms on average reduces the overall computation time by about 10 min. Moreover, the quadratic rather than cubic time complexity makes an impact on the three data sets with larger graphs (AIDS, MUTA, and PROT). On the MUTA data, for instance, Greedy-GED is more than seven times faster than the original approximation. We also observe that the enhanced greedy algorithms, viz., Greedy-Tie, Greedy-Refined, Greedy-Loss, and Greedy-Sort, do not need substantially more computation time compared to the plain approximation using Greedy-GED on all data sets.

The characteristic number $\varnothing o$ measures the overestimation of the assignment costs of one particular assignment compared to the optimal assignment costs. For comparison we take the difference between the optimal sum of costs (returned by BP) and the sum of assignment costs of the plain greedy assignment as 100 %.

---

[2]https://brunl01.users.greyc.fr/CHEMISTRY/index.html.

Table 6.1 The mean run time for one matching in ms ($\varnothing\,t$), the relative overestimation of a greedy sum of assignment costs compared to the optimal sum of assignment costs ($\varnothing\,o$), the mean relative deviation of greedy graph edit distance compared with the original BP-GED in percentage ($\varnothing\,e$), and the accuracy of a 1NN classifier

Data		Algorithm					
		BP-GED	Greedy-GED	Greedy-Tie-GED	Greedy-Refined-GED	Greedy-Loss-GED	Greedy-Sort-GED
AIDS	$\varnothing\,t$ [ms]	3.61	1.21	1.23	1.25	1.24	1.24
	$\varnothing\,o$ [%]	–	+100.0	+99.9	+74.1	+75.0	+72.5
	$\varnothing\,e$ [%]	–	+7.1/−4.1	+6.5/−3.7	+5.8/−4.6	+7.0/−4.3	+5.3/−4.4
	1NN [%]	99.07	98.93	99.20	99.13	98.87	99.27
FP	$\varnothing\,t$ [ms]	0.41	0.30	0.30	0.31	0.31	0.32
	$\varnothing\,o$ [%]	–	+100.0	+99.8	+88.0	+87.0	+86.6
	$\varnothing\,e$ [%]	–	+6.6/−15.7	+6.5/−15.9	+6.0/−17.5	+5.7/−18.1	+5.7/−18.2
	1NN [%]	79.75	77.05	77.20	75.80	76.60	75.95
MUTA	$\varnothing\,t$ [ms]	33.89	4.56	4.68	4.88	4.95	4.63
	$\varnothing\,o$ [%]	–	+100.0	+99.9	+2.8	+15.5	+1.8
	$\varnothing\,e$ [%]	–	+7.4/−3.8	+6.2/−4.6	+5.9/−5.1	+7.6/−4.9	+5.8/−4.9
	1NN [%]	70.20	70.10	71.80	71.60	71.10	72.50
PROT	$\varnothing\,t$ [ms]	25.54	13.31	13.48	13.48	13.52	13.41
	$\varnothing\,o$ [%]	–	+100.0	+94.6	+40.7	+69.1	+9.6
	$\varnothing\,e$ [%]	–	+11.2/−12.9	+10.4/−7.3	+6.2/−3.2	+8.2/−0.4	+1.6/−0.3
	1NN [%]	67.50	64.50	64.50	66.00	64.50	67.00
PAH	$\varnothing\,t$ [ms]	3.30	2.79	2.80	2.82	2.82	2.82
	$\varnothing\,o$ [%]	–	+100.0	+76.2	+42.8	+55.6	+24.8
	$\varnothing\,e$ [%]	–	+22.9/−18.2	+12.2/−13.6	+11.8/−11.7	+12.5/−12.3	+11.9/−11.8
	1NN [%]	63.83	43.62	63.83	62.77	63.83	62.77
MAO	$\varnothing\,t$ [ms]	2.35	1.66	1.70	1.78	1.75	1.79
	$\varnothing\,o$ [%]	–	+100.0	+87.6	+52.8	+50.9	+36.8
	$\varnothing\,e$ [%]	–	+80.3/−9.7	+45.2/−22.8	+29.1/−21.4	+47.4/−33.8	+26.3/−24.2
	1NN [%]	85.29	55.88	70.59	86.76	67.65	77.94

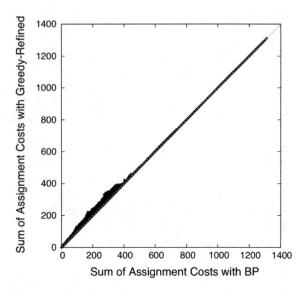

Fig. 6.1 Optimal assignment cost (x-axis) versus greedy assignment costs (y-axis) achieved by Greedy-Refined on the MUTA data set

Regarding the results in Table 6.1, we note that Greedy-Tie is in general not able to substantially reduce this overestimation. Yet, the other refinements return overall assignment sums which are substantially nearer to the optimal sum than the plain greedy approach. For instance, compared with Greedy-GED the difference to the optimal sum of assignment costs is reduced by more than 25 % with Greedy-Refined, Greedy-Loss, and Greedy-Sort on the AIDS data set.

Similar, or even better, results are observable on the other data sets. Note particularly the massive reductions on the MUTA data set using Greedy-Refined and Greedy-Sort. On this data set, the assignment costs produced by these two greedy assignments are essentially the same as the optimal assignment costs provided by BP. This can also be seen in the scatter plot in Fig. 6.1 where the optimal sum of assignment costs (x-axis) is plotted against the sum of costs achieved by Greedy-Refined (y-axis) on the MUTA data set. For larger sums (i.e., sums that are greater than 400), both BP and Greedy-Refined return the same sums of assignment costs, while smaller sums of costs are only slightly overestimated by the novel procedure.

The relative reduction of the overestimation by means of the refined greedy algorithms (when compared to the plain greedy approach) is also illustrated in a similar scatter plot in Fig. 6.2. Here, the optimal assignment cost (x-axis) is plotted against the assignment costs achieved by Greedy and Greedy-Sort using black and gray dots, respectively (on the PROT data set). The improved assignment quality using Greedy-Sort rather than the plain greedy algorithm is clearly observable.

While the sum of greedy assignment costs has to be greater than, or equal to, the optimal assignment costs, the edit distance approximations resulting from any greedy assignment algorithm can also be lower than the distance approximation returned by BP-GED (see Sect. 6.2 for the corresponding discussion). Thus, the characteristic number $\varnothing e$ in Table 6.1 measures both the mean relative over- and underestimation

Fig. 6.2 Optimal
assignment cost (x-axis)
versus greedy assignment
costs (y-axis) achieved by
Greedy and Greedy-Sort on
the PROT data set using
black and *gray dots*,
respectively

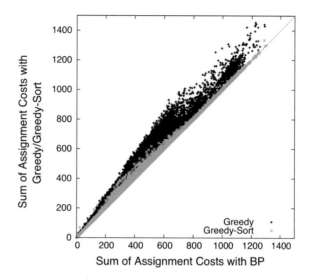

of greedy graph edit distances compared with BP-GED. Note that these two means are only computed on the sets of distances where a greedy approach actually over- or underestimates the original approximation.

Three major observations can be made in Table 6.1 with respect to $\varnothing e$. First, the enhanced greedy assignment algorithms are able to reduce the mean overestimation compared with the plain greedy approach in all cases but one (on MUTA with Greedy-Loss). For instance, the mean overestimation of Greedy-GED amounts to $+7.1\%$ on the AIDS data, while the same parameter is reduced to $+5.3\%$ with Greedy-Sort-GED. Second, on all data sets Greedy-Sort leads to the overall lowest overestimation among all greedy algorithms. Third, the mean underestimation of Greedy-GED is in general further increased with the more elaborated greedy algorithms (observable on all data sets but PROT and PAH).

The reduction of overestimation and the increase of underestimation imply an improvement of the distance quality in general. This improvement by the refined algorithms can be exemplarily seen in Fig. 6.3a, b where the distances of BP-GED (x-axis) are plotted against distances returned by Greedy-GED and Greedy-Refined-GED (y-axis), respectively (on the MAO data set—similar plots are obtained on the other data sets). The decrease of the overestimation and the increase of the underestimation by means of the more elaborated algorithm are clearly observable.

Table 6.1 also shows the recognition rate of a 1-nearest-neighbor classifier (1NN) using the respective distances on all data sets. Note that one could also employ other distance-based classifiers such as edit distance-based kernels [9] for this task. However, we feel that the nearest-neighbor paradigm is particularly interesting for the present evaluation because it directly uses the distances without any additional classifier training.

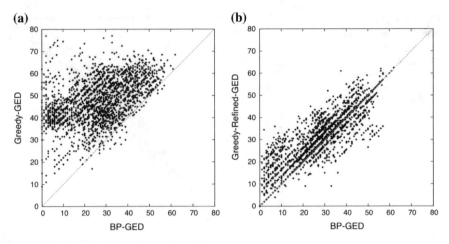

Fig. 6.3 BP-GED (*x*-axis) versus Greedy-GED **a** and Greedy-Refined-GED **b** on the MAO data set

With respect to the recognition accuracy, the following main findings are observable. On four out of six data sets, at least one of the novel greedy algorithms achieves the same result as BP-GED or even outperforms the recognition rate of BP-GED. That is, only on FP and PROT the faster greedy algorithms are not able to arrive at the same recognition rates as BP-GED. Yet, also on these two data sets the classification accuracies of the greedy assignment approximations are thoroughly comparable with those of BP-GED.

In order to compare the five greedy algorithms with each other, we sum up the ranks according to the recognition performance for every algorithm. Greedy-Tie, for instance, achieves the overall best result on FP and PAH $(1 + 1)$, the second best result on AIDS and MUTA $(2 + 2)$, and the third best result on Protein and MAO $(3 + 3)$, leading to a sum of ranks of 12. In Fig. 6.4, the sum of ranks is plotted in a histogram for each algorithm. According to this result, we note that Greedy-Tie and Greedy-Sort generally performs the best, while the pure greedy assignment generally results in the worst classification result.

Finally, we aim at investigating the impact of the node order in the greedy assignment framework. In particular, we want to verify how the distance accuracy can be influenced when the order of the nodes is antecedently altered with respect to the three order criteria described in Sect. 6.1.5. Basically, these criteria can be applied in combination with any of the greedy assignment algorithms but Greedy-Sort (remember that the proposed order criteria sort the rows of the cost matrix with respect to the level of difficulty. Yet, Greedy-Sort operates on a list of costs rather than on a cost matrix).

In preliminary evaluations in [10], it turned out that the proposed reorder strategies superpose the effects of the enhanced heuristics of the refined greedy algorithms and thus neither improvement nor deteriorations can be observed. Thus, we apply the reorder strategies in conjunction with the pure algorithm Greedy-GED. In order to

Fig. 6.4 Sum of ranks of the five greedy approximations with respect to the recognition rate

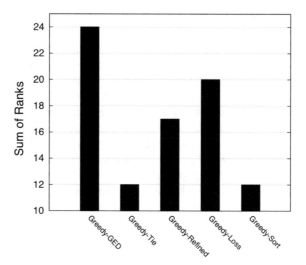

Fig. 6.5 Relative improvement of the three reordering criteria compared with Greedy-GED

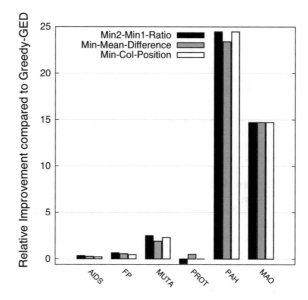

measure the impact of the reordering, we compare the recognition rates of Greedy-GED using a certain order criteria with the original Greedy-GED.

In Fig. 6.5, the relative deviation of the recognition rates from the results obtained by the original Greedy-GED is shown for every data set and every order criterion. We observe that in all cases but one ($Min1$-$Min2$-$Ratio(i)$ on PROT) the classification accuracy can be improved by ordering the nodes before they are assigned in a greedy manner. Note that no substantial differences among the three order criteria can be observed. Yet, $Min1$-$Min2$-$Ratio(i)$ achieves the best accuracy on four out of six data sets. On the last two data sets (PAH and MAO), Greedy-GED with reorder strategies substantially outperforms the accuracy of Greedy-GED. Note that on both data sets Greedy-GED achieves poor results and thus these improvements are rather easy to achieve. Moreover, the graphs from these data sets differ from the other data sets in terms of offering a poor diversity of node labels (the nodes can almost be handled as unlabeled). On this kind of graphs, it is rather difficult to make an assignment based on a greedy choice. Therefore, a sorting criterion that allows to carry out more evident greedy assignments first substantially improves the overall distance accuracy.

Finally, it is worth to mention that Greedy-GED achieves a sum of ranks of 11 with *Min1-Min2-Ratio*(i) and is thus better than all of the elaborated greedy methods described and discussed above. More precisely, on AIDS, FP, MUTA, and PAH, it achieves the overall best classification accuracy; on MAO, it shows the second best performance among all algorithms; while on PROT this combination fails and shows the worst performance among all the tested algorithms.

References

1. J. Munkres, Algorithms for the assignment and transportation problems. J. Soc. Ind. Appl. Math. **5**(1), 32–38 (1957)
2. K. Riesen, H. Bunke, Approximate graph edit distance computation by means of bipartite graph matching. Image Vis. Comput. **27**(4), 950–959 (2009)
3. K. Riesen, M. Ferrer, H. Bunke, Suboptimal graph edit distance based on sorted local assignments, in *Proceedings of the 12th International Workshop on Multiple Classifier Systems*, eds. by F. Schwenker, F. Roli, J. Kittler (2015), pp.147–156
4. K. Riesen, M. Ferrer, R. Dornberger, H. Bunke, Greedy graph edit distance, in *Proceedings of the 11th International Conference on Machine Learning and Data Mining in Pattern Recognition*, LNAI 9166, ed. by P. Perner (2015), pp. 1–14
5. K. Riesen, M. Ferrer, A. Fischer, H. Bunke, Approximation of graph edit distance in quadratic time, in *Proceedings of the 10th International Workshop on Graph Based Representations in Pattern Recognition*, LNCS 9069, eds. by C.L. Liu, B. Luo, W. Kropatsch, J. Cheng (2015), pp. 3–12
6. K. Riesen, M. Ferrer, H. Bunke, Approximate graph edit distance in quadratic time, Accepted for publication in IEEE/ACM Transactions on Computational Biology and Bioinformatics
7. D. Knuth, *Sorting and Searching. The Art of Computer Programming 3, Chapter 5.2.4: Sorting by Merging* (Addison Wesley, Boston, 1998), pp. 158–168
8. K. Riesen, H. Bunke, IAM graph database repository for graph based pattern recognition and machine learning, in *Structural, Syntactic, and Statistical Pattern Recognition*, LNCS 5342, eds. by N. da Vitoria Lobo et al. (2008), pp. 287–297
9. M. Neuhaus, H. Bunke, *Bridging the Gap Between Graph Edit Distance and Kernel Machines* (World Scientific, Singapore, 2007)
10. K. Riesen, M. Ferrer, Predicting the correctness of node assignments in bipartite graph matching, Accepted for publication in Pattern Recognition Letters

Chapter 7
Conclusions and Future Work

Abstract In the previous six chapters of the present book, the general concept as well as recent advances of graph edit distance have been thoroughly reviewed and evaluated. This last chapter first summarizes and comments the main contributions of the present book. Eventually, the main findings—that have been achieved by means of the experimental evaluations carried out in various chapters—are brought together. Finally, we show several rewarding options for further research.

7.1 Main Contributions and Findings

The present book is concerned with the concept of graph edit distance. Graph edit distance is one of the most popular and flexible dissimilarity models in graph-based pattern recognition. Yet, major drawback of this particular distance model is its computational complexity. A recent approximation framework allows the suboptimal computation of graph edit distance in cubic, rather than exponential time. This framework builds the basis for the research project whose output is summarized in the present work.

The main contributions of the book are as follows:

- First, the book gives a thorough introduction into the field of structural pattern recognition with a special focus on the concept of graph edit distance.
- Second, the book provides a proper reformulation of graph edit distance to a quadratic assignment problem.
- Next, it is shown how the quadratic assignment problem of graph edit distance can be reduced to a linear sum assignment problem. In particular, two bounds of the true edit distance, viz., an upper and a lower bound, are derived from this reformulated problem.
- A substantial part of the present book is concerned with one of the well-known problems of the approximation framework, viz., the overestimation of the true edit distance. To this end three different strategies, which aim at reducing the approximation error, are researched and empirically validated. The first strategy is based on post-processing search procedures, the second strategy exploits information

K. Riesen, *Structural Pattern Recognition with Graph Edit Distance*,
Advances in Computer Vision and Pattern Recognition,
DOI 10.1007/978-3-319-27252-8_7

about the centrality of nodes, and the third strategy is based on regression analysis and machine learning in order to improve the distance accuracy.

- Finally, the last chapter of the present book is on the improvement of the existing algorithmic framework with respect to the matching time. While in the original framework the nodes plus local edge structures are assigned to each other in an optimal way, the proposed extension uses various suboptimal greedy algorithms for this task. In particular we propose one basic greedy assignment algorithm and four enhanced versions of this basic assignment algorithm. Four of these algorithms allow the graph edit distance approximation in quadratic— rather than cubic—time (Greedy-Sort-GED works in $O(n^2 \log(n^2))$ time).

Several empirical investigations have been conducted in order to research the benefits and limitations of the novel approaches. In particular, the following main findings have been achieved by means of the experimental evaluations.

- We show that the combination of BP-GED with post-processing search strategies is clearly beneficial as it leads to a substantial reduction of the overestimation typical for BP-GED (regardless the search method actually employed). Though the run times are increased when compared to our former framework (as expected), they are mostly still far below the run times of the exact algorithm.
- The same accounts for the second strategy, viz., the integration of node centrality measures in the matching process. However, the observed improvement is not at the same level of accuracy as the search methods achieve.
- We show that the SVR estimation, in particular in conjunction with the RBF kernel, leads to better approximations of the exact edit distance than both distance bounds on many data sets. Simultaneously, we observe that the post-processing estimation of the distances by means of SVR does nearly not affect the run time of the complete framework.
- The substantial speed up of the novel quadratic time approximation algorithms (compared to the original algorithm) is also empirically verified. We observe speed ups up to factor seven when compared to BP-GED. Moreover, we observe that in most cases the novel greedy algorithms are able to keep up with the existing framework with respect to recognition accuracy using a nearest-neighbor classifier.

7.2   Future Work

Among other possibilities, the following options for further research exist:

- In [1] it has been empirically verified that the distance quality returned by the approximation framework BP-GED is sufficiently accurate for a nearest-neighbor classifier. Yet, it would be worth to analyze the different approximation qualities using other distance-based classifiers such as edit distance-based kernels [2].

- Another application of improved distance accuracy could be potentially found in the field of graph embedding using dissimilarities. The dissimilarity representation [3] has emerged as a novel and powerful approach in pattern recognition in the last decade (see Sect. 2.3.3). Recently, the idea of dissimilarity representations has been adopted to the domain of graphs by the author of the present book [4]. Thereby, the general embedding framework is built upon the approximate graph edit distances of BP-GED. Hence, the question arises whether or not the improved distance quality of the extended graph edit distance approximation framework can support the applicability and accuracy of the dissimilarity representation for graphs.
- Moreover, there seems to be room for further exploiting the upper and lower bounds d_ψ and d'_ψ, respectively. For instance, the development of a certainty measure that depends on the difference $d_\psi - d'_\psi$ could be an interesting option. Clearly, if $d_\psi - d'_\psi = 0$ then $d_{\lambda_{min}} = d_\psi = d'_\psi$. On the contrary, the larger the difference is, the more likely it is that both bounds produce large errors. Hence, one could start exact graph edit distance computation only if the certainty measure is larger than a certain threshold (otherwise, d_ψ, d'_ψ, or an estimation based on both bounds can be safely returned as distance value).
- The reordering criteria in conjunction with the plain greedy algorithm show promising results on all data sets. Hence, it might be promising to develop and evaluate further criteria that can be used to predict the level of difficulty in a certain assignment situation. Moreover, the order criteria are applied only once, viz., before the assignment process is started. It would be interesting to investigate whether dynamic updates of the node order during the assignment process could further improve the distance quality.
- Finally, we aim at generalizing the novel greedy framework in terms of better exploiting the information given by partial assignments during the greedy process. For instance, after a node has been permanently assigned to another node one could dynamically update the estimations of the implied edge costs encoded in the individual entries in **C**. Yet, it is an open research question how these dynamic updates can be integrated in the proposed framework and to what extent this extension might improve the overall approximation accuracy.

References

1. K. Riesen, H. Bunke, Approximate graph edit distance computation by means of bipartite graph matching. Image Vis. Comput. **27**(4), 950–959 (2009)
2. M. Neuhaus, H. Bunke, *Bridging the Gap Between Graph Edit Distance and Kernel Machines* (World Scientific, Singapore, 2007)
3. E. Pekalska, R. Duin, *The Dissimilarity Representation for Pattern Recognition: Foundations and Applications* (World Scientific, Singapore, 2005)
4. K. Riesen, H. Bunke, Graph classification based on vector space embedding. Int. J. Pattern Recognit. Artif. Intell. **23**(6), 1053–1081 (2008)

Chapter 8
Appendix A: Experimental Evaluation of Sorted Beam Search

Abstract In the following paragraphs, the six criteria for sorting the individual node edit operations $(u_i \rightarrow v_{\varphi_i}) \in \psi$ are briefly outlined [1]. All of these criteria can be used to sort the edit operations $(u_i \rightarrow v_{\varphi_i})$ in both ascending and descending order (resulting in twelve differently sorted node assignments).

8.1 Sorting Criteria

In the following paragraphs, the six criteria for sorting the individual node edit operations $(u_i \rightarrow v_{\varphi_i}) \in \psi$ are briefly outlined [1]. All of these criteria can be used to sort the edit operations $(u_i \rightarrow v_{\varphi_i})$ in both ascending and descending order (resulting in twelve differently sorted node assignments). In any case, we use the terminology *Inverse* for sorting strategies that process less-evident edit operations first, while criteria named without the suffix *Inverse* refer to criteria that process evident edit operations first.

Note that three of these criteria, viz., confident, unique, and leader, are also used in the context of predicting the correctness of edit operations (see Sect. 5.2.1).

8.1.1 Confident

The source nodes u_i of the edit operations $(u_i \rightarrow v_{\varphi i}) \in \psi$ are weighted according to $c_{i\varphi_i} \in \mathbf{C}$. That is, for a given edit operation $(u_i \rightarrow v_{\varphi i})$, the corresponding value $c_{i\varphi_i}$ in the cost matrix $\mathbf{C}$ is assigned to u_i as weight. The edit operations of the new assignment ψ' can now be sorted in ascending order according to the weights of u_i. Thus, edit operations with low costs, i.e., edit operations which are somehow evident, appear first in ψ' (*Confident*). Likewise, sorting the edit operations in descending order means that less-evident edit operations appear first in ψ' (*Confident-Inverse*).

© Springer International Publishing Switzerland 2015
K. Riesen, *Structural Pattern Recognition with Graph Edit Distance*,
Advances in Computer Vision and Pattern Recognition,
DOI 10.1007/978-3-319-27252-8_8

8.1.2   Unique

The source nodes u_i of the edit operations $(u_i \to v_{\varphi i}) \in \psi$ are weighted according to

$$\max_{\forall j=1,\dots,m} c_{ij} - c_{i\varphi_i}.$$

That is, the weight given to a certain source node u_i corresponds to the maximum difference between the cost $c_{i\varphi_i}$ of the actual edit operation $(u_i \to v_{\varphi_i})$ and the cost of a possible alternative matching node for u_i. Note that this difference can be negative, which means that the current edit operation $(u_i \to v_{\varphi i}) \in \psi$ is rather suboptimal (since there is at least one other matching node for u_i with lower cost than $c_{i\varphi_i}$). Edit operations in ψ' are sorted in descending or ascending order with respect to this weighting criteria processing edit operations with a higher degree of confidence first or last, respectively (*Unique* or *Unique-Inverse*).

8.1.3   Divergent

The aim of this criterion strategy is to prioritize nodes u_i that have a high divergence among all possible node edit costs. That is, for each row i in the cost matrix **C**, we sum up the absolute values of cost differences between all pairs of node edit operations, i.e.,

$$\sum_{j=1}^{m-1} \sum_{k=j+1}^{m} |c_{ij} - c_{ik}|.$$

Rows with a high divergence correspond to local node assignments that are somehow easier to be conducted than rows with low sums. Hence, we sort the edit operations $(u_i \to v_{\varphi i})$ in descending order with respect to the corresponding divergence in row i (*Divergent*) or vice versa (*Divergent-Inverse*).

8.1.4   Leader

This criterion weights nodes u_i according to the maximum difference between the minimum cost assignment of node u_i and the second minimum cost assignment of u_i. Assume we have

$$\text{min}1_i = \min_{j=1,\dots,m} c_{ij} \quad \text{and} \quad \text{min}2_i = \min_{j=1,\dots,m, j\neq k} c_{ij},$$

where k refers to the column index of the minimum cost entry $\text{min}1_i$. The weight for node u_i amounts then to

$$\frac{\min 2_i - \min 1_i}{\min 2_i},$$

where the denominator is a normalization factor. The higher the difference is, the less difficult is the local assignment. Hence, node edit operations $(u_i \rightarrow v_{\varphi i})$ are sorted in descending order (*Leader*) or ascending order (*Leader-Inverse*) with respect to the weight of u_i.

8.1.5 Interval

First, we compute the interval for each row i and each column j of the upper left part of $\mathbf{C}$ (i.e., for $i = 1, \ldots, n$ and $j = 1, \ldots, m$). We denote these intervals with δ_{r_i} and δ_{c_j}, respectively. Given a row i (or column j), the interval δ_{r_i} (δ_{c_j}) is defined as the absolute difference between the maximum and the minimum entry in row i (or column j). We also compute the mean of all row and column intervals, denoted by $\bar{\delta}_r$ and $\bar{\delta}_c$, respectively. The weight assigned to a given edit operation $(u_i \rightarrow v_{\varphi i})$ is then

- 1, if $\delta_{r_i} > \bar{\delta}_r$ and $\delta_{c_{\varphi i}} > \bar{\delta}_c$
- 0, if $\delta_{r_i} < \bar{\delta}_r$ and $\delta_{c_{\varphi i}} < \bar{\delta}_c$
- 0.5, otherwise

That is, if the intervals of both row and column are greater than the corresponding means, the weight is 1. Likewise, if both intervals are lower than the mean intervals, the weight is 0. For any other case the weight is set to 0.5.

When the intervals of row i and column φ_i are larger than the mean intervals, the row and column of the edit operation $(u_i \rightarrow v_{\varphi i})$ are in general easier to handle than others. On the other hand, if the row and column intervals of a certain edit operation are below the corresponding mean intervals, the individual values in the row and column are close to each other making an assignment rather difficult. Hence, we reorder the edit operations $(u_i \rightarrow v_{\varphi i})$ of the original assignment ψ in decreasing order (*Interval*) or increasing order (*Interval-Inverse*) according to these weights.

8.1.6 Deviation

For each row $i = 1, \ldots, n$ and each column $j = 1, \ldots, m$ of the left upper part of the cost matrix $\mathbf{C}$, we compute the means $\bar{\theta}_{r_i}$ and $\bar{\theta}_{c_j}$ and the deviations $\bar{\sigma}_{r_i}$ and $\bar{\sigma}_{c_j}$ of all entries in the corresponding row and column. Then, for each edit operation $(u_i \rightarrow v_{\varphi i}) \in \psi$ we compute its corresponding weight according to the following set of rules:

- Initially, the weight for an edit operation $(u_i \rightarrow v_{\varphi_i}) \in \psi$ is 0.
- If $c_{i\varphi_i} < \overline{\theta}_{r_i} - \overline{\sigma}_{r_i}$, we add 0.25 to the weight and compute the total number p of assignments in row i that also fulfill this condition and add $0.5/p$ to the weight.[1]
- Repeat the previous step for column $j = \varphi_i$ using $\overline{\theta}_{c_{\varphi_i}}$ and $\overline{\sigma}_{c_{\varphi_i}}$.

Given an edit operation $(u_i \rightarrow v_{\varphi i}) \in \psi$ with cost $c_{i\varphi_i}$ that is lower than the mean minus the deviation, we assume that the assignment cost is low enough to be considered as evident (and thus we add 0.25 to the weight). The weight increases if in the corresponding row only few (or no) other evident assignments are available (this is why we add $0.5/p$ to the weight, where p is the number of evident assignments). The same applies for the columns. At the end, assignments with small weights correspond to rather difficult assignments, while assignments with higher weights refer to assignments which are more evident than others. Hence, we reorder the original assignment ψ in decreasing order (*Deviation*) or increasing order (*Deviation-Inverse*).

8.2   Experimental Evaluation

For experimental evaluations, four data sets from the IAM graph database repository [2] and four data sets from GREYC's Chemistry dataset repository[2] are used. Five out of eight data sets consist of graphs representing molecular compounds from different applications, viz., AIDS, Acyclic, Alkane, MAO, and PAH. A sixth data set consists of graphs representing fingerprint images (FP). The LETTER data set involves graphs that represent distorted letter drawings, while the GREC data set consists of graphs representing symbols from architectural and electronic drawings. For details on the graph extraction methods and the graph characteristics, we refer to Chap. 9.

Major goal of the experimental evaluation is to research the effects of the novel reordering procedures on the distance accuracy. That is, we address the question to what extent the proposed reordering methodologies are able to reduce the overestimation of the graph edit distance approximations returned by BP-GED and in particular by BP-Beam. In order to generalize the results of BP-Beam in [1], the beam search procedure is repeated ten times with random permutations of the node assignments in ψ. Eventually, the mean distance is taken as final approximation result. Moreover, the beam size b is fixed to 5 in all of the experiments.

For the empirical evaluation, we measure the mean relative overestimation $\varnothing o$ (in percentage) with respect to the exact graph edit distance (we take the overestimation of BP-GED as 100%). Obviously, the smaller the $\varnothing o$ is, the better (i.e., nearer to the exact distance) is the approximation.

---

[1]Note that p is always greater than, or equal to, 1 ($p = 1$ when $c_{i\varphi_i}$ is the sole cost that fulfills the condition in row i).

[2]https://brunl01.users.greyc.fr/CHEMISTRY/index.html.

One can expect that the improvement of the distance accuracy is at the expense of a run time increase. Hence, we also aim at investigating how the different reorder strategies (with their different parameterizations) increase the mean run time ($\varnothing t$) compared to the original framework BP-GED and its extended version BP-Beam.

First, we regard the results of the twelve individual reordering strategies shown in Table 8.1. The following major observations can be made. First, we observe that reordering the assignments in ψ before carrying out the beam search results in better approximations than with BP-Beam that uses an arbitrary order of the assignments in 90 out of 96 cases (8 data sets × 12 reordering strategies). Hence, we can conclude that reordering the assignments in the context of beam search is clearly beneficial (regardless the reordering strategy actually employed).

In brackets we show the rank of the corresponding strategy (rank 1 refers to the smallest overestimation, and rank 12 to the largest overestimation on the data set). S (shown in column 2 of Table 8.1) refers to the sum of ranks per sorting criteria over all data sets. By comparing the individual criteria with their corresponding inverse counterpart, we observe that in four out of six cases the inverse version performs overall better. That is, in tendency it seems to be better to process the non-evident assignments in ψ first (this correlates with the intuition that these assignments should be altered in an early stage of the search process). Moreover, the overall winner is *Deviation-Inverse* with a sum of ranks of 18 (Note that this particular ordering criterion is in the top three on all data sets but on Alkane).

Regarding the computation time, we observe negligible differences between the different reordering strategies as well as between the reordered beam search and the original beam search (this accounts for all sorting strategies).

Next, we combine all possible pairs of reordering strategies with each other and take the minimum distance returned by both strategies as final result (that is, we have $12 \times 12 = 144$ different approximations to analyze). For each combination and each data set, we compute the relative rank compared with all other pairs with respect to the overestimation and visualize the sum of ranks for each combination shown in Fig. 8.1.

The first six rows (and columns) in Fig. 8.1 refer to *1. Confident; 2. Unique; 3. Divergent; 4. Leader; 5. Interval; 6. Deviation;* and rows 7 to 12 refer to the inverse counterparts of rows 1 to 6. Hence, the square in the first row and first column corresponds to the combination of *Confident-Confident*, the square in first row and second column refers to the pair *Confident-Unique*, and so on. The darker the square is, the lower is the rank of the corresponding pair of strategies (i.e., the better is the result with respect to the overestimation).

Along the main diagonal, we have the results of the individual strategies (or more precisely the combination of a strategy with itself) and we see that the best individual strategy is the last one, viz., Deviation-Inverse (this corresponds to the findings of Table 8.1). There are two rows (or columns as the matrix is symmetric) that are in tendency darker than the others, viz., row 5 (*Interval*) and 12 (*Deviation-Inverse*). This means that for these two sorting strategies, regardless the sorting strategy used in combination, one achieves accurate approximations (this particularly accounts for *Deviation-Inverse*). Moreover, one also observes that the combination of a specific

Table 8.1 Mean relative overestimation with respect to the exact distance ($\varnothing o$) (including rank) and mean run time for one matching ($\varnothing t$) in ms

Algorithm	S	AIDS		Fingerprint		GREC		LETTER		Acyclic		Alkane		MAO		PAH	
		$\varnothing o$	$\varnothing t$	$\varnothing o$	$\varnothing t$	$\varnothing o$	$\varnothing t$	$\varnothing o$	$\varnothing t$	$\varnothing o$	$\varnothing t$	$\varnothing o$	$\varnothing t$	$\varnothing o$	$\varnothing t$	$\varnothing o$	$\varnothing t$
BP-Beam		21.75	1.82	19.69	1.49	19.77	2.61	20.41	1.41	23.31	8.31	20.55	7.49	42.05	18.22	52.94	47.57
Confident	53	15.81 (5)	1.81	11.99 (2)	1.48	20.57 (10)	2.63	15.37 (8)	1.38	17.35 (7)	8.47	16.69 (10)	7.54	32.13 (4)	17.99	48.85 (7)	47.97
Confident Inv.	49	16.36 (7)	1.83	21.06 (12)	1.49	13.60 (1)	2.64	11.10 (3)	1.38	16.73 (6)	8.51	13.42 (3)	7.59	35.08 (7)	18.14	49.50 (10)	46.15
Unique	50	15.91 (6)	1.81	18.07 (10)	1.49	15.74 (7)	2.65	15.21 (7)	1.38	20.52 (10)	8.45	15.08 (7)	7.50	29.44 (2)	18.28	47.38 (1)	47.78
Unique Inv.	50	16.49 (8)	1.81	14.27 (6)	1.50	14.87 (5)	2.62	12.74 (4)	1.39	16.07 (5)	8.48	16.23 (9)	7.57	33.99 (5)	18.35	49.19 (8)	47.76
Divergent	68	14.03 (1)	1.80	16.29 (8)	1.50	16.68 (8)	2.64	15.92 (9)	1.39	23.40 (12)	8.40	17.84 (11)	7.46	40.95 (10)	18.01	49.19 (9)	48.70
Divergent Inv.	55	21.09 (12)	1.80	16.44 (9)	1.49	15.64 (6)	2.62	12.81 (5)	1.39	14.70 (2)	8.45	13.65 (4)	7.72	41.03 (11)	18.17	48.50 (6)	49.50
Leader	61	15.38 (2)	1.82	14.45 (7)	1.50	21.42 (11)	2.61	16.58 (11)	1.38	20.45 (9)	8.44	13.18 (2)	7.54	35.47 (8)	18.00	49.54 (11)	47.62
Leader Inv.	48	17.52 (9)	1.80	9.11 (11)	1.49	13.80 (4)	2.64	13.09 (6)	1.39	15.89 (4)	8.41	15.62 (8)	7.54	30.31 (3)	18.13	47.73 (3)	47.73
Interval	32	18.32 (10)	1.80	13.64 (5)	1.51	13.73 (3)	2.65	10.50 (2)	1.39	14.35 (1)	8.51	12.54 (1)	7.60	34.59 (6)	18.04	48.27 (4)	47.62
Interval Inv.	66	15.53 (4)	1.81	12.98 (3)	1.49	18.63 (9)	2.63	16.22 (10)	1.39	22.19 (11)	8.38	19.34 (12)	7.45	46.05 (12)	17.85	48.31 (5)	47.84
Deviation	74	20.94 (11)	1.81	13.24 (4)	1.50	21.65 (12)	2.59	17.15 (12)	1.39	20.33 (8)	8.39	14.67 (6)	7.48	39.89 (9)	18.05	52.00 (12)	48.46
Deviation Inv.	18	15.39 (3)	1.81	10.20 (1)	1.50	13.66 (2)	2.66	9.20 (1)	1.39	14.80 (3)	8.53	14.27 (5)	7.58	24.81 (1)	18.14	47.62 (2)	48.36

Fig. 8.1 Sum of ranks for all 144 combination pairs (the *darker* the *square* is, the *lower* the rank and thus the better the approximation)

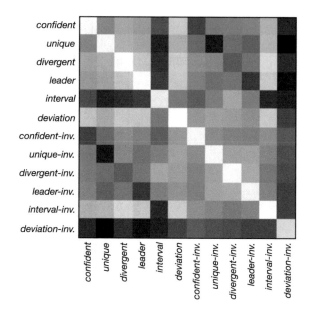

criterion in combination with its inverse counterpart is beneficial in tendency (this can be seen in the diagonals of the upper right part and lower left part of the matrix which are slightly darker than the remaining squares in the corresponding quadrants).

In Table 8.2, the three best combination pairs with respect to the sum of ranks are investigated in greater detail. We observe that on all data sets but LETTER and PAH the overestimation is roughly halved compared to the reference system BP-Beam (on the LETTER data even better reductions are observable, while on PAH the relative reduction is not as large as on the other sets). Yet, this substantial gain of distance accuracy is at the expense of a run time increase. In general, one observes that the run time is approximately doubled using a pair of sorting criteria (this perfectly makes sense as we run the time consuming part of the procedure, viz., beam search, twice with two different assignment orders).

For the last experiment, we iteratively combine all strategies with each other. More precisely, on every data set, we start with the individually best sorting criterion (referred to as *SBP-Beam(1)*). Next, *SBP-Beam(2)* combines the best criterion with the second best criterion on every data set. Then, we iteratively add the next best criterion until all 12 sorting criteria are used. In Table 8.3, the results of this experiment are shown. First of all, we observe that the overestimation of BP-GED can be dramatically reduced. For instance, on the AIDS data set, we observe a reduction of the overestimation from 21.75 (achieved by BP-Beam) to 3.87 % (achieved by SBP-Beam(12)). Similar results are observable on the other data sets. At the same time, we observe that the run time linearly increases with the number of sorting criteria actually employed. Note, however, that the increased run times are still far below the run time for exact computation (except on the LETTER data set).

Table 8.2 Mean relative overestimation with respect to the exact distance ($\varnothing o$) in % and mean run time for one matching ($\varnothing t$) in ms

Algorithm	AIDS		Fingerprint		GREC		LETTER		Acyclic		Alkane		MAO		PAH	
	$\varnothing o$	$\varnothing t$	$\varnothing o$	$\varnothing t$	$\varnothing o$	$\varnothing t$	$\varnothing o$	$\varnothing t$	$\varnothing o$	$\varnothing t$	$\varnothing o$	$\varnothing t$	$\varnothing o$	$\varnothing t$	$\varnothing o$	$\varnothing t$
BP-Beam	21.75	1.82	19.69	1.49	19.77	2.61	20.41	1.41	23.31	8.31	20.55	7.49	42.05	18.22	52.94	47.57
Unique/Deviation Inv.	10.09	3.32	7.15	2.61	9.37	5.01	5.75	2.54	11.69	16.11	9.35	14.38	17.16	35.91	42.73	94.05
Leader/Deviation Inv.	9.87	3.33	5.99	2.64	10.96	4.97	5.35	2.55	11.78	16.11	8.69	14.45	18.12	35.77	43.69	93.66
Unique/Unique Inv.	9.87	3.32	7.93	2.61	8.92	4.98	6.28	2.52	11.54	16.09	9.44	14.37	19.12	35.67	43.27	93.97

Table 8.3 Mean relative overestimation with respect to the exact distance ($\varnothing o$) in % and mean run time for one matching ($\varnothing t$) in ms

Algorithm	AIDS		Fingerprint		GREC		LETTER		Acyclic		Alkane		MAO		PAH	
	$\varnothing o$	$\varnothing t$	$\varnothing o$	$\varnothing t$	$\varnothing o$	$\varnothing t$	$\varnothing o$	$\varnothing t$	$\varnothing o$	$\varnothing t$	$\varnothing o$	$\varnothing t$	$\varnothing o$	$\varnothing t$	$\varnothing o$	$\varnothing t$
A^*	0.00	25750.22	0.00	2535.42	0.00	7770.81	0.00	1.81	0.00	8924.17	0.00	812.77	0.00	13538.46	0.00	30495.54
BP	100.00	0.28	100.00	0.35	100.00	0.27	100.00	0.21	100.00	0.81	100.00	0.65	100.00	0.81	100.00	157.8
BP-Beam	21.75	1.82	19.69	1.49	19.77	2.61	20.41	1.41	23.31	8.31	20.55	7.49	42.05	18.22	52.94	47.57
SBP-Beam(1)	14.03	1.82	10.20	1.51	13.60	2.68	9.20	1.46	14.35	8.57	12.54	7.62	24.81	18.49	47.38	49.81
SBP-Beam(2)	9.83	3.35	5.21	2.68	9.62	5.08	5.74	2.66	10.99	16.43	8.63	14.50	17.16	35.72	42.73	97.42
SBP-Beam(3)	7.40	4.92	3.68	3.82	7.73	7.41	4.57	3.78	8.34	23.94	6.88	21.49	14.63	53.77	40.85	145.46
SBP-Beam(4)	6.59	6.35	3.17	4.98	6.78	9.85	3.82	5.00	7.37	31.34	6.19	28.59	12.86	70.95	40.46	187.76
SBP-Beam(5)	5.89	7.89	2.73	6.39	6.07	12.21	3.30	6.08	6.89	39.23	5.53	35.13	12.38	89.85	39.27	233.97
SBP-Beam(6)	5.51	9.42	2.49	7.21	5.73	14.54	2.94	7.35	6.26	47.70	4.98	42.17	11.44	106.79	39.19	281.09
SBP-Beam(7)	4.91	10.96	2.33	8.28	5.01	16.93	2.34	8.48	5.70	54.63	4.68	49.50	10.92	124.22	38.42	328.01
SBP-Beam(8)	4.52	12.68	2.15	9.50	4.56	19.35	1.88	9.70	5.39	62.42	4.39	56.03	10.30	140.77	38.42	374.35
SBP-Beam(9)	4.26	14.13	1.97	10.50	4.24	21.82	1.69	10.86	5.12	70.91	4.27	62.94	10.04	159.13	38.23	417.19
SBP-Beam(10)	4.08	15.51	1.96	11.68	4.14	24.21	1.58	12.05	5.02	77.84	4.13	69.64	9.95	175.27	37.73	468.53
SBP-Beam(11)	3.94	17.18	1.91	12.88	4.04	26.57	1.46	13.17	4.90	84.96	3.99	77.41	9.77	193.49	37.73	515.74
SBP-Beam(12)	3.87	18.59	1.87	14.40	3.95	28.69	1.35	14.36	4.84	92.37	3.95	84.10	9.64	212.01	37.73	562.24

Fig. 8.2 Gain of accuracy in each iteration of SBP-Beam(i) ($i = 1, \ldots, 12$) for each data set (each bar corresponds to one data set)

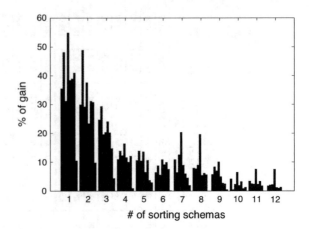

We observe furthermore that the first three iterations lead to relatively large reductions of the overestimation. For instance, on the AIDS data set in the first three iterations, we observe a gain of accuracy of 35.5, 29.9, and 24.7 % from BP-Beam to SBP-Beam(1), from SBP-Beam(1) to SBP-Beam(2), and from SBP-Beam(2) to SBP-Beam(3), respectively. However, using four or more sorting criteria at once we observe that the relative gain of distance accuracy flattens out. This can be seen in Fig. 8.2 where the relative gain of distance accuracy is plotted for each iteration and data set (each of the eight bars refers to one data set). Both the large gain of distance accuracy in the first three iterations and the flattening effect are clearly visible.

References

1. M. Ferrer, F. Serratosa, K. Riesen, Improving bipartite graph matching by assessing the assignment confidence. Accepted for publication in Pattern Recognition Letters
2. K. Riesen, H. Bunke, IAM graph database repository for graph based pattern recognition and machine learning, in *Structural, Syntactic, and Statistical Pattern Recognition, LNCS 5342*, ed. by N. da Vitoria Lobo, et al. (Springer, Berlin, 2008), pp. 287–297

Chapter 9
Appendix B: Data Sets

Abstract In this chapter a thorough definition of the graph data is provided.

The following data sets are employed in the current book for various experimental evaluations. Note that five of these data sets belong to the IAM graph repository for graph-based pattern recognition and machine learning [1]. These data sets have been also used for numerous other empirical evaluations in graph-based pattern recognition during the last years, in particular they are extensively used in a further book authored by the same author as the present book [2].

9.1 LETTER Graphs

The first graph data set involves graphs that represent simple line drawings in the plane. Drawings of the 15 capital letters of the Roman alphabet that consist of straight lines are considered only (A, E, F, H, I, K, L, M, N, T, V, W, X, Y, Z). First, a proto-type line drawing is manually constructed for each class. These letter drawings are eventually converted into prototype graphs by representing lines by undirected edges and ending points of lines by nodes. Each node is labeled with a two-dimensional label giving its position relative to a reference coordinate system. Edges remain unlabeled. In order to obtain a large-scale data set, distortions are applied on the prototype graphs. These distortions consist of randomly removing, inserting, and displacing edges including their corresponding nodes. For each class 150 noisy patterns are generated from each clean prototype resulting in 2,250 graphs in total. In Table 9.1 a summary of the Letter data set together with some basic characteristic properties is given.

K. Riesen, *Structural Pattern Recognition with Graph Edit Distance*,
Advances in Computer Vision and Pattern Recognition,
DOI 10.1007/978-3-319-27252-8_9

149

Table 9.1 Summary of graph
data set characteristics

LETTER	
Patterns	Letter line drawings
Classes	15 (A, E, F, H, I, K, L, M, N, T, V, W, X, Y, Z)
Number of graphs	2,250
Node labels	(x, y) coordinates
Edge labels	None
Average per graph	4.7 nodes, 4.5 edges
Maximum per graph	9 nodes, 9 edges

9.2   GREC Graphs

Automatic conversion of line drawings from paper to electronic form requires the recognition of geometric primitives like lines, arcs, circles, etc., in scanned documents [3]. The GREC data set consists of graphs representing symbols made of such geometric primitives from architectural and electronic drawings. From the original GREC database [4], 22 classes are considered.

The images occur with so-called *salt-and-pepper noise* at five different distortion levels. Depending on the distortion level, either *erosion*, *dilation*, *opening* (erosion followed by dilation), or *closing* (dilation followed by erosion) operations are applied for noise removal. The noise removed image is thinned to obtain lines of one pixel width. To this end, the thinning method described in [5] is applied. Finally, graphs are extracted from the resulting denoised images by tracing the one-pixel wide lines from end to end and detecting intersections as well as corners. Ending points, corners, intersections, and circles are represented by nodes and labeled with a two-dimensional attribute giving their position. These nodes are possibly connected by undirected edges which are labeled as *line* or *arc* depending on whether a straight or curvy line connects the nodes under consideration.

Table 9.2 Summary of graph data set characteristics

GREC	
Patterns	Line drawings of electronic and architectural symbols
Classes	22 (antenna, capacitor, washbasin, etc.)
Number of graphs	3,300
Node labels	Type (end, corner, intersection, circle) and (x, y) coordinates
Edge labels	Type (line, arc)
Average per graph	11.5 nodes, 12.2 edges
Maximum per graph	25 nodes, 30 edges

For an adequately sized set, the five graphs per distortion level are individually distorted 30 times to obtain a data set containing 3,300 graphs uniformly distributed over the 22 classes. These distortions consist of translations and scalings of the graphs in a certain range, and random deletions and insertions of both nodes and edges. In Table 9.2 a summary of the GREC data set together with some basic characteristic properties is given.

9.3 FP Graphs

The Fingerprint data set (FP) stems from the emerging field of *biometric person authentication*. The Fingerprint data set used in our experiments is based on the NIST-4 reference database of fingerprints [6]. It consists of a 2,800 fingerprint images out of the four classes *arch*, *left loop*, *right loop*, and *whorl* from the Galton–Henry classification system [7]. In Table 9.3 a summary of the Fingerprint data set together with some basic characteristic properties is given.

The graph extraction approach pursued for the present data set is closely related to the traditional method based on the detection of *singular points* in fingerprint images [8, 9]. Regarding the fingerprints as orientation fields, where each pixel of a fingerprint image is assigned the direction of the local ridge line, singular points are those points for which it is impossible to determine a unique orientation. There exist two different categories of singular points termed *core points* and *delta points*. Core points are located at the center of a whorl or at the center of a loop. Delta points are at positions where ridges from three different directions meet.

Fingerprints are converted into graphs by filtering the images and extracting regions that are relevant [10]. The basic idea is to detect locations where ridges in fingerprints have almost vertical orientation. It turns out that each core point is connected to a delta point by a region consisting only of vertical orientation. In order to obtain graphs from fingerprint images, these relevant regions are binarized and a noise removal and thinning procedure is applied [5]. This results in a skeletonized representation of the extracted regions. Ending points and bifurcation points of the skeletonized regions are represented by nodes. Additional nodes are inserted

Table 9.3 Summary of graph data set characteristics

FP	
Patterns	Fingerprint images from the NIST-4 database
Classes	4 (arch, left loop, right loop, whorl)
Number of graphs	2,800
Node labels	None
Edge labels	Angle
Average per graph	5.4 nodes, 4.4 edges
Maximum per graph	26 nodes, 25 edges

in regular intervals between ending points and bifurcation points. Finally, undirected edges are inserted to link nodes that are directly connected through a ridge in the skeleton. Nodes are unlabeled, while edges are attributed with an angle denoting the orientation of the edge with respect to the horizontal direction.

9.4   AIDS Graphs

The AIDS data set consists of graphs representing molecular compounds from the AIDS Antiviral Screen Database of Active Compounds [11] provided by the US National Cancer Institute (NCI). Clearly, a molecular structure consisting of atoms and covalent bonds can be represented by a graph in a very natural and straightforward manner by representing atoms as nodes and the covalent bonds as edges. Nodes may be labeled with their corresponding chemical symbol and edges by the valence of the linkage.

Since 1999, the NCI carries out AIDS antiviral screen tests to discover chemical compounds that might be capable of inhibiting the HIV virus. The aim of these screen tests is to measure how strongly the compounds under consideration are able to protect human cells from infection by the HIV virus. Chemical compounds that reproducibly provide a perfect protection from HIV are labeled *confirmed active (CA)*, while compounds that are only able to protect cells from infection in at least 50 % of the cases are labeled *moderately active (MA)*. All of the remaining molecules are labeled *confirmed inactive (CI)*. In total, 42,438 chemical compounds were screened, whereof 406 were found to belong to the CA category, 1,056 to the MA category, and the vast majority (40,976) to the CI category.

The data set actually employed in the present book consists of 2,000 graphs representing molecular compounds from two classes *CA* and *CI*, which represent molecules with and without activity against HIV (400 active elements and 1,600 inactive elements). In Table 9.4 a summary of the AIDS data set together with some basic characteristic properties is given.

Table 9.4 Summary of graph data set characteristics

AIDS	
Patterns	Chemical compounds
Classes	2 (confirmed active, confirmed inactive)
Number of graphs	2,000
Node labels	Chemical symbol
Edge labels	None
Average per graph	15.7 nodes, 16.2 edges
Maximum per graph	95 nodes, 103 edges

Table 9.5 Summary of graph data set characteristics

MUTA	
Patterns	Chemical compounds
Classes	2 (confirmed mutagen, confirmed nonmutagen)
Number of graphs	2,500
Node labels	Chemical symbol
Edge labels	None
Average per graph	30.3 nodes, 30.8 edges
Maximum per graph	417 nodes, 112 edges

9.5 MUTA Graphs

The MUTA data set is similar to the AIDS data set in the sense that also molecular compounds are considered. *Mutagenicity* is the ability of a chemical compound to cause mutations in DNA and is therefore one of the numerous adverse properties of a compound that hampers its potential to become a marketable drug [12]. The Chemical Carcinogenicity Research Information System (CCRIS) database [13] contains scientifically evaluated test data for approximately 7,000 compounds. The data set used in the present book was originally prepared by the authors of [12]. From this data set we use 2,500 chemical compounds in total. In order to convert molecular compounds of the mutagenicity data set into attributed graphs the same procedure as for the AIDS data set is applied. The mutagenicity data set is divided into two classes *mutagen* and *nonmutagen* of equal size (1,250 mutagenic elements and 1,250 non-mutagenic elements). In Table 9.5 a summary of the Mutagenicity data set together with some basic characteristic properties is given.

9.6 PROT Graphs

Proteins are organic compounds made of amino acids sequences joined together by peptide bonds. In fact, a huge amount of proteins have been sequenced over recent years, and the structures of thousands of proteins have been resolved so far. The best known role of proteins in the cell is as enzymes which catalyze chemical reactions. There are about 4,000 such reactions known. Yet, the experimental determination of the function of a protein with known sequence and structure is still a difficult, time and cost intensive task [14]. Being able to predict protein function from its structure could save both time and money.

The PROT data set employed in the present book consists of graphs representing proteins originally used in [15]. The graphs are constructed from the Protein Data Bank [16] and labeled with their corresponding enzyme class labels from the BRENDA enzyme database [17]. The proteins database consists of six classes (*EC1*,

Table 9.6 Summary of graph data set characteristics

PROT	
Patterns	Proteins
Classes	6 (EC1, EC2, EC3, EC4, EC5, EC6)
Size of *tr*, *va*, *te*	200, 200, 200
Node labels	Type (helix, sheet, loop) and amino acid sequence
Edge labels	Type (sequential, structural) and length
Average per graph	32.6 nodes, 62.1 edges
Maximum per graph	126 nodes, 149 edges

EC2, EC3, EC4, EC5, EC6), which represent proteins out of the six enzyme commission top-level hierarchy (EC classes). The EC numbering of proteins is a numerical classification scheme based on the chemical reactions they catalyze. That is, two proteins having the same EC number catalyze the same reaction. For instance, proteins from the EC3 class are hydrolases meaning they use water to break up some other molecule.

The proteins are converted into graphs by representing the structure, the sequence, and chemical properties of a protein by nodes and edges. Nodes represent secondary structure elements (SSE) within the protein structure, labeled with their type (helix, sheet, or loop) and their amino acid sequence. Every pair of nodes is connected by an edge if they are neighbors along the amino acid sequence (sequential edges) or if they are neighbors in space within the protein structure (structural edges). Every node is connected to its three nearest spatial neighbors. In case of sequential relationships, the edges are labeled with their length in amino acids, while in case of structural edges a distance measure in Ångstroms is used as a label.

There are 600 proteins totally, 100 per class. We use a training, validation, and test set of equal size (200). The classification task on this data set consists in predicting the enzyme class membership. In Table 9.6 a summary of the protein data set together with some basic characteristic properties is given.

9.7   GREYC Graphs

Finally, we make use of of four data sets stemming from the GREYC's Chemistry data set.[1] All of these data sets are rather small and consists of graphs that represent chemical compounds (thus, the same extraction method as for AIDS and MUTA is used).

The *Monoamine Oxydase* (*MAO*) data set is composed of 68 molecules divided into two classes, viz., 38 molecules that inhibit the *monoamine oxidase* (antidepressant drugs) and 30 do not. The *Polyciclic Aromatic Hydrocarbons* (*PAH*) data set is composed of 94 cyclic unlabeled graphs. All atoms are carbons, while all bounds

---

[1] https://brunl01.users.greyc.fr/CHEMISTRY/.

Table 9.7 Summary of graph data set characteristics

MAO, PAH, Acyclic, Alkane	
Patterns	Chemical compounds
Classes	2 (MAO), 0 (PAH, Alkane, Acyclic)
Number of graphs	68 (MAO), 94 (PAH), 150 (Alkane), 185 (Acyclic)
Node labels	Chemical symbol (MAO, PAH, Acyclic), none (Alkane)
Edge labels	None
Average per graph	18.4/20.7/8.2/8.9 nodes, 19.6/24.4/7.2/7.9 edges
Maximum per graph	27/28/11/10 nodes, 26/34/10/9 edges

represent aromatics. Note that few acyclic bounds connect some atoms to cycles. The *Alkane* data set consists of 150 purely structural graphs. That is, the nodes refer to carbons only. Finally, the *Acyclic* data set consists of 185 molecules with heteroatoms (acyclic ethers, peroxides, acetals and their sulfur analogues). In Table 9.7 a summary of the GREYC data set together with some basic characteristic properties is given.

References

1. K. Riesen, H. Bunke, IAM graph database repository for graph based pattern recognition and machine learning, in *Structural, Syntactic, and Statistical Pattern Recognition*, vol. 5342, LNCS, ed. by N. da Vitoria Lobo, et al. (Springer, Berlin, 2008), pp. 287–297
2. K. Riesen, H. Bunke, *Graph Classification and Clustering Based on Vector Space Embedding* (World Scientific, Singapore, 2010)
3. F. Shafait, D. Keysers, T.M. Breuel, GREC 2007 arc segmentation contest: Evaluation of four participating algorithms, in *Graphics Recognition. Recent Advances and New Opportunities*, vol. 5046, LNCS, ed. by L. Wenyin, J. Lladós, J.M. Ogier (Springer, Berlin, 2008), pp. 310–320
4. Ph Dosch, E. Valveny, Report on the second symbol recognition contest, in *Proceedings of the 6th International Workshop on Graphics Recognition (GREC'05). Graphics Recognition. Ten years review and future perspectives*, vol. 3926, LNCS, ed. by L. Wenyin, J. Lladós (Springer, Berlin, 2005), pp. 381–397
5. R.W. Zhou, C. Quek, G.S. Ng, A novel single-pass thinning algorithm and an effective set of performance criteria. Pattern Recognit. Lett. **16**(12), 1267–1275 (1995)
6. C.I. Watson, C.L. Wilson, *NIST Special Database 4, Fingerprint Database*. National Institute of Standards and Technology, March 1992
7. E. Henry, *Classification and Uses of Finger Prints* (Routledge, London, 1900)
8. M. Kawagoe, A. Tojo, Fingerprint pattern classification. Pattern Recognit. **17**, 295–303 (1984)
9. K. Karu, A.K. Jain, Fingerprint classification. Pattern Recognit. **29**(3), 389–404 (1996)
10. M. Neuhaus, H. Bunke, A graph matching based approach to fingerprint classification using directional variance, in *Proceedings of the 5th International Conference on Audio- and Video-Based Biometric Person Authentication*, vol. 3546, LNCS, ed. by T. Kanade, A. Jain, N.K. Ratha (Springer, Berlin, 2005), pp. 191–200
11. Development Therapeutics Program DTP. AIDS antiviral screen, 2004. http://dtp.nci.nih.gov/docs/aids/aids_data.html
12. J. Kazius, R. McGuire, R. Bursi, Derivation and validation of toxicophores for mutagenicity prediction. J. Med. Chem. **48**(1), 312–320 (2005)
13. Chemical Carcinogenesis Research Information System. http://toxnet.nlm.nih.gov

14. K. Borgwardt, C. Ong, S. Schönauer, S. Vishwanathan, A. Smola, H.-P. Kriegel, Protein function prediction via graph kernels. Bioinformatics **21**(1), 47–56 (2005)
15. K. Borgwardt, *Graph Kernels*. Ph.D. thesis, Ludwig-Maximilians-University Munich, 2007
16. H. Berman, J. Westbrook, Z. Feng, G. Gilliland, T. Bhat, H. Weissig, I. Shidyalov, P. Bourne, The protein data bank. Nucleic Acids Res. **28**, 235–242 (2000)
17. I. Schomburg, A. Chang, C. Ebeling, M. Gremse, C. Heldt, G. Huhn, D. Schomburg, Brenda, the enzyme database: updates and major new developments. Nucleic Acids Res. 32:Database issue, D431–D433 (2004)

Index

© Springer International Publishing Switzerland 2015
K. Riesen, *Structural Pattern Recognition with Graph Edit Distance*,
Advances in Computer Vision and Pattern Recognition,
DOI 10.1007/978-3-319-27252-8

Printed in the United States
By Bookmasters